ISLAND YEARS
ISLAND FARM

Frank Fraser Darling

LITTLE TOLLER BOOKS

This paperback edition published in 2011 by
Little Toller Books
Ford, Pineapple Lane, Dorset
Island Years first published in 1940 by G. Bell and Sons
Island Farm first published in 1943 by G. Bell and Sons

ISBN 978-1-908213-01-3

Text and photographs © The Estate of Frank Fraser Darling 2011
Introduction © Iain Stewart 2011

Typeset in Monotype Sabon by Little Toller Books
Printed in Cornwall, UK by TJ Books

All papers used by Little Toller Books
are natural, recyclable products made from
wood grown in sustainable, well-managed forests

A CIP catalogue record for this book is available
from the British Library

9 8

CONTENTS

PREFACE

Alasdair Fraser Darling

IT IS EARLY IN THE MORNING in July 1938 and my father is shaking me awake in my bunk where I have been enduring seasickness for several hours. He pushes me up through the hatch on to the deck of the Fishery Cruiser – I shall always be so grateful for that. Before us was the great 350 foot east cliff of North Rona almost hidden by the sea birds flying all around us, screeching, squawking, croaking in a deafening sound. Now seventy years later that memory is still as fresh. Then, one night, we are sitting in the ruins of the old village on North Rona listening to the 'churring' of the Leach's fork-tailed petrel. The pace and the noise quickens as their famous aerial dance begins. There is the musty smell, the brush of wing on cheek. Even now I am one of few people privileged to have witnessed this event.

So how did it come about that my parents and I found ourselves on this desolate island fifty miles north of the Scottish mainland?

My father was born in June 1903 in Yorkshire and grew up in Sheffield. His mother instilled in him a great love of nature from an early age, taking him on early morning treks to the local woods, bird watching and looking for nests, or on to the moors looking at wildlife and plants. He was devoted to his mother, a remarkable, brave and doughty lady who never doubted his ability. I too loved my Granny Harriet dearly.

His thirst for knowledge led him to read Charles Darwin's *Origin of Species* aged fourteen, just sixty years after it was first published. By then he had also become a rebel. Deeply unhappy and bullied at school, he refused to be confirmed in the Anglican Church because he could not accept the then orthodox teaching of Creation. Nevertheless, he always retained a deep sense of God – it was his reverence for what he saw that was sacred and good in this fragile earth, and mans' failure to be a careful steward that moved him in his work as an ecologist. And I sense this reverence for life inspired in him a great empathy and compassion, for people and animals alike.

On his fifteenth birthday, in 1918, my father left school and went to work as a farmer's boy in the High Peak in Derbyshire. They were hard days but he loved the life and described with great excitement and pride the first time he led out the horses with a loaded wagon. He learnt much, including the art of dry stone walling – a skill he valued throughout his life. Three years later he entered Sutton Bonington Agricultural College, where he met his first wife, 'Bobbie', my mother, who became the other central character in this story. She was studying for a Dairying Diploma – born and bred in London, her mother came from a farming family at Dunton Bassett in Leicestershire.

The story of their lives together from the mud of Buckinghamshire to the North West Highlands reveals a dream to live on an uninhabited island. They were married in 1925 and in 1928 (just after I was born) they moved to Edinburgh where my father became Director of the then Imperial Bureau of Animal Genetics. But in his heart was a longing to study animals in their natural environment, 'social biology', instead of studying them in a laboratory. The red deer was his choice, and a good one at that – little was known about its social life although it was known, even then, to have a major impact on habitat. The award of one of the first Leverhulme Fellowships in 1933 enabled him to put his ideas into practice, and this study from 1933-36 homed his scientific skills as well as indulging him in what he loved: exploring the high tops and living alongside the deer, observing and interpreting what he saw. We are now so used to television showing animals in their natural environment that it is difficult to appreciate just how groundbreaking his work with red deer was, and how derided it was by the scientific establishment of the day.

We moved to Brae House, Dundonnell, during this time. There were no shop for miles, no sanitation, no cooking facilities, water had to be carried from the burn, and there were a lot of fleas! But as a five-year-old I just loved living there, which is a tribute to my mother's ability to make such a happy home. In fact, none of this would have been possible were it not for my mother. There we were, either living in a bare house or in a bell tent on an uninhabited island – the later huts sound like luxury – and she was running a household, producing three meals a day with adequate variety, cooking bread on top of a primus stove, seeing to the needs of a small boy, and generally making sure there was comfort against the harshness of the weather and the land.

My daughter recalls looking with amazement at the lists her granny made, with menus for each day extending for several months ahead, notable for their detail and accuracy! Right into her old age my mother always declared vigorously how much she had enjoyed this life, and how much better it was than working nine to five in an office. One proof must surely be that for me these years were supremely happy, living in a secure and loving family where there was always good food and plenty of it!

Even though I was an only child with no other children with whom to play, I was never lonely and invented my own fantasy world. There were recurring criticisms about taking a child to such isolated places, especially North Rona, but the alternative would have had me farmed out for months at a time. The one experience I had of this, when my parents were on a lecture tour, was a very unhappy one. I can only be deeply grateful for their decision to take me with them to the islands. I did not begin formal schooling until I was nine but thanks to my mother's teaching with, as she used to say, 'a book in one hand and a ruler in the other', I found the intricacies of learning Gaelic at school a bigger challenge than arithmetic!

But I had my uses on Rona too. Hitched to a rope I would clamber round the cliff edges catching fulmar chicks for my father to ring. These chicks would eject the most foul smelling, fishy orange liquid all over me – my father expressed more concern for the poor little chicks than for his son looking for a pool in which to wash himself!

Island Years was published in 1940, at the beginning of the Blitz, and its popularity was exemplified by one correspondent who wrote that during an air raid he would get under the bed with his torch and the book and was able to forget what was happening outside. *Island Farm* was published in 1943, after four years of war in a tired country with only glimpses of eventual victory in sight. It was a tale of two people (I was more peripheral by then, being at boarding school) having no option but to earn their living from the croft and whatever income my father could earn from his writing. They worked incredibly hard physically. Every page describes digging, mulching with seaweed, building byres and shedding, carrying loads of basic slag and coral sand on to the hill so that Cnoc Glas (Green Hill) could be green once again. There was no idle sitting and watching wildlife now, and the onset of war induced in my father a deep sorrow. He hated war and the attitudes it encouraged, but he was not a pacifist and realised well enough that this war was necessary. He always held a deep anger against the politicians who had let this conflict happen.

For me, I could not wait to return from school and take up my routines on the croft. The calves and their care were my responsibility as well as mucking out the byre. In the summer I would be out fishing while my lobster creels produced a regular harvest. I would roam the bays on the west to salvage useable driftwood and other items blown ashore, including lots of sailors caps. It was a good life for a lad with no chance of boredom.

My father used to keep voluminous notes in his daily journals on all their island expeditions and he started this again in 1941. After about six months it peters out, the entries becoming shorter often recording just the jobs done that day. I have the impression that sheer physical exhaustion was taking its toll. By 1942 my mother and father had got as far as they could in developing Tigh an Quay without further help. During this time my father had written a good many articles about farming practice in the West Highlands, and through all his books and articles runs a thread of interaction between humans and the environment. The war forced him to study this in relation to the West Highlands, which he had described as 'a devastated terrain' or 'a wet desert' due to deforestation and overgrazing. Sadly, by the time *Island Farm* was published, their marriage had ended and they went on to live their separate lives.

Yet, the work my mother and father did showed how fertility could be created with good agricultural husbandry. His influence spread and resulted, in 1944, in the then Development Commission of Scotland commissioning

West Highland Survey: an essay in human ecology, a five year study of all aspects of the West Highlands. The results of this massive survey were of no interest to the Government in 1950, but his ideas caught the attention of those in the USA and Africa who were concerned by similar problems on a much larger scale.

In 1949 he was awarded a Special Research Fellowship by the Rockefeller Foundation to travel across the USA, bringing his West Highland experience to bear on their problems of deforestation and erosion. What he had to say so impressed his hosts, the Conservation Foundation, that human ecology became a subject of serious study. In 1956, he was invited to East Africa to advise on similar problems of wildlife resources, loss of habitat and land use. His visits to Africa from 1956-61 covered Zambia, Tanzania, Kenya, and Sudan. He was deeply involved in the creation of their National Parks.

The BBC Reith Lectures of 1969, *Wilderness and Plenty*, were the culmination of a life's work, the harbinger of what is now a concern to us all, climate change and its consequences. Sadly, ill health prevented him from continuing to contribute more and he died in October 1979. He has been called a prophet for the way he interpreted what he saw and its implications for our planet and ourselves. But it was the life in the West Highlands of Scotland that he describes in *Island Years* and *Island Farm* that was the inspiration.

Sadly, my father and mother separated after leaving Tanera Mòr in 1943. She was heartbroken when he died and insisted on coming to his memorial service, saying she would come in quietly on her own and stand at the back. But my father's third wife, Christina, made her very welcome and they became good friends – somewhere I have a photo of them knocking back the sherry! My mother never remarried but led a fruitful life working with youth clubs, particularly in the Highlands, and became the warden of a house for youth groups in Argyllshire. She retired to Lincolnshire at sixty, where she enjoyed a happy twenty years looking after her garden and was active in the community, particularly with the Women's Institute. She died in 1987, aged eighty-seven, and is buried here in Caythorpe.

West Coast of Scotland

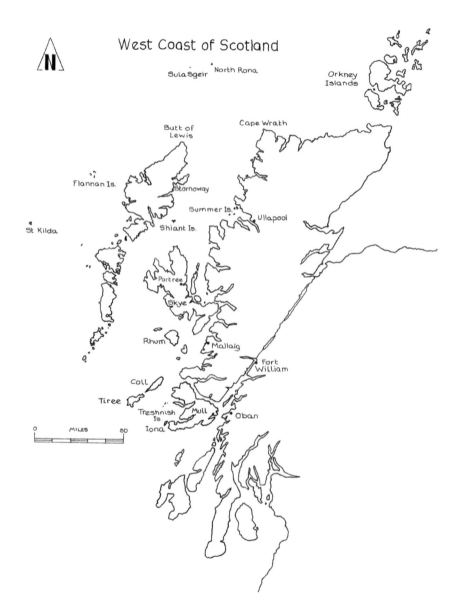

INTRODUCTION

Iain Stewart

To the casual outsider, the Highlands of north-west Scotland are a magnificent wilderness. Bens and glens wrapped in heather and tradition. Rivers that run with plaid. Scenes of untouched nature, pure and wild, which left Lowland Scots proud and more alien visitors awed. But it was all a delusion. A romantic idyll of the sublime and picturesque carefully cultured by a Victorian nobility that adored the landscape but did precious little to protect it. What they did protect was game, and with the spread of deer forest and grouse moor the postcard country became sterilised of its ecological richness. The loss of such natural resources came at a cost for those that lived scattered amid the mountains. For those communities the land had long had an intrinsic value and an enduring purpose; woods were cut and planted, ores were mined, gentle slopes were farmed, seas were fished. This utilitarian world of profit and subsistence conflicted with the mystical notion of the Highlands as heritage, a place for idle amusement and preservation. Tugged by the twin tensions of use and delight, the Highlands remained beautiful but largely abandoned. A moribund landscape with precious little money and precious few people. But that was fine: after all, less people meant more beauty. Perfect for shooters, anglers, walkers and climbers, and ideal for the passing tourist trade. Beautiful, but dead.

It was to this scene that Frank Fraser Darling arrived in the 1930s, a young, compulsive and charismatic ecologist who blended hard science with romantic tradition. His doctoral studies at the University of Edinburgh on the genetic make-up of Blackface sheep had instilled in him a love of wild places and passion for scientific endeavour, but it also introduced him to the depredations imposed on the Scottish landscape. He described how 'two centuries of extractive sheep farming in the Highland hills have reduced a rich natural resource to a state of desolation.' This was a theme to which he would return to again and again. The Highlands, he would argue, had once been a rich natural system – almost a living thing in its own right. And an essential part of that system was man. The traditional ecology of the Highlands was one in which people were bound to their habitat just like any other animal, and the habitat was bound to them. The trouble was, after centuries of land clearances the Highlands were empty. Not just empty of life – devoid of mammal predators and birds of prey – but empty of people.

The importance of people in the affairs of Scotland's natural world was a notion that seemed to grow gently on Fraser Darling. His early years, much of it narrated in *Island Years*, were spent in the wilderness studying the social life of red deer, seabirds and grey seals. In their social orderliness he saw human qualities, none more so than among the grey seals of North Rona. On this remote speck of Hebridean gneiss a hundred miles west of Orkney – surely one of the barest places in Scotland – he built a research station to observe their sea behaviour. His station, on the edge of the vast and cacophonous summer breeding colony, was a set of timber huts enclosed in a tumbled-down sheep pen. In this small stone enclosure he lived for a year with his wife Bobbie and their nine-year old son Alasdair, delighting in the wildness of the place, especially the savage beauty of the Atlantic breakers that pounded the rockbound shores. But special reverence was given to the grey seals, 'the people of the sea'. He noted reverently how the Gaels had 'invested them with a half-veiled but occasionally irruptive humanity.' That apparent human nature was most expressive in the seal pups, for 'there is no creature born, even among the greater apes, which resembles a human baby in its ways and cries than a baby grey seal.' Decades later, Fraser Darling's powerful evocation would find a very practical application. In the late 1970's, when grey seals were blamed for falling fish stocks and fishermen in Orkney successfully petitioned the government to sanction a cull, environmental groups like Greenpeace stirred popular dissent with the emotive imagery of the all-too-human helpless seal pup. The approach worked; Downing Street received 14,000 letters in protest and announced a halt to the cull. By the end of that decade the much-hunted grey seal had been embraced as a treasured part of our natural heritage, our very first environmental icon, a powerful eco-symbol. It is a designation that must have sat uncomfortably with the man that first brought them to the world's attention. 'Sentiment,' Fraser Darling maintained, 'is a dangerous basis for conservation.'

Fraser Darling knew these dangers all too well. His ability to evoke human qualities in the species he was studying, though making his writings exceptionally popular, gained him little respect from his academic peers. Moreover, although he spent much of his time toiling in the remote outposts of Scotland, living amongst the wildlife that he was observing, his science was deemed intuitive at best, and not empirical enough for the mainstream ecological science. Quite simply, he had gone native. And yet it was his hands-on determination to demonstrate in a real and pragmatic way that Highland ecosystems were undernourished and needed careful tending that led to his most telling and enduring legacy. The seeds of that legacy would be sown at Tanera Mòr, in the Summer Isles. Fraser Darling went there in 1939 to prove that it was possible to croft. Official wisdom saw crofting as unable to provide more than a subsistence livelihood. But Fraser Darling laid the blame for this on two centuries of sheep farming and deer forest which had stripped the soils of their vitality. He set about renourishing the land with seaweed, industrial slag and manure.

After four years of hard work, the island farmstead blossomed. Cows thrived, sheep prospered, and the quality of the grasslands round about were restored. Corn, potatoes, swedes, cabbages, kale, carrots, cauliflower, broccoli, lettuce and onions sprouted from the supposedly barren ground. His efforts, magnificently chronicled in *Island Farm*, quickly gained him a reputation and he began to focus his attention on the wider ills that bedeviled the Highlands. At the end of his Summer Isles 'experiment', Fraser Darling was eager to extend his ecological regeneration to a bigger problem – the depopulation and economic decline in the West Highlands.

In 1947 he was commissioned by the government's Scottish Office in

Edinburgh to write a formal report on his assessment of the fertility and future of the western Highlands. He delivered it three years later – *The West Highland Survey: an essay in human ecology* made for depressing reading. The Highlands were a devastated countryside, he wrote, a 'wet desert'. It was an ecosystem dominated by bottlenecks – log jams of nutrition in which the natural cycles had stalled. They had stalled because the food chain was full of missing links. Entire species had disappeared. The loss of trees had led to the loss of woodland ants which once processed leaf litter; earthworms were absent too, impoverishing the soil further. A crumbly, fertile mould had been transformed into a dense rubbery peat which locked away its nutrition. Not only that, but once naked hills were cloaked in strong, woody heather (too thick for its own seeds to reach the earth) and riddled with the burrows of rabbits, whose populations had exploded as their natural predators were exterminated. For Fraser Darling, Scotland had become a desolate nation, a shadow of its former self, paying the price for past human want. Its sterile landscape was a direct consequence of human exploitation and mismanagement. The majestic Highlands had been systematically asset-stripped. Little wonder they were empty. What they needed, more than anything, was people.

It is said that Fraser Darling never received any sort of acknowledgement from the Scottish Office that the West Highland Survey report had arrived, let alone been read. Its message – that there could be no cure unless the misuse of the land over the previous two centuries was reversed by fewer sheep, more cattle and the regeneration of its forests – fell on deaf ears. In a political context that was becoming dominated by agricultural subsidies and a drive for hydroelectric transformation of Highland glens, it was heresy. In a scientific context in which humans were largely ignored in ecological studies, it was folly. The report was quietly shelved, its publication delayed for five years. When it did see the light of day, none of its recommendations were implemented. It was as if the report and its contents had never happened. And yet, of course, it had. The 'human ecology' that Frank Fraser Darling first explored in the highlands of Scotland soon found root in a more fertile environment in North

America, where a stronger environmental consciousness was growing. His emphasis on the totality of the relationship between man and the natural environment gained academic credibility and political momentum. The unorthodox views of a pseudo-academic 'crank' gradually shifted to the environmental mainstream and began to influence a new generation of conservationists, many of them back in Scotland.

In early 2010, when BBC television produced the landmark series *Making Scotland's Landscape*, it was infused with the ideas of Frank Fraser Darling. Most Scots believed that their Highlands were a natural wilderness. What they did not grasp was the fact it was entirely man made. Our grand industrial heritage came with a heavy environmental price: deforestation and the subsequent loss of native wildlife. In the ancient past we were stewards of the landscape, but modernity has detached us from it. *Island Years* and *Island Farm* are a remarkable portrait of a family adapting to isolation and the extremes of nature, in a land shaped by an unceasing and intimate relationship with its people.

Iain Stewart
Plymouth, 2011

PROLOGUE
Nostalgia

I WONDER MORE as I grow older how great the influence of nostalgia is on the course of our lives. How far does it make a man creative, or does it become his token of defeat? The Scottish people, to which the half of me belongs, has a traditional nostalgia: surely in no other race are found at the same time such power for successful action and such nullifying defeatism. Burns Clubs outside Scotland, and the most active ones are outside Scotland, are plain expressions of nostalgia. Elderly men who have left their country gather together to sing the old sweet songs of Border and Island, and it is doubtful if they will ever go back again to stay; they are dead to Scotland, and other countries have reaped the drive of their transplanted will.

I have suffered this sweet and bitter longing and have replied by coming back and shedding worldly comforts. I wanted in those earlier days to live by my science, working as it wished to work. For to me science and art are not far from each other; each is creative and concerned with discovery. I thought of W.H. Hudson's work which I loved so much: was it not all nostalgic writing? Was his work not the reaction to the boundless freedom he had known, a freedom lost when he was cooped in the Bayswater Road?

There was Fiona Macleod also, that strange figure who lived in several worlds, masculine and feminine, urban and Hebridean, intellectual and primitive. Much of his writing is nostalgic and it cast a spell over me as I emerged from adolescence. He says somewhere that his picture of the Gael is not a complete one, nor a true one. He has taken one facet of the complex Gaelic genius and has exaggerated it, or at least dimmed the others: his critics have it that he thought he was showing the whole man. Sometimes I had to put those books at the back of the shelves, for an essay like *The Mountain Charm* was too strong wine.

I knew an Irishman once who was farming in Buckinghamshire when I was working in that county in an agricultural advisory post. I was little more than a lad and he was a man of over forty, yet we became friends in that time because we were both like fish out of water. He was longing for the green country of County Clare and the sea mist coming in from the Atlantic, and I was dreaming of the little islands and the same rain-soaked wind from the sea. He could not go back, for he was one of those Anglo-Irish whose house had been burnt over his head and his land confiscated. It was he who introduced me to the delights of Somerville and Ross.

We both loved cattle and horses and would spend hours talking points and pedigrees among his animals, but ever and again this talk of the beasts would bring us to the land on which they fed, and soon it would be the West of Ireland or the Highlands and Islands of Scotland. The older exile was patient with the daydreaming lad, and the mud, the eternal soul-clogging mud of the Vale of Aylesbury, isolated them.

'If a man has not got where he wishes to be by the time he's forty, he is a failure altogether and he will never be getting there. Do you hear me?'

Indeed I heard him, and his saying has welled into my mind many a time in later years as a truth few learn soon enough in their lives. There was another thing he said in that soft voice of his which had yet a strange sharpness and clearness of diction. 'As you stand here, boy, in this sink of mud from which there seems no escape, remember this: if you want to reach your island farm, and you must get there while you're young or never at all, do something towards getting there every day. Never let one day pass but you save a penny or a pound or make yourself abler to live that life.'

The Irishman has passed out of my life, but perhaps we met when we needed each other most, and his message has stayed with me through the years. I have tried since to find him, but he is gone and his acres are farmed once more by a man of the Vale who can live in that mud.

There was a time in my stay in Buckinghamshire when I was in danger of not heeding the Irishman's message, but was content to dream nostalgically. I was by this time a factor of an estate and, having come from a harder country, life seemed comfortable and easy. I was sitting in my kitchen one night before a roaring fire which made the red tiles of the floor and the brass on the walls flicker with comfort and of something that was England. England! For me no supercilious and envious Caledonian contempt: I love her dearly. She is my England too. Life seemed good as I sat there in a wheelbacked armchair, tilted gingerly on its two back legs as is my way. Poised there, the tips of my slippered toes lightly touching on the hob, and dreaming into the midst of the burning wood, it was as if a voice spoke in my mind. 'You are wasting your time,' it said, 'you are twenty-four years old and the girth of your middle will soon be as great as that of your chest. Get up from your dreaming; act; move away from here.'

I had been married over two years and our child would soon be born. Surely this was no time for moving. And yet, before the baby was three months old we were in Scotland again, our two or three hundreds of capital providing the means of life while I worked for a Doctorate of Philosophy in animal genetics at the University of Edinburgh.

The doctorate came in two years' time. For me it was a happy time, enjoying to the full and romantically the Edinburgh of my fathers, working on something new with the Mountain Blackface breed of sheep, and travelling the hill districts of Scotland. I was working under a brilliant man who fired my imagination and opened for me new gates of the mind. There was a constant stream of new faces and stimulating personalities.

It was not a happy time for my wife; she saw much more than I did of that Portobello flat with its one virtue of facing the sea. She had all the irksomeness of urban life which we had never known before. The baby was a skinny and nervous creature in the early months of his life; Bobbie devoted herself to him and made him a fine child, and she never let the baby and the work he caused impinge on my life. I think in the interest of my own affairs I grew unduly selfish and got farthest away from Bobbie in that time. She could not walk the Pentlands and Moorfoots with me nor spend the weekend birdwatching in Aberlady Bay.

And yet there was the bond of the island, if a little dim. One day there came someone to call on us; she was a Shetland lady who had been a friend of Bobbie's mother. We talked long together of the islands, for the nostalgia was in her also, and she taught me much in the years before she died. Her nephew, Stephen Saxby, came from Unst to study in Edinburgh, and the island bond made us friends. I went to his home in the North Isles for one of the most wonderful months of my life, for it was May and bird time, but Bobbie was back there in the Portobello flat, half living. Each little island we explored I considered as a possible home, though it were bare and far in the sea. They were not all idle thoughts, for I learned things by thinking like that, but I felt all the time it would be in the West I should settle and not in the North.

I learned from the example of Stephen's father the value of a life of service in the islands. He is the doctor in that farthest north bit of Britain, and I saw the devotion of the people to him and his family. A doctor is a fortunate man because he can minister directly to his fellow men; a farmer and biologist is in a less good position from that point of view, but I saw in many ways that a man living in remote islands need not bury himself and be lost to the good of his fellows. An island life need be no selfish life.

I was appointed Chief Officer of the Imperial Bureau of Animal Genetics in the autumn of 1930, which meant money coming in instead of the poverty we had endured until then. We moved to a larger house in Broomieknowe which had an interesting garden and outbuildings. The stage seemed set for a pleasant spell of life, but it was not to be just then, for I suffered a sudden and terrible unhappiness in the loss of a friend, from which it took me a long time to recover. It was now the islands pulled at my heartstrings, and within a month I was walking through Mull and Iona, a very lonely man. An Iona green with spring did much for me then, and a walk through Glen More in the darkness, but my trouble needed time to be healed.

Bobbie worked for my good then as never before, and two or three friends among whom I worked helped me also. Those dear folk did what they could and I warmed in their love, but I knew it must be within myself the battle must be won. When it was over I found myself in rather an easy world in which the house at Broomieknowe was the centre. We had our dogs and I my mice, and we entertained travelling scholars a good deal. Broomieknowe was full of friendly folk who were kind to us.

Most days I walked the five miles into the Research Institute with my dogs alongside me. My room was at the top of the building, with a circular window facing west, so that the shape of the Pentlands was my constant companion. Sparrows and starlings sat on the windowsill and chattered about the life outside, and over the paddocks below me wheeled flocks of peewits, crying to me of farther fields. Springtimes were not easy to bear, though I would rise early and spend an hour or two before breakfast bird-nesting in Polton Park on the banks of the Esk. I do not think I tried or knew how at that time to understand the foibles and mannerisms of the rather artificial society in which I found myself.

Here was I, a fellow who had overcome much to be a farmer, living in the country where I belonged, sitting with white hands in a room in a town. It had all happened imperceptibly, losing sight of the goal for the sake of expediency. I began to feel the lack of discovering for myself, though trying to write a history of genetical science masked it for a time, until I realised that my history fell far short of my intentions. It was leading me deeper and deeper into the dust of the bookshelves and did not compensate for the loss of work with my hands as well as with my head.

Holiday times found me disappearing for a week or more into the Cairngorms, to Skye or into the high hills of Appin and Lorne, living hard and uncomfortably, but for the moment joyously. These sallies forth did little more than make me determined to overcome present difficulties and make the Highlands my home. Ever since childhood I had had the power of dissolving into a background of woodland and hill and of becoming at one with the creatures I found there, and now these moments were poignant. It was never difficult for me to stalk deer or to find weasels and hedgehogs whose lives I could watch intently for some short episode; and I have spent hours which were almost mystical in the bed of a woodland beck where the growth of fern and honeysuckle has met above my head, watching the passage of spiders and insects among the liverworts and cross-leaved mossy saxifrage. Tiny silent lives, but not passing unknown.

There was something wrong with my science now; it had lost the simplicity of the wondering child which I think is the approach of the greatest men of science. I did some work on animal behaviour for my own amusement but realised that if it was to be of permanent value and not just anecdotal, I must get away from the artificial atmosphere of experimentation under laboratory conditions. I began to see that if I was constructive enough in my thinking, the goal of the island and the life of the man of science need not be incompatible.

At this time I received a gift which brought the island nearer: some old friends gave me £100 to be used for the island when one should come my way. Islands do pass through the estate markets from time to time, but most of them are well-established homes and farms beyond my small means. There was one of 1400 acres which had a good house and natural harbour and carried a stock of Blackface sheep which made me open my eyes, so good were they. The island also carried a big fold of Highland and Galloway cattle. How dearly I would have liked that place at that time, but it was far beyond us, even with the estate market at rock bottom. A good island farm of 400-1500 acres off the West Highland coast was worth from £2 to £3 an acre and the stock had to be bought on the top of that. This particular island was eventually sold for less than £2 an acre, so low were prices at that time. An uninhabited and houseless island of 100-300 acres is worth about £1 an acre, and it was something of this kind we hoped might come our way. But small properties are not common in the West Highlands. Small islands belong to large estates, the owners of which are not generally disposed to part with one small portion for what is to them an inconsiderable sum. This is only reasonable.

I remember as a lad thinking I would like the little island of Inchkenneth, west of Mull. Was this because of its romantic history as the burial ground of chiefs and kings, and because Doctor Johnson was so hospitably entertained there? That island has had several owners since Sir Harold Boulton, composer of the *Skye Boat Song*, died. But when I came to know it I coveted it no longer, for it lies below the great precipices of Ardmeanach. The south wind comes tumbling down those 1700-foot cliffs, lays flat the corn and rips slates from the buildings unless they are cemented.

And then, strangely enough, there came into the market a little island not far from Inchkenneth – Little Colonsay. It was 150 acres in extent and had some sort of a house on it. Bobbie and I were about to have the first holiday together and alone for seven years, so we decided we would spend the time walking through Mull and Ulva and would look at Little Colonsay on the way.

It was a magnificent holiday: the rain fell at night and we had fine days of early June sun. We walked down to Cragaig on the south shore of Ulva to meet John McColum, the lobster fisherman, who, though now living at Cragaig, had spent most of his life in the house on Little Colonsay and was generally known as Johnny Colonsay. He was a fine man to whom I warmed immediately; his smile was slow to come, his look direct and his dignity and courtesy would have graced a king. McColum, and so near Iona: it is a rare name and I have met no other men spelling it so. John McColum said little enough to us about the island except that the landing was poor, but he happened to have with him a garrulous old man dressed in Sabbath blacks. From him we learned that the rats had put Johnny Colonsay out of the island, and a good many more things not likely to give us too rosy an idea before landing. The wind had been fresh before starting and had meant a hard pull out of the landing at Cragaig before John McColum could raise his sail. Then suddenly the boat was a stern dead thing no longer; she leapt forward, spray flying and gunwale down on the water. John McColum sat silent and unmoving in the stern, one hand on the tiller and the other holding the straining sheet. The two-and-a-half miles over to Little Colonsay, through the skerries and shallow channels that are characteristic of that stretch of coast, were all too short for us. Not only was the sailing stimulating, sea-starved as we were, but John McColum's skill was a thing to watch of itself.

The island itself was of the same tabular formation as the western side of Mull. The lower plateau immediately above the sea was boggy, and then, set above miniature cliffs, was the higher plateau of good dry grazing. It was up here we met a small herd of wild goats. The house was set to the north-east and had evidently been built with pretensions which somehow had not quite materialised. It had four large rooms with expensive-looking

Victorian mouldings round the ceilings. The door had nearly gone; at least, there was room beneath it for a sheep to enter the house. The walls had lost their paper, but in the kitchen, where Johnny Colonsay had evidently lived in bothy fashion, there were newspapers pasted on the walls. These are always readable, and this old copy of *The Oban Times* contained an account of the burning of the MacBrayne steamer in Oban harbour several years ago. Everywhere showed the presence of rats in great numbers – holes in the walls, floorboards gone; the derelict character of the place made Bobbie shudder. I found an abandoned copy of the Bible in Gaelic, and since that day I have come to look upon this battered and lonely Book as part of the tragedy of a deserted island. In each such crumbling ruin I have found a copy of the Book: I confess I have been touched in a way reason cannot justify. Here was an age-old companion of private hours of devotion, now lying desperately alone. A worn out mass of paper and printer's ink – but a loved book is more than that, and this was a Book of books.

We put up our little tent outside that night though the wind and rain would have made the house a welcome shelter: the rats were too much for us. It was a pleasant enough island we thought next day as we worked round its shore, climbing little cliffs and lying in the sun in a tiny bay of shell sand on the south side, but we were disappointed to find no seabirds nesting. I think we knew even then that the place would not be ours. I remember laughing aloud when I got back to Edinburgh and saw the agent, who asked me in what condition were the bathroom and hot water system. The only water was a tiny surface well fifty yards from the house.

Bobbie and I continued our way through Mull, ever reluctant to be working eastwards to where we should catch the boat. It was the *Lochinvar* and I found no pleasure in gazing at the highly coloured exploits of that hero painted on panels in the saloon aft. There he was on a chestnut horse, the lady pillion, galloping hard across a bog where any man with feeling for a horse's legs would have got off himself and walked.

Oban quite depressed us, though it had had power to charm us even at six o'clock in the morning when we had been starting our holiday. I felt I could not look out of the window of the train until we had passed

Crianlarich, so bought a copy of *The Listener* to read. The editorial page bore a long comment on the institution of the Leverhulme Research Fellowships, which were to be awarded to senior workers who wished to do a particular piece of work, but who were normally prevented from doing it by routine duties. I read through the announcement again and showed it to Bobbie. 'I'm going to get one of those,' I said.

'You never were blessed with modesty, Frank,' she answered with a smile that took the sting out of it, and would have dismissed the subject there and then but I said again: 'I'm serious; I tell you one of these Fellowships is going to set us free; it is the rising tide to be taken at the flood.'

I thought about it all the way home, allowing myself to look as long as I wanted into the Forest of Blackmount and at the fine cones of Stobinian and Ben More, growing surer of the scheme of research that had lain at the back of my mind for years. When I got home I put the scheme down on paper and it looked good; then I slept on it, reread, polished and extended it slightly, though paring down words wherever I could to make the short synopsis both precise and concise. Now it looked better still and I was ready to go with it to a friend in the University who might act as a referee. Bobbie was rather nervous about this impulse of mine, suddenly leaving a land of dreams and trying to become real.

'If you don't get this Fellowship and your application becomes known in high places, you'll lose your job,' she said.

This was true enough, I thought, especially as I had always shown myself to be of the non-acquiescent type in a job which had all the fetters of the Civil Service about it. I had fought and won a few battles, and was continuing to fight because I felt myself suffering an injustice. That is not a thing to be discussed here, but I had to admit to Bobbie that to let it be known I was eager to leave the job and was positively trying to get out, would be to light a match in an explosive mixture.

'But after all, Bobbie, I'm not going to fail, and I would rather take the bull by the horns anyway.'

'Well, if you do, I expect I shall be following you.'

My friend in the University, who must be nameless, settled my mind, but with more solid reasons than I had given.

'Apply now, this time,' he said in his practical incisive way; 'these Fellowships are a new thing and the selection committee have no precedents to govern them in their choice. They come to these very open terms of reference as free men. This scheme of yours is something new and I think they will react to it favourably. I will back you as far as ever I can.'

And he did. The application was sent and I put it outside my mind and got on with my job. To think more about it when I had done my best would have been a waste of energy and unfair to those for whom I worked.

I was in Cambridge six weeks later when a telegram came from Bobbie saying I had been awarded a Leverhulme Fellowship. Emotions welled up within me, emotions of relief from nervous tension not admitted, of gratitude, pleasure and anticipation.

The weather that week was all that an English summer could be, with long days of brilliant sunshine and cool leafiness. I walked along the Backs by the Cam; trees, water and fine buildings took on a dreamlike quality; then I went into the loveliest building in the world for me and attended Evensong in King's College Chapel. The great organ, the high vaulted roof and impression of space and peace affected me in the same way as when I lay as a child under the foliage on the banks of a woodland burn. I became one with that great place in the chanting of the psalm and came forth humbled. There can be few moments like that in any man's life. And that evening I remember my host filled my cup of joy by playing a long Beethoven sonata on his piano. My sensitiveness was heightened; each bar and chord cut clear into my mind as it had never done before, and I was touched with the inspiration of the master.

The months which followed held much happiness for Bobbie and me though they were not without their trials. Clearing up one life before embarking on another quite different one holds many depressing moments; ties are being broken, ties which we may be glad to break, but which hurt nevertheless when the break comes. There was also the task of preparation. Bobbie and I bought an old car and came north in a snowstorm to look for a house; we had left Broomieknowe before it was light; the Stirling road was a misery of sleet, Drumochter was thick with snow and I had difficulty in keeping the windscreen clear. Glorious, because enthusiasm was driving us forward; and then, when we came to the birch woods before Garve and later to the great pass of the Dirie Mor, the snow hardened and the sun came out to make this one of the best of all worlds, the world of freedom ahead.

We slept in the car that night well wrapped in sleeping bags and rugs, and the first thing we saw when we woke the following morning was the Brae House, Dundonnell.

'That is exactly the sort of house,' I said. 'Wouldn't it be perfect!'

It was empty. The floors were rocky and the walls terribly damp, but there it was, the house under the bruach, backed by trees of many kinds and looking across to An Teallach, the highest point in my new territory. By nightfall of that day we had arranged to rent the place, and that is how we came to live in the house from which we watched the deer and in a later time hatched our island ploys. For now I saw that this forest on the north-western seaboard would be the gateway to the islands for us. This life would be part of a training which it was obvious we must undergo before we bought an island for ourselves. I never lost sight of that, and when the island years themselves came, years of living rough and alone, there was always the feeling that it was a period of training, a moulding and hardening of character and ability. For island life is in the heart of many folk who have not considered how different it is from the one they are leading.

I have come back to a real country where the joys and discomforts of living have given zest to my mind. Now I know that if I am to interpret life in men and animals it must not be from the attic or suburban study, but at the time and from the place where my life is lived. If I write well enough to please me it is when I write out-of-doors among loved things; and as I write now, in the calm of an October sun, the sea at my feet and the collie lying beside me. The cows are grazing near, the sound of the plucked grass a comfortable undertone in my ears. Sometimes one of them will come across and lick me with her rasp of a tongue – her affection makes bearable the smart. The night watches give me no inspiration to write unless I am outside, and then I can but see and feel the beauty of the night; it is too dark for writing.

Eilean a' Chlèirich

Tuill an Chlèirich

Hidden Loch

Cauldron

East Cave

Geodha Fada

Lochan Tuath

Exchange

Àird Glas

Lochan na h-Àirigh

Lochan Fada

Hut

Lochan à Gleann

Lochan Iar

West Landing

South Cave

Àird Beag

N

0   MILE   1/2
      1/4

EILEAN A' CHLÈIRICH

PREPARATIONS

THE BRAE HOUSE of Dundonnell in the north-west corner of Ross and Cromarty is one of the finest houses in the land – from a man's point of view – and that, perhaps, is an important qualification. But for the moment accept a description flavoured by the masculine bias which is more concerned with the outside of a house than its inside.

The house nestles white and snug into the southern race of a precipitous and wooded hillside, and this is the first and only dwelling seen by the traveller new to the glen, who has come over the long, dreary pass of the Dirie Mor and the narrow, winding and atrociously surfaced road of the Feighan. Twenty miles from Garve railway station land you at Braemore with the Dirie behind. Woods and rhododendrons are before you, and the seductive view of Strath Mor, Loch Broom and Ben More Coigeach in the far distance gives the newcomer the false idea that the wilder part of his journey is over. But the signpost says fourteen miles to Dundonnell and this road is not going into the big strath at all. The traveller is on the Destitution Road, so called because it was constructed in the famine years of 1847-48 as a means of providing work and food for the stricken crofting population of the West Coast. There are twelve miles to go before the next smoke rises from a chimney.

Some people call it the Desolation Road, doubtless because they have let their impressions colour their memory. I suppose it is desolate to one who sees scenery as a picture without the detail. The high hills are in front and to the left hand – the Forest of Fannich, the double spear points of Slioch looking very near beyond Loch a' Bhraoin, and then, as you turn away somewhat surprisingly from that glen, the spiry ridges and pinnacles of An Teallach. You have left the trees and are on a high moorland scarred with black gullies showing the grim, whitening skeletons of the trees which once were part of the ancient Forest of Caledon. It is not always raining up there, but it is very often, and the road seems never-ending. Feighan House, just past the summit, is like an empty skull showing black holes where once were windows and door. Tramps find it a useful port of call for a night's rest, and they are gradually burning up the mantelpieces and any other removable woodwork. The bogwood would burn longer and better, but that would mean work to get it.

Feighan means bog, and this bog and this house have an unpleasant history if all you hear is true. Feighan House was once an inn placed on the old drove road. I was going to say the drove roads were the arteries of the Highlands, but that would be bad physiology; arteries carry newly charged red blood from the heart to the extremities of the body, but Scotland's heart has been pulsating weakly since a long while, and what has come north and westwards along the drove roads these two hundred years has been poor anaemic stuff. Let us rather call them the veins and drainage channels of the Highlands. Great herds of cattle, slowly driven by a wild crowd of men, left the country west and north of the mountain backbone and disappeared into the hungry maw of the South. Year after year the cattle walked away and later the sheep, and now the men have gone as well.

The inn of Feighan was a halt for the drovers going and coming. They drank strong spirit in a place which the law did not reach, and if some of them disappeared and were not heard of again in their own time, they may turn up yet in those black gullies where the peat is disintegrating. Such then is Feighan, and now, the house well past, the road runs alongside a flat where the deer graze in the evenings and from where a walker may see a golden eagle soaring nine days out of ten.

I love this road myself, not for its own sake but because it is the road to home and the wild country it pierces is the bulwark against what is to me the less pleasant world of the east and south. Many, many are the times I have come tired over this stretch and in the half-light of evening, not grudging the badness of the road, yet with relief and joy crossing Feighan Bridge from where the road drops steeply under the great rampart of the Black Rock and enters the glen.

Here are the birch woods again, and after a few precipitous twists of the road the glen opens before the traveller now hungering for something kind. An Teallach appears in full grandeur above the foreground of trees, then the wooded sweep of the strath, and when the hills rise again on the

northern side in slopes of great beauty there is the little white house less than a mile away, a cheerful man-made thing in a big landscape – just a little West Highland house and nothing more. When I first came into the glen and saw the house where we should live, I remember saying to myself it would be a bad day when I should drive out of the glen to leave it. And now it seems that day will never be, because we have left the glen seawards to settle on the island of Tanera Mòr.

As you leave the road which goes on a mile or two more to the head of Little Loch Broom, and climb towards the Brae House, you will see that it is set in no garden but is almost part of the hillside. There is one door and five windows which are all too small when you are inside for long. A Highland house which is not a mansion does not usually have more than one door, for though two doors may have social advantages when you leave the level of simple folk and begin to climb in the world, they create draughts of wind so the house is never warm. And you never yet met

Highland folk who liked a cold house.

The beasts of the hill come about us; the roe deer very often, summer and winter; red deer in the very bad weather of winter, though more usually in spring when the grass is shooting well but the nights yet cold; wild cats in autumn and winter, and especially if we leave open the henhouse door at night; rabbits always; the wood mice or long-tailed field mice come inside in waves, and charming as I find them, they have a wretched habit of emptying jars of jam and marmalade in the store press; house mice are rare and not encouraged; weasels are never far away, and we have had the pleasure of one living under the house. Our red squirrels are delightfully tame and are to be seen at all times of the year.

Bird life is varied and pleasant; the eagle and the buzzard are often overhead, and peregrine falcon and sparrowhawk are not uncommon. Chaffinches take the place of sparrows about the door and are much to be preferred. Goosanders and mergansers come up the glen on their way to the freshwater lochs where they breed. There are both tawny and barn owls in the glen, and in wintertime you may find a tree gay with a flock of four kinds of tits, treecreepers and goldcrests.

The rock behind us gets all the sun and no north wind. There is hardly a month in the year when a primrose cannot be found somewhere in the sheltered nueuks, and once in the midst of a hard winter, when all else seemed frozen, I found a plant of the delicate and feathery herb Robert in flower.

So much for the man's view of the place. Marian Fraser Darling, usually known as Bobbie and who as my wife is the mistress of the Brae House, would tell you another side of the picture. The burn is forty yards away and dries out sometimes in summer. Not only must water be carried into the house but it has to be thrown out as well! And once inside, you will see that the walls are so permeated with damp that wallpaper will not retain its original colour for more than a week or two, and only with periodic help will it stick to the wall at all. The floorboards are warped and lie open, and when we first went there it took us nearly two years to get topside of the fleas. The boarded ceiling flakes whitewash into your soup if someone should tread incautiously overhead. Our fireplace is a natural gem, just an open hearth with two stone hobs, so impossible to keep clean that we never try – so why grumble, says the masculine element.

Despite these interior shortcomings, it is a house where people are happy. It is Alasdair's background, and the child dearly loves the place to come back to after a spell among the islands or at school. This house has seen our

hopes grow, watched our work being done and our island ploys hatched. Here have come new faces, for it is known we keep open house when at home, and some of these acquaintances have ripened into friendship after hours of good talk which have stretched into the early mornings.

The one fault of the Brae House is that you cannot see the sea. It is necessary to climb a hundred feet through the bracken and up the cliff by the waterfall, and then a long view stretches away north-westwards. Flat parks and woods of the strath, and then the wrinkled saltings at the head of the Loch; green strips here and there by the sea's edge, and little white dots which are the houses of the crofts; and behind these on either side of the long sea loch the hills rise steeply, getting browner and more bare until the summits seem to be just naked faces of the red Torridonian sandstone.

The steep hills make Little Loch Broom a dangerous place for a boat when the winds blow, but from this perch behind the Brae House the sea looks calm enough until you put a telescope on it. If the day is clear you can see the Outer Hebrides and pick out the shapes of the hills in the Forest of Harris. And from farther up the hill, where the view is unhindered, the crofts near Stornoway, over forty miles distant, are visible through the glass. There is an island between there and Little Loch Broom, and its long shape cuts off part of the Hebridean view. It is about eighteen miles from this rock behind our house, and now, after our years of island life, I do not care to look at it through my glass, for if I see the surf beating up in white puffs, distorted by mirage, I am reminded of anxious days of wishing to get there and knowing the swell would not allow; and if the sea is flat calm and the sun shining, I wish I was going anyway.

The island is Eilean a' Chlèirich, a rugged little half-square mile of varied country, lying remote and uninhabited by man. It seemed heaven on earth to us when we first landed there, and each year when we went for odd days we would say – if only we could live there. The quietness, the numbers of birds and the beauty of the little freshwater lochans hidden away from the wild ocean, all pulled at our heartstrings. Was it the job of work or our own desires which drew us there to live in 1936? Call it fifty-fifty and let us not give way to introspection. The scheme of work on the social behaviour of birds looked quite good on paper, and as we had at that moment no income from research fellowships we had only ourselves to satisfy.

We were satisfied and we began to plan.

Bobbie is an excellent quartermaster; I conceive the ideas and rough out the ways and means, and she fills them in to the minutest detail. Then we go through the lists together and think of the thousand and one things which might happen but which we hope never will. When we embark on these ploys we certainly do not seek adventure, for to our minds adventure often means incompetence somewhere or carelessness at some earlier time. Living on uninhabited islands is no lark but a responsible task, especially so when you add to the possibilities of trouble by taking a child. Alasdair spent his eighth and ninth birthdays on Eilean a' Chlèirich, and since then has been on two other island expeditions. If I describe this first move to isolation in some detail it is because our growing-pains may have a value for someone else, and there is always a certain interest in seeing how things get done on an empty purse.

A man should never wait until he sees money running along in front of him so that he may follow. It is man that leads and money follows. I would say to Bobbie, if the work is worthwhile it will gather its own support, and if it isn't we shall go down the nick, and good riddance. But before the summer was out we had a fellowship to live on and research funds to supply us with the instruments necessary for measuring weather in relation to the behaviour of the birds.

First of all, what were we going to live in? As we were going to Eilean a' Chlèirich early in April, which is still wintertime in the West Highlands, it would be good to have a rigid structure. This idea was dropped because we had not money enough for a hut, and what was equally important, it was unlikely that a hut could be got over and landed so early in the year. We decided on a waterproofed bell tent with a collection of small tents, which had been used as bases for my work in the deer forest, for stores. It did not take us many weeks to grow wiser to this extent – if you are going to spend several months on an island where there is no covered shelter, it is necessary to have as good a tent for stores as for your own living. Two or three small tents are not enough, for canvas flaps and tends to loosen in a wind unless it is raining as well, and then it seems to find the corner of a packing case to chafe against. The canvas wears thin and admits the rain, and you find yourself in all kinds of trouble.

A bell tent is a very well-designed piece of work. The whole strain is in a downward direction on the pole, and in windy weather the tent has a compensating, self-strengthening action. At least this is the theory. It works in practice until you get winds of force ten on the Beaufort scale. We modified our bell tents on the next expedition by fitting intermediate guys all round and four long guy ropes of heavier type to the apex. These had a line steadying effect, and for future trips they will always be fitted. Its faults are those common to any shelter made of canvas and rope, and in long stretches of rainy weather the wish for a window becomes acute.

Then sleeping arrangements: lying on the ground is fine for a week or two when you are moving on each day. But for a more or less permanent camp in all weathers, warmth and comfort at night go a long way towards successful work during the day. Sometimes the weather causes you to lie up for a day or two, and then the psychological factor cannot be ignored. Discomfort added to the closeness of living and the makeshift character of many camp arrangements tend to shortness of temper.

We bought ourselves Hounsfield beds made of light tubular steel and strong canvas. They bend and give to the stresses of the body and are not as flimsy as they look. We put thin kapok mattresses on these beds and each of us had an eiderdown sleeping bag. We have no cause to regret our choice, for this equipment is still standard for our island expeditions, and as far as the time spent in bed is concerned, we have never had a cold or physically uncomfortable night.

Bobbie made lists of rugs, deckchairs, books to take, pens and paper, cutlery, crockery, cloths and cooking utensils; everything to be packed in boxes which would be useful as seats and cupboards on the island. We also wrote on all the boxes with a blue pencil a complete list of what was inside them. Even with all this care it was a fortnight before we could find the Primus prickers! A large order was sent to one of the Glasgow stores for groceries to be dropped by the *Clydesdale* at Scoraig. These were sent in tea chests, and we felt at fault for not having asked for the groceries to be packed in smaller boxes. As it was, we had difficulty in landing the heavy tea chests on Eilean a' Chlèirich.

Cooking can make or mar camp life. Fires are all right for boiling water or frying, but we had to think of good sound meals and baking bread over a long period. We took a Hestia oven, two Primus stoves and a Valor heating stove. Yeast came from the Postal Yeast Company of Hull with the launch which was supposed to visit us fortnightly. We have read and been told of yeast being maintained as a culture in lonely places where fresh yeast cannot be got, but we have met no one yet who can tell us how they themselves have maintained a clean and satisfactory culture in the West Highlands. Our own efforts have not been successful, and the probable reason is that we have no means of keeping the yeast culture at a constant temperature. The yeast from Hull keeps for a fortnight without deterioration. Dried yeast tablets have never worked with us, and the bread made with them has been like lead. It was something of a problem, then, in 1938, to think how we could make bread on North Rona* during six months of complete isolation. The Postal Yeast Company kindly helped us out by supplying tinned flaked yeast made by the Distillers' Company. This handy stuff is packed in half-pound airtight tins and keeps for at least eight months.

We could have carried a wish for simplicity to the point of building a stone oven to be heated by driftwood and peat. But the peat should have been cut the previous year and the oven would need to be built. I have seen attempts at these things from time to time, and think them as well left in the realm of storybooks. A good outdoor oven which will be economical of fuel and will not burn food on one side and chill it on the other needs careful engineering and a good time to build.

The problem of fresh food is linked with that of cooking, especially when you have to think of a child. We decided to take our goats and hens and let them take pot luck of the place. Islands are usually better grazing grounds for animals than the adjacent mainland. The reason for this, off the West Coast of Scotland, is that the small islands have less rainfall than the mainland and the ground is well manured by the birds which draw their food, rich in lime and phosphorus, from the sea. Also, being well out in the sea, temperature is more even than on the mainland and the grass comes earlier.

Green stuff was impossible to get. We could not make a garden in a few months, there are not enough nettles on the island for a boiling, and Bobbie will not face up to very much in the way of seaweed. Alasdair and I used to chew dulse and enjoy it, and there was something pleasant about going down the rocks to the world uncovered by the low spring

* North Rona is called Rònaigh Tuath in Gaelic.

tides where the dulse grows, iridescent as the wings of a tropical butterfly. We did sow lettuce and mustard and cress in a box, but the hens found it before it was ready. A case of apples and oranges was included with the stores, and Alasdair and I took a little chickweed and sheep's sorrel now and again. The crowberries ripened at the end of June and were plentiful for a month and more. We would pick a handful, crush them in the mouth for the sweet juice that was in them, and spit out the flinty seeds before their bitterness reached our taste.

Sea fish is a great luxury to us, though we live near the sea at Dundonnell. The fish come into the Loch late in the year and sometimes not at all, and there are not the men and boats to go far out in the Minch. We are in the position, then, of seeing herrings sporadically hawked on the West Coast from Dingwall on the East. Eilean a' Chlèirich is well out, and the tangle grows thick round the island to form good cover for the lythe or pollack and the saithe when they come. We took our long bamboo rod, hanks of line and gut and a varied lot of white flies, spoons, rubber eels and plain hooks.

The question of contact with the mainland in case of emergency exercised us for a long time. We must have a boat of sorts, if only to fish from, and in which to poke about the inlets of the island coastline. A little nine- or eleven-foot dinghy would not be a big enough craft to cross to Scoraig or Achiltibuie in safety, yet anything larger than that could not be got out of the water at the island, for the landings are bad and there are no anchorages. We decided on a rubber or canvas kayak. These craft may look frail but they are easy to handle in the water, and because of their low centre of gravity and absence of keel resistance they ride the sea with a high degree of safety.

We bought this boat, the bell tent and several other oddments from Messrs Thomas Black and Sons of Greenock, and we shall not forget the delightful afternoon they gave us looking over the factory where, in an earlier day, sails were made for the Clyde clippers. Indeed, sails are still made there and a reek of wood tar and rope is about the place. Colza oil lamps hang obsolescent in the windows, and dusty binnacles look as if they were forgotten. You could sense the continuance of hereditary craftsmanship as soon as you got inside the door. Each expedition since then has been helped by Messrs Black, and when we went to North Rona in 1938 they went so far as to accept the onerous duty of seeing a large part of our gear and stores aboard the cruiser. In the ordinary way, this is a task which every expedition should do for itself.

There was also the formal matter of getting permission to squat on Chlèirich for six months. The proprietor had already given me his good will, and when I asked the grazing tenant, Donald Fraser, I made a lasting friendship, for his desire was as keen as my own to keep the island as a sanctuary for the birds that live there. When I went round to see him that day he was rebuilding his house and was limited to one room which itself was stripped to the stone of the walls. He was busy and I had much farther to go myself, but we found the talk too good. Donnie and I sat before the peats for a couple of hours and his mother plied us with cups of tea.

It is one of the tragedies of this remote North West that the fishing has declined along with other economic and social conditions of the crofting areas. We are short of safe harbours, of boats and of men to make up crews. At that time, the spring of 1936, there was only one boat on this lochside with an inboard engine – a launch of twenty feet long which was probably never built for work off this awkward coast. This was owned by our friend Scoraig, who keeps the store in the small isolated community of that name. I walked down the track on the north shore of the Loch and found Scoraig behind the counter of his shop.

Here in this little whitewashed building is none of your chromium-plated shop fittings and aids to selling. This is a man's shop. You can buy butter and sugar there, and crockery and stuffs, buckets and girdles and rope and tackle. There are shelves and benches of bare deal, hooks from the rafters for stuff that will hang, and the stone walls and the window are hygienically festooned with cobwebs to catch the flies. It is such a shop as a man lingers in unashamed to discuss the affairs of the world.

Scoraig listened patiently to the scheme, and with a grave face. He never raised an eyebrow in surprise, and naturally he would not be telling me outright that he thought it madness. He merely commented on the earliness in the season to be landing on Chlèirich, and indeed there would be no eggs yet. That was so, admittedly, but in extenuation I said there was as much to watch in bird life before the eggs appeared as afterwards.

'Ay, ay,' was all he would say to that.

Money is an awkward subject to discuss between gentlemen, more especially when the gentlemen are Highland. Both Scoraig and I knew what would be a fair rate for the ferrying, but good taste forbade our stating the sum baldly thus early in the conversation. We never haggle here so much as politely shuffle round a point, so great is the distaste for the mention of money. We talked for an hour about the sea, the island and the crofts, and as we were walking out of the shop the awkward words stumbled from our lips. We were in complete agreement, and that was a big fence over.

The packing for our shieling summer was as difficult as a total removal, for we had to pick and choose and eliminate drastically. There is always most trouble with those Last-Minute-Things. We had to get the bell tent to the island, put it up and fill it with things not needed at home, such as my scientific instruments, bins of flour and meal, and some of the stores. March was a lovely month on our coast, but I was too busy with my work on the deer to leave for the island at that time. We feared for what April might bring, and sure enough the north-west weather came with the new month and put a great swell on the sea. It was difficult to be knowing what Scoraig was thinking of the weather each day, because there is no such thing as telephone or telegraph down the lochside and there is no road along the north shore beyond Badrallach. I would go down the strath each morning to a place half a mile beyond the boathouse on the Loch and put my glass on the stone slip which is Scoraig pier eight miles away. Sometimes figures moved at the shore, and sometimes mirage and rain distorted the field and I could see nothing.

Wednesday, 8th April, was a morning of mist, rain and north-west wind. The Loch did not look good, but Scoraig and young Iain from Rhirevoch were at the boathouse with the launch at half-past eight. It rained hard while we loaded the launch, but I was well pleased with Bobbie's packing of the stuff and felt there was no need to bother. Then Scoraig knelt before the engine and the ritual of starting began. I am one of those people who exert a bad influence over any engine with which I come in contact. Animals I can charm, but to a machine my name is Jonah. I have sat on the verges of many a roadside and rolled in a boat on half the lochs in Scotland with engines which 'have never been like this before'.

'She wasn't coming too well at all,' said Scoraig.

I grunted.

He turned and turned at a handle, the shape of which appeared to me to violate every law of mechanics and levers. Starting handles are usually like that, hopelessly inadequate in size, shape and grip. I still have a scar on my chin from one of them which hit me ten years ago, and I hesitated about helping now. But Scoraig is elderly and he crouched lower in the boat to rest and get his wind back. I offered to take a turn, but the handle came out and hit me a sound crack under the jaw again. It was a matter of knack evidently, and I left it to Scoraig after that. Iain sat in the stern and grinned all over his face.

Why engines do start, when previously they have refused to, is a mystery to me; this one did in its own good time, and the launch made a brave sweep and a white wake out into the middle of the Loch. The rain stopped and Eilean a' Chlèirich shimmered in the sunlight and shower. This was fine; something getting done at last. But the engine, 'she was but firing on the one cylinder'. We put in to the Badluchrach shore, and John Macleod came down from the crofts. He tested the plugs by pressing his thumb down on top of them while the engine was running. I was silent in admiration of this Spartan method. Then he brought out the inevitable bit of string and tied wires here and there. We got under way at half-past twelve, firing on two cylinders, which happily was the total number.

The swell was more evident when we came to the mouth of the Loch and it was considerable by the time we were out past Cailleach Head. We looked forward and backward until Eilean a' Chlèirich looked nearer than the mainland. Then we looked back no more.

The sky became leaden, and when we turned in to the east bay of the island, Acairseid Eilean a' Chlèirich, the swell was beating up white on the rocky coastline. The cliffs are sheer below Àird Glas and there are spiry stacks of red rock standing off from the land. They looked threatening today and the thud of the swell echoed between the stark walls of the bay. On the northern side there is a hole running into the cliff, and with this heave on the sea, and in this state of the tide, the hole filled with air as the swell dropped. Then the air was greatly compressed as the sea rose, so that a cloud of spray was shot out each time with a tortured scream of sound. An otter ran down the tiny shingle beach into the sea. Who were these people coming into his world at this season of the year? Beds of tangle appeared and disappeared in the water in an oily, secret way in the rise and fall of the swell. It seemed alive, and once I saw a long tail come out of the water and return, slimy and silent. A catfish. The swell was as much as ten feet; far too much to think of landing.

We had trouble starting the engine again, and the quarter of an hour lying about on the swell did not make me feel better. Forward motion in a small boat in a rough sea is a fine thing to experience, but lolling about from side to side in a deep swell is the finish of many a good man's equanimity. We came round the south shore of the island and tried the west landing, but the swell was just as bad there. To the north-west high waves were breaking over a point of rock, and it is only when you are at sea level in a small boat that you can judge the height of waves at their true worth. Scarts and cormorants flew over us in clouds, ruffled at our intrusion, and settled on the rocks sloping up from the sea. In the meantime our engine had stopped. The next half-hour of swell and stench of spent oil broke down the reserve I had maintained until now.

We tried the south landing by the cave, just for the sake of trying, and we were becoming hopeful when a big wave nearly put us up the beach. We pushed off as hard as we could and made for home – after another quarter of an hour's prostration before the engine. Scoraig was as patient as ever. What was time to him? Iain grinned widely, as he always did. It was a miserable task unloading the boat at Scoraig's pier, and as I came home to Dundonnell I wondered if we should ever go to Eilean a' Chlèirich. Good days were few now, and before we could go ourselves this first load must be landed.

Saturday, 11th April, came in sunny and fine, and I thought it a good day to walk down to Scoraig and arrange for another try to the island on the Monday. But the Loch looked so calm and inviting that I went along the south side as far as Badluchrach in our old car. John Maclean ferried me over a dead-calm sea to the north shore. Scoraig was filling bags with seed oats when I walked up his pier at nine o'clock. Yes, he was thinking to be trying it in the morning time but now he was thinking not. Would I like to try? I said yes, so we launched the boat, loaded up, fiddled about and had a cup of tea. At five minutes to eleven we were in the boat and starting away. Mistress Scoraig came running down to the shore and called in Gaelic. Scoraig's face became a little longer as he turned to me.

'A party was saying we shouldn't be going today.'

'Well, it is your boat,' was all I could say.

'Och, och,' said Scoraig, 'we will be getting out of the Loch and seeing what Cailleach is like.'

He shouted back to the Mistress, and it was the long face was on herself now; then we were soon out of the Loch and rounding the point. There was a fine breeze by now and the sun shone to make the sea a deep blue. The spell I had exercised on the engine earlier in the week had passed, for the launch went forward without a misfire. We sat back to enjoy the sea. We watched the guillemots skimming the sea and the dinghy we were towing, which pulled at the painter like a young horse on a halter. We were under the island in little more than an hour, making for the west landing. The anchor was dropped two hundred yards from shore and we began lifting cases from the launch into the dinghy. Three trips should empty her. The swell was bad enough as we drew in, and the little boat bumped badly on the rocks.

It was good to have my feet on the island again. While Scoraig and Iain went back to the launch for more gear, I carried loads over the boulders and up towards the ruins of the old shieling. The sea had begun to whip up white; I knew Scoraig would be anxious to get back as soon as he could, and as I was not staying on the island this time, I had no wish to linger after the warning we had been given.

It is not always easy to put up a tent of any size in the West Highlands. You may find a flat place, but will it be dry enough? If there is a flat and dry place, will it be sheltered, and is there depth enough to take the pegs? I was thinking of such things as I made my way to the place of the old shieling, which would be the most likely to provide a site.

But my eyes were here, there and everywhere, not wishing to miss anything of the island's life. A flock of purple sandpipers scurried over the barnacle-covered rocks at the sea's edge, and when I came in sight of the ruins twelve greylag geese rose from a patch of green grass. Eight more were swimming on Lochan na h'Airidh. A snipe flew out of the rushes and rock pipits undulated in flight round about me. The sun was brilliant, making the lochan a deep blue. The goat's-beard lichen clung to the rocks, a dull pastel green, and the grass was a dull parched green as well. But the patches of crowberry were a darker and livelier green, and as a background for all of them the rocks showed a bright red in the sunlight. I wanted to drop the gear and look at everything, but beyond the lochan I could see the blue expanse of the northern ocean flecked more thickly with white wave crests. And there was work to do.

I chose a position on a little knollie that was flat and dry, from which we could see the lochan and the sea. It was not as sheltered as I should have liked, but there was nowhere else as good and dry. Iain helped me put up the tent. We left the guys fairly slack because of probable rain before we came for good. Then we ran back to the shore, where Scoraig was having to hold the dinghy off the rocks and having to take her farther and farther out on the receding tide. Had he not done this, she would have been lying among the big boulders and we could not have got her afloat until the next tide came in. He was wondering what on earth Iain and I had been doing all this time, though we had worked as fast as hands could.

The north wind was strong, but not too strong to prevent us having the sail to help the engine. We were going at a good rate, and we should have covered the eight miles from Eilean a' Chlèirich to Scoraig in under the hour had not the tow rope of the dinghy broken. Running before the wind was fine, but turning back to catch the dinghy and make her fast was not so good. The engine took a quarter of an hour to start, and I was thankful, if the boat had to pitch about, that I could get the wind in my face.

When we got under way a kittiwake followed us, coming within two or three feet of our heads. How easy the flight of those grey wings! How white and round was her head and how wise-looking her black eyes! Scoraig watched her for a long time and turned to me.

'Man, is she no bonny?'

Then he asked me how old I thought the bogwood was. In an unguarded moment I answered as truthfully: about eight or ten thousand years. A look of doubt and some sorrow crossed Scoraig's grave face. I knew I had uttered heresy by indirectly questioning the time scale of the Old Testament – I was on the edge of dangerous ground.

Strings of guillemots and razorbills passed us, flying with swift wing strokes close to the water. Sometimes a puffin flapped by in his own clownish way to make us smile. Scoraig and Iain put me off on the Badluchrach shore, and I was back home at Dundonnell in time for tea.

THE JOURNEY

From monday morning, 13th April, we had to hold ourselves ready to start for Eilean a' Chlèirich. We were dependent on the state of the sea and what Scoraig thought of it. We would be up fairly early each morning to run up the brae behind the house and throw the glass over the Loch. Was it calm? Was there a sharp line across the mouth of the Loch, which meant that the sea was much rougher outside in the open Minch? Was the surf breaking in a white on the shores of Eilean a' Chlèirich?

Monday and Tuesday were no good at all, so we let the hens loose and did not pack the Last-Minute-Things. Wednesday seemed good and I went down to the boathouse. Soon the wind got up and it rained hard. I came home and let the hens out once more. By this time the food problem was growing troublesome at home, for you cannot be in a state of indecision about moving from a place for three or four days without your resourcefulness being taxed. We are ten miles from a shop at Dundonnell and only dry goods can be bought there.

Thursday morning was good at half-past six, as spring mornings often are, but at nine clouds were gathering. Scoraig was to be seen coming up the Loch at ten o'clock. We had enough small baskets of oddments which had to go out of the house with us, but these things, apparently, were of little importance compared with the stuff Alasdair suddenly decided he must take with him. There was Willum, the cloth-stuffed squirrel, a tiny Cairn terrier and a spaniel in a model dog basket, several varieties of small boats and a broken, antique camera which was a treasure retrieved from a lumber room during his recent visit to Edinburgh. These things had to be stowed with the utmost care in the car and in the boat, for be it known that stuffed squirrels breathe the same air as you and I do and their emotions are similar to ours in that they must not be crushed, turned sideways or upside down. But the car did get us and our gear to the boathouse eventually.

Scoraig had a load to land at Badrallach. We saw him put in there, but mist and sleet showers soon hid the other side of the Loch. The north-west wind was increasing. It was our good friend Hector Morrison who suggested we should go down to Scoraig anyway, and if it was good weather we could go straight away from there on the next day without the delay of the boat's journey up and down the Loch. Scoraig thought it was a good idea also, when he came across from Badrallach, and away we went in the rain and sleet. This shower did not pass as the others did, and the wind freshened again. It was magnificent going, nose into the rough sea, but that day we were not out for the blow. The goats were wet through in the bow of the boat, and the spray drenched us all sitting abaft the engine. Bobbie looked at me and raised an eyebrow. Yes, we were both thinking of the drying out of bedding and so on when we got ashore. But we had no wish to spoil the fine sense of well-being of the moment. Alasdair was enjoying it too, and he cracked jokes with his new friend Iain.

When we came to within a mile of Scoraig the sun came out and the wind slackened; and in the way of this country our clothes were blown dry by the time we drew up under the concrete pier. Scoraig suggested we should put our animals in his warehouse-cum-barn; and for this we were glad because it was obvious there were more stiff showers to come from the north-west. The goats munched some oat straw and the hens were put into a large packing case, for the building was not bird-tight. The canary, which was now singing very loudly, was hung high in the rafters because of the rats.

Scoraig and its headland seem very much out to sea after Dundonnell, where the hills are close about and the beautiful peaks of An Teallach are our southern horizon. Bobbie and I walked along the short turf by the shore and went to look over an empty croft. Here in the open fields we heard the skylark for the first time that year, and the sound was good. We cannot keep our larks throughout the year; they come in April to the fields of the crofting townships on the coast and by September they are away again. Thrushes were perching on the more prominent rocks, lacking trees for a stance, and singing of a new spring. Life presses upwards against the weather, as it were, at this time of year. But spring comes late to this north-west country, and undue haste on the part of living things in their efforts to reproduce means tragedy. The year before, I had seen the frog spawn killed and thousands of mother frogs as well by the frost. Our immigrant birds, therefore, must learn a patience against which their bodies rebel.

I rose early the following morning to look at the sea. It was calm and the sun shone, and yet I could tell the sea was not settled. An occasional burst of surf showed white on Eilean a' Chlèirich. Scoraig rubbed his chin and thought he would wait and see 'what like was the day'. So I milked one of the goats and put them out to graze for the morning; they, philosophical creatures, concerned themselves with filling their bellies. Scoraig decided to go at half-past twelve. We reloaded the launch and got under way, goats, hens, canary, bedding, child and all.

We were barely out of the Loch before the wind increased. Before we were off Cailleach Head the weather was a thoroughgoing squall. Rain, hail and sleet beat down on us under the force of the wind and we were drenched with spray from the bows. The little launch would rise over the crest of a wave and come down with a terrific slap into the trough. She was not a heavy craft, and the force with which she struck the water each time made the water spurt up through the seams. One or other of us was baling all the time. One goat lay down on the boards; the other stood all the time and shivered as the spray broke over her. The hens sat huddled together and did not express their emotions. I was most sorry for the canary, for although we had put him where he would get least of the weather, some of it was reaching him now and he and his cage were wet with sea water. He crouched over his seed trough, his little wings drooping low. Bobbie did not smile at me now; yesterday was a joke coming down the Loch, but this was not funny.

I began to feel my responsibility heavy upon me. There were those who thought I was wrong to take a wife and child to an uninhabited island at this time of year, and to live in a tent at that. Were they right and I wrong? I looked at these two and these animals under my care, and all looked unhappy. I asked Scoraig to turn back if he could and to try later. Scoraig said he was not wishing to turn the boat just now and would rather keep her nose into it. Obviously he was right and we kept going for the shelter of Bottle Island. The slap in the trough of each wave was monotonous and we dared not go fast.

I fell to wondering what would happen if the engine failed. At that moment it coughed and spluttered and I jumped forward to the carburettor lever. It was not my engine, but I was more nimble than Scoraig and I was frightened at the idea of it stopping. Then, looking forward, I saw that the screw cap was off the paraffin tank in the bows. I climbed over the gear to look for the missing cap. Happily it was down on the boards and had not been left on the small decked bow, otherwise it would have fallen off into the sea long before now. Scoraig was at once surprised and relieved. So were we.

We were now lying under Bottle Island, and Scoraig asked me if I would rather wait a while before striking across to Eilean a' Chlèirich. I wondered. If we did wait I should be soon no man at all lying around on this dreadful swell, and I felt there was a lot of work ahead of us. The worst was over, so I asked him to go ahead for the south cave, for it was obvious that neither the east nor the west landing would let us in today. Since we have lived on the island and I have known this stretch of water better, I have seen how with a north or north-west wind, the sea bores through between Bottle

Island and Eilean a' Chlèirich. From the summit cairn you can see a great semicircular series of deep waves riding through the two-mile strait. The launch had now to cross these. We did not ship nearly so much water from the long deep waves as when we were heading up from Scoraig. Each wave as it came across us seemed to climb up the gunwale, but they never came nearer than two inches of it, for I was watching most carefully. This to me is one of the mysteries of boats.

We were soon under the south-east point of Eilean a' Chlèirich, and Bobbie and I will not easily forget the relief of being on a comparatively calm sea. Back where we had come were the white-capped waves, and here, close under the land, there was no wind at all. And when we anchored off the south cave and stopped the engine, the silence was sheer luxury.

'I don't care if we live here for ever now,' said Bobbie.

Scoraig thought he, Iain and I should go first to try the landing before the Mistress. So we loaded the dinghy not too heavily and pulled over. I jumped into the surf and held the stern of the boat while Scoraig and Iain got out the stuff. I carried the gear over the clean rounded boulders of Moll na h'Uamh to the cave while the dinghy went back for Bobbie and Alasdair. When they came I lifted each of them through the surf.

The goats looked expectantly over the gunwale of the boat to the island and they seemed as keen as we were to be ashore. The sun came out to make the surf sparkle as it crashed on those round boulders. This little pocket of the coast was quite out of the wind and we felt actually warm. We took the goats to the flourish of grass above the cave, where they began grazing immediately. Here on the islands, and on the south side particularly, the grass is earlier than on the mainland, and this green bite was a treat for the animals. The canary, being a thoroughly hardy bird, was put down in the sun to dry. He preened his feathers and within ten minutes was singing in that great voice of his which experts tell us is much too loud for a canary.

There is but one thing to do for people of our country after this kind of experience – to make a cup of tea. I climbed over the big ridge to the nearest lochan for water while Scoraig and Iain got a fire going with heather shaws and driftwood. Bobbie found food from among the Last-Minute-Things and it smelt good. Alasdair began exploring as soon as he had settled all his treasures into the cave.

Scoraig, refreshed and rested, looked over a much calmer sea to Little Loch Broom. It was four o'clock and time for him to be moving. He gave us a warm farewell and we could see he had misgivings about leaving us alone on this 'wild island'. He had called it that from time to time, but today he had climbed to the ridge while the kettle was boiling and had looked down over the maze of little hills and lochans.

'Man,' he had said, 'I like the feel of this place. I'm thinking I could have lived here had I been younger.'

Now he shook hands solemnly and I pushed the dinghy through the surf. We watched him kneel at the engine, looking meanwhile for the tell-tale puff from the exhaust which would show it had started. There it was now, and Iain was standing in the bows hauling in the anchor. They went away with a waving of hats, and we waved handkerchiefs in return from the sea's edge till we could see them clearly no more.

'This, you might say, is where we start work.'

As we looked at each other we realised suddenly and forcibly what there was to be done by dark. Our first load consisted of the hens, the white goat which had kidded earlier and was agile, and a basket of ready-to-eat food. This was the beginning of a back-breaking job, for the climb from the cave to the ridge is two hundred and fifty feet and very sharp. From the ridge we passed down a rough and stony way to the strip between Lochan Iar and the sea. There was the sea pool to walk round, and over two little ridges until we came to the old shieling and the tent by Lochan na h'Airidh.

The one-time inhabitant of Eilean a' Chlèirich was an outlaw, put out here by the people of the mainland under the old clan law for sheep stealing. It has always struck me as a most sensible thing to have done with that man. Here he had to work out his own salvation, and from all accounts he became a reasonable member of society. He brought a wife here and had children. They grew up, married and had children also, and as far as I can find out, it was this third generation which left the island about eighty years ago. The family was now accepted by the crofting community of Lochbroom and was under no stigma. Descendants of the Eilean a' Chlèirich family still live in the parish of Lochbroom, and one of them came over with Scoraig and the mails one day during our first summer. It was his first visit to the island of his forefathers.

Well, on this stormy April day of our landing, when we had carried two or three loads from the south cave to the camp, we were able to imagine vividly the feelings of the outlaw when he was planted on Eilean a' Chlèirich. Perhaps he had carried things over this ridge to the place where he had built the little house in drystone, but I am certain the folk would not have set him down with as much gear as we had. From the ridge to the foot of Lochan Iar you can see that boulders have been rolled out of the way and that hollow places have been built up with stones to make a very rough track down the steep brae-face. Now, through disuse over a period of nearly a century, the path is difficult to see under its covering of grass and crowberry, but it is the way you would take instinctively to cross the ridge. All the gear from the south cave came down the outlaw's path on our backs. We made four journeys the first night, and it took us four days more to get everything over to the tent.

Morag the little brown goat was very heavy in kid. It would have been cruel to walk her that mile to the tent, so I made her comfortable by the cave where she would have most shelter. It was dark before ten o'clock, by which time we had put things in temporary order at the camp and I went over to the cave again to see that Morag was all right. She had started to kid. I waited with her a while until the white, drop-eared male kid was born and getting to its feet. Morag, it seemed to me, had a better place for the night than we had ourselves. I left her lying down and content, and as I came over the ridge in the darkness I was cheered by the triangular shape of light which was the tent. Bobbie's shadow moved to and fro as she busied herself making comfort for all of us.

We slept solidly because we were dog-tired, and when I woke at seven o'clock it was to think immediately of the little brown goat. I would get up and slip over to her before breakfast, but I fell asleep again until half-past eight, when Alasdair was awake and anxious to be up and doing. What with one thing and another it was nearly ten o'clock before I reached Morag. She was lying chewing her cud in her own quiet, untroubled way exactly where I had left her, but there was no sign of the kid until I looked about and found a hole in the rocks six feet away. He was down there and dead, and another one, a nanny, had gone the same way, though she had wedged by the neck nearer the top. She was still breathing as I lifted her out.

I blamed myself then for not coming immediately when I woke first at seven o'clock. This is the sort of occasion when reason does not order behaviour. We had brought the goats for milk, particularly for Alasdair, and the decision was made long before that we must kill the kids. We were, indeed, short of milk and we could not have kept this kid, but now when the little mite was cold and in such dire straits I could do nothing else than put it inside my shirt to try to warm it back to life. I was half successful and brought it to the stage of sucking when I held its head to one of Morag's teats. I was angry with myself. Morag would not walk a step back to the camp and I had to carry her all the way. When I say she would not walk, I mean that she would neither drive nor be led, nor even stand. First I would carry the kid for fifty yards, vainly hoping she might have enough maternal feeling to follow. Then I carried her as far as the kid, and so on. Her motherly sense had evidently not been excited, and she made things harder for me and added to my irritation by going downhill each time I went forward with the kid.

Morag throve and milked well for a goatling that summer, but the nanny kid lived only through that night. I was both sorry and glad, for we should have been sorely put about had it lived. Nevertheless, I was left feeling that tragedy had visited us at the beginning of our venture and that it might have been prevented if I had been more careful.

It is a thought which appals any research worker if he suddenly asks himself how many hours he devotes to his actual research. They are extraordinarily few, because research not only demands its own routine duties of recording, reading, getting things assembled and so on, but there is the irksome business of caring for the physical body which even the most intellectual of folk must continue to carry around with them.

In those early days I was itching to be exploring and to be watching the birds which were so tantalisingly close. Sometimes I did snatch a couple of hours, though I felt as if I had gone on strike by doing so. But there was a fireplace to build, a trench to dig round the tent, a table to make from driftwood, some sort of shelter to make for the goats and hens as the weather became devilish, and there were all those things to carry over from the south cave. We lived hard those days and felt we were getting topside of things. We even went to the length of building a turf shelter as a place of retreat should the tent blow down. I put the canvas and rubber kayak together one afternoon, trying to follow the instructions, which said the job would take twenty minutes. It took me two and a half hours, and I never took down that portable canoe again. It went about with us as it was and finished its days on North Rona in the late autumn of 1938 when the seals broke it to matchwood.

The first day of May was gloriously calm and mild. When you have had a long period of wind and wild weather and it is followed by a perfect day, activity seems to be frozen and all you can do is to lie about and heal your battered self in the quiet of it all. This morning had brought the welcome sound of common sandpipers to the lochans, that long-continued piping which is as moving to me as any music Pan himself might make. The sun shone through the canvas of the tent in the early hours, and I lay basking in it and listening to the sandpipers before I rose.

This was not all, for the eider ducks had come onto the freshwater lochans and were courting. To me the croon of the eider drake is a sound of the north and of spring. 'Ooh-*ooh*-oh' calls the drake with a lift and drop of his head; 'ooh' answers the duck with little more than a chuck of her beak. I lay there listening and content, and would not have changed places with anyone in the whole world.

How lazy I was that day! I rubbed my chin and realised I had not shaved for a fortnight. 'Well, you'll look a bit less of a mess if you do, certainly,' was the compliment from Bobbie.

Oh well, there was no hurry anyway, but it was placed on the mental list of things to do. We were sitting over lunch when I heard what I thought was very much like a human voice. Impossible. No, not quite; there it was again; good God! I think you have to have lived alone for a long time to appreciate the primitive terror which the unexpected sound of the human voice can bring. At that moment the roots of my back hair tingled, and possibly it rose a little as the novelists tell us it does under the stress of circumstance. Anyway, the lunch went dead on me and I keeked out of the tent door like a frightened rabbit. There were two men and a boy a hundred yards away walking towards the tent; I sat down again and murmured the news. We heard them go to the edge of the lochan and begin talking loud enough that we should hear them, and only then did I go out to greet them. I was grateful for such a charming way of calling on a household where you cannot knock on the door. There was nothing to do but make the best of my face and remember it was only one of three. Our visitors were neighbours from Lochbroom and had come over in their yacht on this first good day of spring.

Our next visitors came a fortnight later and were of quite different type. I was walking along the coast to the north-east of the island one unpleasant rainy afternoon after a cold spell of weather of which that first day or two of May had been a false harbinger. I was surprised to see a forty-foot East Coast type fishing boat lying offshore and a launch from her shooting lobster creels. This was something new indeed, for there is no such outfit on our coast. There was a definiteness about the behaviour of the men which seemed foreign to the leisurely way we do things here. The launch and I reached positions where we could hail each other.

'Where are you from?' I yelled.

'*Bluebell*, of Wick. What are you doing in a place like this?'

'Staying here for the summer and doing a bit of work.'

'Well, there's been no summer yet! Where can we come alongside and give you some crabs?'

I pointed to the east bay, Acairseid Eilean a' Chlèirich, and ran round the cliffs towards a place on the north side of the bay which is known as the

Exchange. This is a very interesting and puzzling phenomenon. At this point you will find that the swell does not break and does not rise and fall with the same depth and suddenness as elsewhere. It is usually possible for a man to get ashore there from a boat or for goods to be thrown one way or another, but it is a long way from the habitable part of the island and we could not have got our heavy gear ashore there when we first came. Nevertheless, it was an excellent place for the East Coast skipper and me to exchange greetings. Here was one of those grand Scandinavian types of men to whom the sea is a footpath and to whom physical conditions make very little difference. Times were bad on the East Coast, so four of them had made up a crew and were trying this new venture of lobster fishing on the West. They were a fortnight out from home and had come in this little boat through the Pentland Firth and round Cape Wrath. He threw up to me four big cock crabs and I asked him to come ashore in the evening and take some hens' eggs back with him. He said he would the next day when he came to lift the creels.

Bluebell lay in the west bay the following evening and I paddled out to her in the kayak. What men, I thought! The boat was never fitted out for more than overnight fishing, yet these fellows under the stress of the times had improvised bunks and cooking arrangements and were doing a month's trip in waters they had never visited before. This was the first time out and lobsters seemed scarce. Paraffin, also, was 8½d. a gallon over here and only 6d. in Wick. Doubtful if the trip would do more than pay its way, but it was better than doing nothing at home. And yet when the skipper and two of his men came ashore they brought some little soles for Alasdair and small lobsters for us, and it was with difficulty we were able to persuade them to take some eggs back with them. They were sure we should need them all, living so far away from things.

The skipper was particularly anxious to hear the shipping forecast at nine o'clock, and as he sat on a packing case with a mug of coffee and a biscuit in his hand, and the cultured tones of the announcer came through, he exclaimed: 'Well now, this is the first touch we've had with civilisation for a fortnight!'

EILEAN A' CHLÈIRICH

THE NAME OF THE ISLAND means the Isle of the Priest or, more correctly, of the cleric. This name goes back to pre-Reformation times because Sir Donald Monro, High Dean of the Isles, mentions 'Na-Clerache' in his famous manuscript of 1549. Probably the island became a place of retreat from the religious establishment on Isle Martin at the mouth of Strath Kannaird, and was thus used from a very early time. Some day, perhaps, we shall find some tangible evidence of clerical occupation, but as it is unlikely that the place would be very suddenly relinquished, artefacts will not be found easily.

The south cave above the boulder beach of Moll na h'Uamh is wide-mouthed and not very deep. It is fairly dry and the floor is covered with a very thick layer of powdery earth. The whole floor is in the nature of a kitchen midden and we have dug into this enquiringly for things of interest. Bones there are in plenty and even bits of antlers of red deer, but no artefacts. Miss Margery Platt of the Royal Scottish Museum, Edinburgh, kindly identified some of the bones from a bagful we sent, and gave the following list of species: grey seal, ox, sheep, red deer, pig (which is most surprising, especially as there were relics of two pigs, one with a milk molar in the lower jaw), dog; and of birds, oystercatcher, song thrush, skua (unidentified species), guillemot, lesser black-backed and herring gulls, shag and fulmar petrel.

This list is really thrilling to anyone working on the birds of the island and interested in the present distribution of birds in Scotland. Guillemots do not breed on Eilean a' Chlèirich or anywhere in the neighbourhood, but they are common on the sea in spring, so perhaps they were obtained from the sea rather than from the breeding ledges. All the same, I have not heard of these birds ever being caught on the water and it would need a fairly crafty fellow to do it. There are no skuas in this area now, though I cannot see why. And lastly the fulmar petrel: before 1878 the only certainly recorded British colony was on St Kilda; after that date the most completely recorded colonisation has taken place and a few years ago the birds came in small numbers to Eilean a' Chlèirich. Yet it seems at the time of the kitchen-midden folk fulmars were obtainable.

Sometimes, as I have scratched about in that cave, I have wished it possible to call up visions of its long history – if I could but speak to those old folk who fed on seals and skuas and fulmars.

Eilean a' Chlèirich has two wild mammals apart from the grey seal – the pygmy shrew and the otter. The island is an otters' paradise, for there are not only innumerable small caves about the coast in which they can lie, but there are the eight freshwater lochans and many dry cairns of rocks where they can breed in peace. The dry, powdery mould of the south cave often shows the claw marks of the otter and the furrow made by the long and powerful tail. Naturally I like the otters, but a population of twenty or thirty of them can do a lot of damage to the avian inhabitants. The birds I have seen affected happen to be two of my favourites – the greylag goose and the tiny storm petrel. There are not many geese, and that makes it all the more serious when an otter puts a goose off her nest and takes the eggs. The little stormies are numerous and the otter seems very clever at catching them. He bites off the head, and the tail with the legs attached, eats the body and leaves the wings. Each year you will find remains of one or two newly killed storm petrels in the south cave.

I never cease from wonder at the storm petrel. How does it manage to survive and increase? Think of a bird of such small size and slender build living from October to June on the face of the mighty ocean, never coming to land. Perhaps the very smallness of its bulk saves it from being buffeted, so that it walks the waves in freedom or sits on them as lightly as a cork. One of these mites nested in an accessible place in the outlaw's shieling, so that we were able to take an occasional look at her and her egg. One large white egg, an egg often cold and taking five weeks to hatch; then a helpless chick taking three months to fledge, a chick which receives no aftercare from its parents, but which is just left in the dark and bare cavern where it was hatched. It must come forth into the world of its own initiative and face the stormy ocean in autumn. What a tenuous thread is this for the survival of the species! Often have I lain out of a summer night by the outlaw's shieling to hear and see the stormies. It is a fleeting glimpse, for the birds are black and they do not fly until the night is at its darkest. It will be a grey day for me when I know that never again will I go to sleep to the churring song of the stormies. It, like many other bird sounds, dwells deep in the mind.

The climb from the cave to the summit cairn on the ridge at 252 feet is a steep one whichever way you take it, but it is always worth the effort. The character of the island can be best seen from there and the distant view is the finest I know. This is an easy thing to say – the finest I know – but I have now lived on other islands with magnificent views and the West Highlands are very well known to me. The view from the summit cairn of Chlèirich is the finest I know. As you cannot see all ways at once, it would be better perhaps to say there are two main views – to the east and to the west, the mainland and the Hebrides. Seven o'clock of a fine June evening is the best time to see the mainland, for the sun is behind you and still high enough to shine into the corries of the high hills. The whole range from the Reay Deer Forest to Torridon is visible and those hills nearest are among the best – Quinag, Suilven and Stac Polly, with the rough coastal foothills of Archaean gneiss in the foreground; Ben More Coigeach (Beinn Mhòr na Còigich) and the magnificent range of An Teallach; you can see the summits of that great country round Mullach Coire Mhic Fearchair, Ruadh Stac and the Maiden; and continuing southwards Slioch and Beinn Airidh Charr. It is a fine picture, but better still when you happen to know the individual corries and slopes. I have lain on the summit cairn of Chlèirich and lived earlier years over again.

When the sun has at last fallen on this same evening it is well to turn about and look upon the long, purple line of the Outer Hebrides. It is hard to tell where Lewis disappears into the sea where the sun has gone already, but after the thin line of that northern peninsula the Forest of Harris rises a bold shape, topped by Clisham. Farther south again, North Uist is just visible beyond Rhudha Hunish, which is the northern point of Skye. Here is none of the detail lately seen in the mainland hills; just the remote, violet, swelling and fading line with which the imagination can run riot.

Eilean a' Chlèirich itself is seen to consist of two main masses cut by a principal glen running slightly south of west to north of east. The southern mass consists of the ridge on which is the summit cairn. The climb was steep from the cave, but the slope was gentle compared with the northern face of the ridge, which is sheer in many places. The rock of which the island is formed is Torridonian sandstone, but the complex out here is smoother and redder than that of the mainland. The strata are tilted to form rugged cliffs on the northern faces, and the southern ones slope unbroken into the sea here and there. This northern face of the ridge is of extreme beauty, especially when seen of a fine March evening, for then the sun is low and throws the fluted columns into sharp relief, and the redness of the sun makes the rock face shine an amazing vermilion. It is in this cliff that the peregrine falcon has her eyrie, alternately with a place over the sea. She also has eating places at several points, and I, clambering about, have found many remains of little auks left by the falcon. We do not see these little birds on the coast every year, but there were large numbers in the winter of 1936-37.

The eastern end of the southern half of Chlèirich opens to form two low corries ending in steep boulder beaches to the sea. The floor of each corrie is a flat peat bog of several feet thickness. I, the farmer at heart, the man who has always had the urge to carve out a new farm, play with the idea of starting from scratch on Eilean a' Chlèirich. These two flat areas, well sheltered from the raking west and south-westerly winds, should become my cornfields. I would run surface drams to the boulder beaches, burn the herbage in the dry days of March and April, bring boatloads of shell sand from the beaches of Tanera Beag and spread on the charred surface, then plough and, by whatever means I could, get muck on to it. 'But it wouldn't pay' screams your up-to-date expert. No, it would not *pay*. What a debt we owe to the men who first broke the earth's surface! Probably they had not brains enough to realise it 'wouldn't pay'. Modern agriculture follows the enlightened dictum of the man from the Middle West who said, 'Posterity never did nothing for me'. And for all my brave talk, those fine flat bogs of Chlèirich will continue to grow their sour crop of sedge, interspersed with cross-leaved heather and a clump of common reed where the water gathers.

The slopes of this southern half of the island drain easily, and being covered with good black peat they grow fine heather. Rowan and birch trees would grow in many places if the sheep gave them a chance. Think of this island as it must have been when the first man landed on it – a tiny Highland world of hills and wooded glens and lochans to mirror the green fringes. Two shallow lochans cover part of the floor of the main glen and end westwards in a narrow boulder beach running to the sea. They are the least interesting of all the lochans, and rarely are any birds to be seen about their shores other than the common sandpiper. Some time I hope to see whooper swans come there, for since I have known the island these lochans have come to grow a wealth of *Sparganium*, and one day I shall take some water lilies there to plant. The fringes of these two lochans are lined with otter tracks constantly used. There is also a cairn on the southern edge where the animals breed; a patient observer prepared to wait all night on the rock a hundred feet above may be lucky enough to see the family gambolling on the grass in the early hours.

North-west of these lochans is another little range of hills, and at their northern foot is the longest loch on the island, Lochan Fada. This stretch of water is of exceptional beauty. The water winds before you, and the hills either side frame the distant view of the mainland – high, rocky mountains with white specks of crofts at their foot. Several beds of flags grow on the edges of this lochan, and here and there the banks are too steep for sheep to climb down and nip the aspen poplars. Some of these little trees reach a height of ten feet, and isolated though they may be by miles of sea and moor from others of their kind, their leaves are grazed each year by caterpillars of the poplar hawk moth. At the foot of the trees and at several points round the loch are large plants of the luxuriant royal fern

Osmunda, and what adds further to this subtropical place in the senses of the foliage-starved islander, the honeysuckle climbs about the trees and shrubs of willow.

There are times when we, as island dwellers who have known hidden, tree-shadowed pools in softer places, wish to turn away from the wildness of the west wind and the tortured sea, and it is then the beauty of Lochan Fada has great healing power. I have never known a July without great gales and rain from the south-west, just the time when the honeysuckle is sweetest. How little do we use our sense of smell for the enrichment of experience! Wild hyacinths or bluebells grow in a patch of vivid green halfway along the northern shore of the lochan, and many an idle quarter of an hour have I spent there in late May when the flowers have added another blue to those of lochan, sea and sky.

As I have lain on the hillside above this lochan I have had a glimpse of the haven it must be to some birds. I have seen a solitary shape fly in from one of the other islands two miles away, a greylag goose weary from a long spell on her nest. Her wingbeats sound rhythmically as she circles and descends into the quiet air over the lochan and between the hills.

Then with a final rush of water against feet and feathers she comes to rest on that still surface. There is beauty in the way she sips eagerly at the fresh water, leans into it and throws it over herself. Rarely have I seen a bird unconsciously express the feeling so vividly, of refreshment which must have flowed through her. She rests content on the water for a quarter of an hour before rising again to return to her long vigil. These are the moments which give me the most pleasure in bird watching, moments of spontaneous and revealing behaviour which carve deeper into the mind than hours of observation *ad hoc* from a hide. I should like to share them, so that wild geese would be no longer creatures to be thought of in conjunction with guns and punts and chilly dawns. This is noonday, and this one goose is without suspicion.

There are five more lochans on Eilean a' Chlèirich, each with its own charm and marked individuality. Lochan Bheag, set high in the little range of hills north of Lochan Fada, gives exactly the impression you get from coming suddenly to an unexpected loch on a high moor. It is quiet and unfrequented except by a pair of common sandpipers in the summer. Sometimes I seek it for its upland character when the sky is very blue and dotted with sharp-edged white clouds. North again and a little eastwards is the Hidden Loch, and I call it that because its discovery is my one small addition to the body of geographical knowledge. It is by no means the smallest loch on the island, and even the One-Inch Ordnance Survey map shows all the others. But the Hidden Loch is not shown on any map except mine. It is 140 yards long and 80 yards wide, roughly triangular in shape and 11 feet deep at its deepest (sounded by an illustrious discoverer when messing about with kayak). The lochan is enclosed by little hills, and if you were making a circuit of the coastline and plotting a rapid survey from high points, as the surveyors did, no doubt, the loch would be lost entirely. An otter lives there, but it is rare to see any birds swimming on it or working its steep shores.

Lochan Tuath, or the north loch, is not far away but is of quite different character. This loch lies high, gets a lot of wind and does not give the impression of quietness. It is beloved of the eider ducks in spring and summer, and most of the eiders' nests are round its shores, hidden in the heather. The wild geese commonly come to Lochan Tuath, and it is practically the headquarters of a colony of lesser black-backed and common gulls. The colonies of gulls are an outstanding feature of the avian fauna of Chlèirich. Six species of gull breed in Britain, and four of them on this little island of less than half a square mile. When the young birds appear, the lochan is in the nature of a thoroughfare and a training ground for flight. And, of course, there are the ubiquitous otters and common sandpipers. It is the kind of place where something is always happening. The lochan is 21 feet deep in one place.

Lochan Dubh Medhonach, the little black middle loch, lies westward of Lochan Tuath and twenty feet below it, taking the overflow from its big sister. The special beauty of this loch for me is that it gets very little wind, and as you lie quiet and sheltered in the heather by its shore you are quite out of sight and sound of the sea. You are in a little cup of the island's hills, and from the south shore of the lochan there rises a sheer bluff of rock about forty feet in height. A thick green willow bush reaches forth over the dark surface of the water. Seeing what there is to see in scenery is something of a practised art; a painter concentrates your attention on his picture by framing it, and if you look over a limitless scene you will find it difficult to fully appreciate any single part of it. You must look at the small in scenery sometimes and have it framed off from the outer world. Thus the beauty of the little dark loch, where I love to watch the tiny breezes crossing its surface in rapid, shimmering patterns of silver. No far horizons lure the eye from this play of water, air and light.

When this lochan has water to spare, the overflow falls another fifty feet to Lochan na h'Airidh, the loch of the shieling. I called it that because of the remains of the outlaw's little house at the southern end. Here is another hub of the universe, a stretch of water much frequented by herring gulls, black-backed gulls, eider ducks, oystercatchers, greylag geese and cormorants fishing for eels. It is also the loch from which we take our water supply. Little bays and points make this a happy playground for Alasdair and his kayak. From this flagship he inspects fleets of driftwood boats and

dockyards of original if not orthodox construction, and from its southern margin he can see the great ocean to the north and the sea bounded by the sands of Mellanudrigill to the south-west. It is near to the heart of the island and a happy place. This lochan provides the deepest sounding of any on Eilean a' Chlèirich – 23 feet – under the steep hill on the east side. One or two royal ferns are beginning to grow on the shore of this loch and we have transplanted a few more because we like them, but I believe your pukka plant ecologist surveying the island would frown on. But consider the whims of elfish folk who love little islands as an ecological factor affecting species distribution? That would explain for flags growing in the tiny burn which runs from Lochan na h'Airidh through a little green flat below the shieling, and then loses itself among the stones of the storm beach above the west landing.

The place of the shieling, the burn and the little green flat are the heart of the island. You would not think of living anywhere else. The outlaw chose well, but he was not the first man to build here. When, in preparation for our second year, I drained that acre of ground, the foundations of an earlier building appeared from the grass at precisely the spot where we were going to put up our hut. These were nearly twenty feet long, pointing east and west, and we have wondered if it may have been an early chapel used by the clerics in retreat. The doorway was evidently at the west end, a queer position for any ordinary human dwelling. As I dug those open drains to the burn I cut through a roadway of shingle leading from the building now gone.

The Scottish naturalist Harvie-Brown paid several visits of a few hours each to Eilean a' Chlèirich, and the place fascinated him so much that he wrote some pages about it in his *Vertebrate Fauna of the North West Highlands and Skye*. On his first visit he saw what he thought was a stone circle on the west bank of the burn and in the little green flat. He found it had disappeared next time he was there and, imagining it to be of too great interest to be lost, he returned with an excavation party. The stones had evidently sunk into the turf, which had become much more boggy than on his earlier visit. He dug them out and replaced them in circular form on the east side of the burn where the ground is firmer; they lie there still, and as the sheep graze over them, the stones do not disappear. The hole made by Harvie-Brown's party in excavation became a little wet place with a clump of rushes, much beloved of the snipe. As we lay in our tents thirty years after Harvie-Brown's bit of fun, we used to hear the snipe come down to that hole, 'chick-chacking', every night at about five minutes past ten. So do our deeds live after us; Harvie-Brown would have liked to hear this, but he has been studying the natural history of Elysian Fields these many years.

A botanist would divide Eilean a' Chlèirich into two main zones by drawing a line from the south-west point to the north-east point. Heather is dominant to the south, but to the north and west it gives way to a wealth of crowberry, sheep's fescue grass, buck's-horn plantain and sea pink. This is a herbage floor of great beauty for the senses – the crowberry is kind to the foot, an aromatic scent rises from it, and its darker green against the grass is pleasing to the eye. How can anyone write of the profuse growth of sea pink flowering in late May and in June without lyric fervour? Chlèirich is a fairy garden of colour, blowing in a heedless world year after year. That north-western half of the island is gay by the end of April when the dwarf willows are in flower. There are several species present of this numerous family, and each flowers profusely. The bumble bees come to the golden heads shining from the drab herbage and give a breath of summer while it is yet far away. The wheatears recognise the difference between the north-western side of the island from that of the south-east, for they come to the northern and western parts and almost leave the rest of the island untouched. It would be impossible to pass through the springtime country of the sea pinks, where heaps of lichened stones add their saffron and green to the brilliance of the whole, without seeing the wheatears. They are brilliant also, and no bird more graceful. The Gaelic name for this bird is beautifully descriptive; even the sound of *clachoran*, the little one of the stones, gives an impression of the little flights from stone to stone, the bowings and bobbings and the flirp of the wheatear's tail. The birds come in April and leave gradually in August.

One day in that first summer on the island a brown-sailed boat came into the west anchorage, and like an animate figurehead leaning over the stem was a laughing child, her eyes the colour of sunlit sea and fair hair streaming in the light breeze. She disappeared into the island when she first landed, but in a quarter of an hour she was with us again with the island in her hand, at least its distilled beauty. There was the bright green and red of bearberry, the three purples of bell heather, ling and rinze heather; there was a sprig of white heather, a flower of the golden bog asphodel, and from somewhere thus late in the season she had found a silvery head of bog cotton. A rich posy of colour from what is called a barren island.

Eilean a' Chlèirich repels from the sea but invites from within. Six miles of coastline round half a square mile of island seems impossible at first thought, but there it is, and exploration of every cleft and sea cave has taken a long time. Some of those caves can never have been entered before by man, for alpine rope is a relatively modern production and the men of past times left the cold reaches of dark sea caves severely alone. There is one cave running into the cliff from one of the little boulder beaches to the south-east, hidden from the sea and easily missed from the land. It shows signs of human occupation in that the boulders inside are built into the form of a small circle. The cave is a narrow, eerie place – water dripping from the roof in one place to form an ochreous stalagmite, ferns growing in the dank floor with their light-starved fronds reaching piteously to the opening; and when I shone a lamp into the rickle of stones I saw three toads sitting there like statues. Small eyes gleamed in the strange light and their throats pulsed every few seconds, the only signs of life.

This cave was, I believe, a store for smuggled whisky in the bad old days of not so long ago. Many a nostalgic West Highlander in Glasgow has sipped the raw spirit distilled on Eilean a' Chlèirich and imagined he has felt the breath of his home air. The cave may have been the store, but the actual distillation took place by the tiny burn running from Lochan na h'Airidh to the storm beach. The broken iron 'pot' of the smugglers is still there, but the 'worm' is somewhere in Lochan na h'Airidh, lost for all time probably. The legend of the capture of the smugglers is funny.

These men had some sheep on the island, and the attention paid to the animals was remarkable. Every week or two the smugglers would be going over a dangerous stretch of sea in a small boat to look at the sheep. One young man got himself married and, like all women of the West Coast, his wife looked anxiously to sea those times her man was out. When a squall blew up and the boat disappeared in the murk this new wife was frightened. She was panic-stricken when it did not show up again after the sky had cleared. She called out the men of the township, exciseman and all, and they rowed the eight miles in the longboat. There was no boat drawn up at the usual landing and no sign of the men. The crew began rowing round the island and then saw the small boat hauled up and neatly made fast in a tiny bay of rounded boulders. A nod was as good as a wink to the gauger, who leapt into the surf, went into the mouth of the cave and found the gentle shepherds far tasted in their own brew. Even the most indulgent and understanding of excisemen could not overlook that.

Indeed, this sort of whisky is raw stuff. A pedlar with whom I talked one day in Uist described it to me in a phrase of delightful restraint. Stricken with a cold, he had begged a night's rest in a widow woman's byre and she had given him half a bottle for a cure. 'You will understand,' said he, 'that in the light of that dirty lamp I couldn't be seeing the colour of it whatever, and believe me, I could not get away under three days.'

Some way north of the east anchorage there are two dark geos.* It is a bad place for swell in there, and it is doubtful if you would persuade anybody to take a rowboat in. A kayak is much better. The light fades as the walls of cliff steepen, and once the cave proper is reached you can paddle on for fifty yards to reach a boulder beach. You wait for a slackening in the swell, which pounds with a frightening roar in here, and then quickly in you go, jump into the surf and lift the little boat high before she breaks herself on the boulders. Eyes are now getting more used to the dim light, and you see, as you climb up these round boulders, every step resounding like a shot, that the high roof and narrow walls converge to an arch about fifteen feet high. Once through, the cave opens again into another large chamber thirty or forty yards long. Spring tides have been right up here and there is a large unpicked assortment of timber. I delight in beachcombing, and on my first visit of discovery I greedily loaded my kayak with wooden rollers and towed spars round to the east landing.

I never went there again during our first year, but in 1937, when Kenneth McDougall was with us, he and I went in together for a fuller exploration. He is a bolder fellow than I am, and when he found a hole through which he could creep at the far end of the cave he went down it and I followed. All was quiet and dark, for we had brought no torches. I meekly follow. After hands and knees for fifteen feet we found ourselves in another chamber, and on again to still another and much larger one. Here we were indeed in the hollows of the hills. The matches did not burn well and were getting few. I got the fright of my life when we went up the wrong hole and found it a cul-de-sac. Damn adventurous folk who go caving with a box of matches, and that not full! We retraced our steps, if they are steps on hands and knees, and found the right hole. Thank goodness!

When we got back again to the outermost cave, where the dim light was ineffably welcome, it was to find the swell much increased. We had to wade

---

* *Geo* or *geos* is a shortening of the Gaelic word *geodha*, which means small gully or chasm and is from the Scandinavian *gjá*.

a good way out to get the kayak launched again. Two days later found us in the cave once more with torches and a ball of string. We measured the cave as being 134 yards long – quite inconsiderable to a potholer or speleologist, but exciting enough for me. When those terrific spring tides had entered the cave, how long, long ago we do not know, they brought oak timbers through to that farthest hall of Pluto. Years and years of that still, dank air and the complete darkness had wrought a strange change in them. They were spongy and tough, like rubber.

There is a long slit in the cliffs running in from the north coast of the island, and even when the sea is moderately calm the water bores into there and crashes dully far in at the head of a sea cave. It is a horrible place at the best of times. One morning it was the calmest I ever knew, and I had been fishing in the Cauldron, as we call that northern bight of Eilean a' Chlèirich. I looked into the mouth of Geodha Fada: how calm it was! Too narrow to paddle, I pulled the kayak along by putting hands out to the side. The sky disappeared. Here was I in a large cave floating on a floor of deep water. I could see dim corridors leading far away inland and no beach anywhere. And then, right up there where I could not see, there was a horrible deep boom. I could not hurry out of here; the way out to the kind light of day seemed endless. No boat could get in, and no one could climb into the place on a rope. I had looked where no man had looked before, and I do not think it is myself that will be going again.

There is a terrible place called Tuill an Chlèirich – the priest's hole. It is a sea cave of undetermined length, in the roof of which a large chunk of rock has sloughed away to form a sort of skylight. The sea never calm inside It seems to gather, gather, gather in the mouth of the cave and then rush forward into it in romping fashion. Several seconds later you hear a dull boom, smothered by the length of the passage. When the seas are big the boom is like a cannon shot and the rock trembles palpably. There is no place on Chlèirich I like less than this. God made me for the daylight, I have decided, and to enjoy the sunshine. The fair face of Eilean a' Chlèirich is good enough for me.

THE EVEN TENOR

THE NORTH WIND was still blowing in June, and especially one sunny afternoon when we were lazing in the sunshine in the lee of the old shieling. It was cold if you put your nose up into the wind, but June sun is hot anyway if you can eliminate the wind, and we were basking in it to the point of semi-unconsciousness. The West Highland June draws living things to abandon. There is enough of wild weather in the year to keep crofter folk battling with it one way or another, but the prodigality of June sunshine calls a lull. Southrons remark on those lazy West Highlanders sitting around in the sun when they should be cutting peats. This is not laziness but a therapeutic necessity. It is an art which reaches its aesthetic zenith in the sun and laziness of the northern June.

Is there any light quite like this June sun of the North and West? It takes trouble out of the world. It makes the warmth of the heart.

We heard voices from round the knollie which hides the west landing, and then came Scoraig and Iain and our friend Kenneth McDougall. We had expected no boat today and were completely caught out. The big fair head of Dougal was all smiles and white streaks of dried salt from the spray they had shipped on the crossing.

'Absolutely magnificent,' said Dougal, 'God, what a country!'

'The point is, how long can you stay?'

'Best part of a fortnight.'

It seemed the best of all possible worlds. Who was more welcome than Dougal? He was not only the friend of Bobbie and me, but the personal possession of Alasdair, almost.

Lily came into our lives that first evening Dougal came. We were going to the summit cairn for a general look round when I heard an awful to-do in the neighbourhood of the lochans under the ridge. The wind had dropped and the loud, raucous cries of birds which we now heard sounded worse for their echoing in the glen. I ran along by myself to see what was happening and saw the unpleasant picture of two greylag geese standing back to back with tiny goslings at their feet. Each goose was facing a heron, and these piratical wretches were trying to get the goslings from under the parent birds. The geese were doing the right thing, standing back to back, but the herons were very cleverly trying by feinting tactics to make the geese both turn one way, and one of the herons would make a quick dart with that javelin of a beak in an attempt to steal a gosling. I did not watch this for long, for the geese had only three babies left of their brood, and these were the very birds of the island in which I took most pride and wished to preserve.

The herons flew up with that deceptive slow flapping of wings which hides the speed of their movement, and were gone. The geese turned to what they considered a new enemy, and I found myself in a quandary. If I just left them alone I knew the herons would be back before long; if I took all the goslings to rear I should bereave the geese. I compromised and took two goslings, but I have always regretted since not taking the three, for the parents did not manage to rear their one child.

Two wild goslings fresh from the egg are an enormous responsibility. I looked at these beautiful mites of green down which I must now mother as well as their own parents, and put doubt aside. I gathered eider down from old nests, put it in a box with a hot-water bottle for the night time, and in the day I carried the goslings inside my jersey. Bobbie had the good idea of cutting grass small and floating it in a shallow dish of water, and this started them grazing on their second day of life.

Geese have a faculty of becoming 'fixed' on a foster mother in a very complete manner. All were kind to the goslings, but they took little notice of anyone but myself. I learned much of child behaviour from them in that first fortnight of their lives, and I saw things which I never should have done in the ordinary way. Sometimes I would take them to some fresh grass at the head of Lochan na h'Airidh where I would lie silent as they grazed about me. It was revealed to me then how other birds were taking an interest in these babies. On one evening alone there came a rock pipit, a female wheatear and a snipe. The pipit and the wheatear hovered above the goslings, not in any animosity, but in interest. The snipe walked up to them, her beak and head extended inquisitively. The goslings took no notice as the snipe walked round with short, quick steps. I would be wrong to say that bird expressed wonder, but that is how she looked, and because of my relations to the goslings I felt that for the moment I had entered a world from which we are nearly always barred.

One of the goslings died at a fortnight old through having picked up what I did not know we had in the place – a drawing pin. This placed an even greater responsibility of companionship towards Lily on my shoulders, for I was beginning to realise that if you rear a gosling in this way you make it human and deprive it of kinship with others of its tribe. As time has passed this has become the more plain; Lily is a personal person, not a goose any more. She takes no notice when other geese fly over, nor will she associate with other tame ones we may have about the place.

The bond of utter dependence on me as a mother slackened suddenly at eight weeks old, but not the joy of my companionship, which she sought on all occasions. She would sit on my lap each evening after a supper of bread and milk and run her beak through my hair. The anecdotal Reverend F.O. Morris in his classic work on British birds mentions the preoccupation of a tame goose of his acquaintance with its master's hair. The delight of Lily's friendship with me has made me decide that when I can settle for a long period in one place I shall rear a whole brood of greylag goslings from the eggs and carry out a minute study of the social relationships which ensue from contact with me as a mother goose.

I believe it was while Dougal was still with us in June that we seriously thought of spending another year on Eilean a' Chlèirich. Supposing we got the Fellowship for which we hoped and were to build a hut. We could then come earlier in the year and record the very beginnings of the seasonal influx of the gulls to their breeding grounds, and make a more valuable study than we should have this year. Were Dougal to come as well, we could do a parallel study on the cormorants. He said little then, but he joined forces with us before the year was out.

Everything seemed late in that spring of 1936 and it was not until the beginning of July that the fish were about the island in any quantity. We began then to supplement our feeding very largely with fish and were glad of the excuse to get out in the kayak in the late evenings. Nevertheless, 1936 was not a good year for fish and there were many unsuccessful hours spent working the west coast of the island where most of them seemed to be.

Bobbie and I were traversing the south side of Eilean a' Chlèirich one early June evening when the weather was calm and sky and sea leaden. It was not a pleasant evening for such a time of year, but the dullness suddenly went out of it when a swallow flew near us. We watched its slim beauty in entrancement, for we had not seen a swallow for some years. The bird perhaps recognised us as being of the species under whose eaves it was accustomed to breed, for it came back again and again, flying within three feet of us. Then it was gone. Next year, when we had the hut and a wireless aerial led across to the top of the outlaw's ruin, two swallows came for a space and rested on the wire, twittering a soft song from russet throats. Would that our hut had a deep eave and a support for a swallow's nest, and that we had a small patch of clay to give it the material for building!

I know that we had many a wild gale in that summer of 1936 and that I was often out slackening or tightening guy ropes and looking to see that the child was all right in his little tent. What can sleep like a young thing? I was amazed and grateful for the power that kept Alasdair asleep and unaware of the tumult round him. Though we can remember these times, the impression remaining uppermost in our memory is of sunshine and long hours idly looking over the sea. There were days when we could explore the coastal cliffs intimately in the kayak; rare days those, of absolute calm and broiling sun, but they have so filled our minds that they are not rare now. How lovely it was to be in the kayak at low tide on such a day, seeing the wonder of the strange world of the cliff foot. We would have to pull our way through the glossy tangle now half exposed and giving off that strong, tonic scent which you can smell sometimes in iodine. There are shiny masses of red and gold sea anemones, and tiny, silent seas caught up as pools in the rocks for the few hours of the ebb tide. How grateful we were always for the sun! Island sun tans darker than the mainland sun, and we have been so deep a brown that people have grinned when they have met us. It is doubtful whether any other place in Britain gets more actual sunlight than we do in June, or May and June together. Eight and a third hours a day average for a month is a very high figure – half the total possible sunlight for this latitude.

You may think I write a great deal about lying in the sun and doing nothing; and when exactly, you may ask, do I do any work? Well, if you would hear the birds singing their sweetest it is not in the hot sunlight of the afternoon you would be listening. That is the time when the birds are least active, and so are the seals and the deer. I follow their example and take a siesta whenever possible. But at dawn and sunrise and in the forenoon I may be found at work; and again when the heat of the day is past and I am soaked in sun and sloth you may find me becoming active until the darkening. It is remarkable how much outdoor work you can accomplish in our country after ten o'clock at night in June. All the same, says your practical man, it seems to me you have a jolly good time of it, and it all sounds just what I should like myself if I didn't have to chain myself to the serious things of life. Of course I am having a good time of it, for the simple reason that I am doing the job in which I am most interested. You've been lucky, says the man in the bowler hat, I should like to live on that island free from all care as you seem to be. Perhaps. I did not get to this island and this job of work just by saying I would like to go. There have been sacrifices to make somewhere.

Most people do seem to demand a reason, or at least an excuse, from the man who lives on a small island without human neighbours, for he is deemed asocial and is failing to be regimented in a country seething with people. Freedom seems to be playing a losing battle these days, and we who love her must be prepared to make sacrifices, to see clearly and with single-mindedness. That bowler-hatted fellow may say my love of islands shows frustration, or even fear, and that my desire for quietness is really a veiled attempt to escape from reality.

Look at the question this way: sincerity must be the standard of action unless self-respect is to be lost. I, the complete egotist if you will have it so, feel that the way and surroundings of my own life are of immense importance to me, and consequently, but to a lesser extent, to my fellow men. My wish is to serve, to give, to seek and interpret. I find truth in the wilderness, though another man may find it in the press of humanity. In my view humanity spoils when it packs, and I find myself moving to the fringe. Natural scenery is spoiled as well, water becomes unfit to drink without treatment, animals which give pleasure disappear or are exploited for profit, and everything takes on a soiled, secondhand character, all of which is unpleasant. On an island I can be scrupulous about these things without having my efforts rendered void. There is a cleanness about things here which means much to me, and I can respect cleanness in my comings and goings about the place. If I make the birds tame I can do so without wondering if I am increasing their chances of getting shot.

There is a strong spirit of revolt in the younger generation of us against the increasing complexity of our civilisation, and some feel we must make a move towards simplicity. Conventions and petty luxuries which soon become necessities can absorb much of a man's earning power and leave him little time to live the life he might have chosen. Unfortunately, there are many who cannot be as simple as they would wish, for the world has got hold of their bodies and their existence depends on their remaining a drop in the vortex. Every move towards simplicity demands a greater personal ability in doing things with head and hands, and on a coordinated strength of the organism as a whole. The type of simplicity I seek – hard living by mountain and sea – is not everybody's choice; obviously it could not be without general famine and starvation, but it is one form of friction on soul and body that they shall not rot.

It is not frustration, then, which makes me seek an island, but a refusal to be frustrated. This way of living is not an escape but a goal which has been sought. To this end I have sacrificed money and comfort. I must admit, all the same, that I cannot enjoy comfort for long before I am yearning for the wilderness again. Now, with worldly goods worth about a couple of hundred pounds, I find myself one of the few really successful men. But what about your wife and child, says that bowler-hatted fellow, are you so wrapped in your own conceit that you have no thought for them. Bobbie can answer for herself, and she says that life is altogether fuller since we came back to the field to do our research and left the laboratory. A child of ten or eleven can answer for nothing but the moment – in which Alasdair himself is happy. I have a feeling that the island years have given him a background which in later life he would not be prepared to trade for the pounds in money I might otherwise have left him.

The fact remains that I draw many good things from the civilisation questioned, and while I continue to do so something must be returned. There is such a thing as ethical economics which demands service to his fellows from every man. Unless you walk out naked and alone into the jungle and live on what you can catch, you are partaking of the goods and services of society. If no service is given in return, the conscience is soon bankrupt.

To this end I sincerely believe in the cultural value of work which reveals the ways of life in animal societies. When man can look upon animals as sentient beings, often with vivid personalities, he will consider them less as material to be exploited. When life is respected in lowly forms, our human society will be a better one in which to live. It is not killing that is our sin, but killing thoughtlessly, needlessly and for fun. And now, Mr Man-in-the-bowler-hat, shake hands with me, please, and let us part as friends. If you should ever get the length of Tanera Mòr, there is usually a fly cup of tea going. You have not really had a fair chance to answer me back.

That first summer wore on seeing us become more and more adapted to our island life, and anxious to come back to the island at the end of January, 1937. News came in one of the mails that we should have a Research Fellowship for one year at least, but with any luck, for three. We were quite agreed that it would not do to face the worst part of the Highland winter – from January to the end of April – in a tent.

We designed a sectional hut ten feet by eight feet, with plenty of headroom for tall folk like ourselves, and it was made for us by Messrs Cowiesons of Glasgow. It was to have a deep shelf running the whole length of the hut above the window; half the window was to open inwards from the top; there was to be a rain-shedder above the window and door, and a shutter to the window. That order went away in August and we began to prepare the site.

The little flat beside the burn running from Lochan na h'Airidh was a little meadow at one time. By 1936 it had degenerated to bog, but there was no doubt it had been drained at one time and that I could drain it again now. I dug half a dozen open parallel drains to the burn, with immediate and surprising effect, and a circular ditch round the place where I intended to transfer the tent. From this a drain led into the main drain of the system. We pulled all the grass from the patch where the tent would be, and left the site to dry off for a while.

One night brought a south-easterly gale, a dry one, which gave us no sleep at all. We decided to go down to the new and sheltered place the following afternoon, for the wind had dried the ground beautifully. We looked at the weather and said it would rain in two hours. Could we move all our gear about seventy-five yards in that time? It was worth trying. The work took us exactly two hours going as fast as we could, and the rain began in about two hours and five minutes. So we had five minutes to get tea ready in a very delightful atmosphere of calm and security. The rain came softly with no wind, and gradually increased in intensity. By nine o'clock we said it must stop soon; can't go on at this rate. I was improving the drainage from the circular tent ditch to the main drain at ten o'clock and was working in the nude, for I should have been wet through in no time in clothes, and things are such a nuisance to dry in a tent. Wear nothing, and you need only a towel to dry yourself when you come in.

I think it must have been about one o'clock when I dug a deep, narrow hole in the floor of the tent so that we could bale out as soon as it filled and thus keep the bedding more or less dry. But it still kept on raining.

We were tired from the last night's gale and slept from sheer exhaustion and because the monotonous patter induced sleep. It was still raining when we woke in the morning, but not so hard. I rose to see what our island world looked like after such a flood. My drains were working like mill races, and there was some kick to be got out of that. At the foot of the burn where it disappears into the high ramp of the storm beach there was a loch of about half an acre in extent, complete with gulls swimming on it; the burn itself was running like a real burn and the sound was pleasant. The overflow from Lochan Dubh Medhonach into Lochan na h'Airidh comes down a rock face at one point, and this was now a rushing waterfall audible from the other side of the loch. The goats looked utterly miserable, for they are dry-weather animals for preference.

Rubbish such as small trees, heather and a good deal of hay drifted over the eight miles of sea from the mainland and littered our coasts. I realised then what an effect such a flood as that might have on the distribution of plants from a mainland to islands offshore. But we were lucky to get off with two inches of rain that night, because they had five inches at Gruinard House, eight miles away. And they were not at the centre of the cloudburst, which seems to have been on Druim na Fuadh, the road leading from

Gruinard to Little Loch Broom. The waters there reached such magnitude and velocity as to wash away the road at half a dozen places and make a jagged furrow several feet deep. A large part of a field at Muncastle became a shingle beach.

Shortage of food is a most unpleasant thing to experience on a small island because, first, your appetite is large and nicely whetted, and second, there is no way of getting a supply quickly, nor does the uncertain state of the sea allow you to say when you will get it. We had planned our amounts rather carefully in that last month because we did not wish to carry much back with us. Imagine, then, the sudden advent of a young man we hardly knew, from the Continent. He jumps ashore and shakes hands and turns about to tell the launch to call for him in a week's time. That young man started with a severe handicap. I might have helped him up with his gear to the camp, but I noticed with some apprehension that he was travelling light. He was one of your real open-air boys, the rough stuff. Had he brought food with him? Not much – half a loaf – he was going to eat whelks and *Boletus* fungi; that was what was so extraordinary about the English, they didn't understand the wealth of natural food going to waste around them. Oh!

Tent? Yes, here it was. He had cycled through Scotland, but do you know the Highlanders were so hospitable, the tent had not been undone from the parcel in which he had bought it. I showed him the place I would like him to use for his tent and began helping him put it up. The material was like a coarse butter muslin and the poles rather thicker than a matchstick. The neat little price label still hung by its slip of thread and flirped in the breeze; a real lightweight this. We let him have one wet night in it and then gave him Alasdair's tent. Alasdair came in with us and could not help being the nuisance any third party would be in a tent, even if he was our own bairn. I explained to the visitor the peculiar set of circumstances under which people lived on a small island, and that to avoid personal frictions as far as possible we made a point of taking our siesta quite alone. The idea never got through; he talked to us in his monotonous drone every afternoon. The British have never learned to be sociable.

The whelks and winkles were never in danger, and the population round our shores continued to creep about the barnacled rocks and among the seaweed. The *Boletus* fungi waxed into their short period of ripeness and waned into glutinous blobs. We saw the butter disappearing and the flour supply going low. We learned that indigestion was a myth; what you should really do was to get your belly tight every meal; never get up from the table with an appetite. Oh!

Fishing became sheer necessity and the sea was kind. We caught lots of large, oily mackerel. Now then, thought Bobbie, I'll just feed these into the hopper and see how the machine will take them. They were grand mackerel, weighing a pound apiece and more as they came from the sea. Now, I am considered a biggish fellow, carrying fourteen stone when I am lean, but I cannot get further than one large mackerel. Our visitor consumed three, completely and with relish; and half a dozen raisin fritters as well. We stared in admiration and with a new respect. I expect the British simply have not got the digestions.

The boat did come a week later, and though a big swell was running we bundled our friend into it somehow. He wrote us a charming bread-and-butter letter afterwards; it had been one of the best holidays he had had, and never had he been better fed.

For some days after that we were actually tightening belts against hunger, for Scoraig had not come with anything for us. Supposing this calm weather suddenly stopped and we had a week of gales. It was 30th September now, and October is one of the stormiest months of the year. I felt justified in going the eight miles to Scoraig in the kayak.

The sea was flat calm, with trailing banks of mist drifting about in the early morning. I paddled all the way at my best pace and did the journey in a little over an hour and a half. Scoraig was away to Dingwall for a day or two, but Mistress Scoraig fitted me out with bread, butter and a jar of jam and one or two other oddments. It was still calm as I set forth on the return journey, but a north wind began to blow when I was halfway; not a serious wind at all, but enough to frighten me. The muscles of my back seemed about to crack as I paddled without ceasing, and I wondered

how much way I was making. The north point of Eilean a' Chlèirich and
the south point of Ghlas Leac Bheag gave me a good bearing. As long
as I was seeing less and less sea between them I was getting on. There,
they joined, and Chlèirich seemed to creep along the length of Ghlas Leac.
And now Chlèirich was giving me some shelter, the fear was gone and I
felt exhilarated. Bobbie was delighted, and after some mackerel we simply
gorged on bread and butter and jam. The butter was Mistress Scoraig's
own make, full-flavoured and tasting its best, as bread and butter does
when eaten out of doors. On this occasion we followed our recent visitor's
advice in not getting up from the board with an appetite.

We felt autumn coming upon us and that we should be glad when the
hut came. When that was erected and all stowed inside, our season's work
would be done. Our neighbour, James Macleod of Tanera, brought it one
evening, laid across the decks of his big teak launch. Donnie Fraser was
with him and in a state of tearing eagerness for work. It was a ticklish job
getting the sections ashore, especially those of the roof and window; one
dunt through the felt would mean the rain coming in and a great deal of
trouble repairing the damage. It was nearly dark when they left, but all the
sections were down at the site and if the weather would let them come two
days later we could get it up and return to Dundonnell.

The weather fortunately continued good, though autumn was subtly
making itself felt in other ways than the departure of the birds. The gulleries
have lost their shining newness of spring and look decrepit places. No birds
singing except the indefatigable wrens. The bracken was not growing green,
uncurling frond after frond in the June sun; it was browning and falling
back to earth. The bents and deer's-hair grass browned also, and the wind
whistled in a different way through the wilting swords of the flags at the
lochan's edge. A swell would come on the sea with little provocation and
took a long time to go. Now, if the skies and seas were grey we could not
feel, as we did in the spring, that the weather would get better; there would
be no improvement, nights would draw in and lengthen the time we should
be confined to the tent. Life would be harder for the child and for us.

James Macleod and Donnie Fraser came in that first week of October, but not alone. There must have been eight or ten of the lads and lasses from Coigeach all ready to help and all primed for a good day's fun. The hut shot up into position, the lining was fitted and wires slung over the top and suspended with boulders. We put what we could inside, and the rest was carried to the landing by the willing hands. The goats were excited, and Lily, not being sure if she liked all these strangers running about, would be happy nowhere but on my knee. It seemed as if we should never get off that night; when we were all aboard, James found that his exhaust was leaking into the boat, and that meant going back to the hut for tin and wire to bind round a pad of cotton waste. No one wished to spoil the general sense of well-being with a consciousness of time, even if we could not get to Dundonnell boathouse by dark. What was that floating on the sea a quarter of a mile back? Round we go to pick up a worthless fruit crate and add it to the present congestion of folk, goats, hens, canary and so on. Gaelic songs rose to heaven all the way, and I could not help contrasting this happy journey of fulfilment with the one in the spring when the weather seemed against us and so much had yet to be learnt.

But we had confounded the Jeremiahs. We had neither come home after the first fortnight on Chlèirich, died of rheumatism or pneumonia, nor had we said 'Enough is as good as a feast'. On the contrary, we had made new friends and welcomed old, got some first-rate research results and gained a Fellowship which would greatly ease our finances. Bacon said that man conquers Nature by obeying her, and that is our own attitude. It is best to treat Mother Nature as a foster-mother and accept her discipline; only a topsy-turvy world treats her as a serving wench.

Our homecoming was the more pleasant because our friend Elsa Graham Dow had taken possession of the house a week or two before, and now she had a meal on the table and a cheerful fire in the grate. Kenneth McDougall had cycled in that very evening, and he had come to stay for a year or more, he said. Alasdair went to bed as soon as we could get him there, and we should have followed soon after. But the sweetness of good-fellowship was deep upon us all until the early hours of the morning.

SECOND YEAR

WAITING IS THE HARDEST JOB. Inactivity, uncertainty, inability to get going, not because you are not fit and ready but because other factors are holding you back. Each day the following February we used to go up the back of the house with the telescope to look as far as Chlèirich. What else did we see but a great surf breaking on the cliffs of that island? One day was reasonably calm, it was the 17th, and we felt sure James Macleod and Donnie Fraser must be coming . We looked out and – yes, there was a boat in the mouth of the Loch; but our wild hopes sank within us when we got the boat focussed and saw that it was not the one for us. It speaks well for the characters of Bobbie, Dougal and Alasdair that none of us was sharp-tongued in that time; I know I felt irritable enough sometimes.

When the boat did come for us eventually we did not hear until one o'clock in the day, when we had given up hope. Now we were to go, the going was a nuisance; hot stew on the table for lunch, and Bobbie's birthday plum pudding. We had awful indigestion for the rest of the day. Goats, hens, geese, canary, bedding and a thousand and one things had to be taken to the boathouse, and it took us four journeys with the car, two of which were made before the boat came. There were James Macleod, Donnie Fraser and Donnie (Beag) Macleod on board, all in a cheerful frame of mind. We worked as fast as possible, but even so it was half-past four when we got away, by which time the wind had freshened from the east and was following us down the Loch. Dougal was forrard, Bobbie and Alasdair aft where it was warm, Donnie Beag took the tiller, and James, Donald and I sprawled on the only other vacant place, the decking over the engine amidships.

What a great length of a loch it is! I unconsciously noted the landmarks showing the stages of the journey – the Ardessie point on the south side, then Cadha na Muic on the north side; then Scoraig, where we saw the Macivers outside their house waving to us. There was something warming about that. When we got out beyond Cailleach Head we felt the great swells coming down from the north, and Ghlas Leac Bheag kept appearing and disappearing as we topped them and fell into the trough again. Several little auks were on the sea that day, and we realised their small size only when some razorbills came by as we were looking at them.

The darkness was coming down as we neared Chlèirich, and we could make out no details. The launch went round to the west landing and anchored off because James would not take her close in, seeing the swell licking up white everywhere. I did not count how many dinghy loads came from the launch, for I was busy getting stuff above the tidemark on the pier rock. I had come ashore with the first load, which had included a pair of Chinese geese in their crate. There was a bit of trouble in landing them, but we looked at it in this light: if we dropped the crate overboard and gradually hauled it ashore, everything should be all right. For the crate would float and the birds could swim. All the same, there was considerable hissing going on as we got the crate on to the rock. It was rather a nightmare pulling heavy boxes and perishable stores out of the dinghy and dragging them up the slippery seaweed-covered rocks in the dark. Obviously we must let James and his crew away immediately the last dinghy was emptied. That pier rock looked like the Caledonian Market just then.

It had been our intention that Alasdair should go back with the launch to Achiltibuie to start school there, but we did not like the idea of his going off to new surroundings at that time of night, so we said no. Instead we put him down in the lee of the cliff, put some rugs over him and a cushion under his head and told him to lie quiet. Dougal, Bobbie and I began sorting the perishables from the non-perishables, making a neat heap of the former over which we could put a tarpaulin. There was no moon, but it was not a dark night, for Venus was very bright, throwing a golden path along the sea, and before she had set in the west Sirius was high to the south.

It was long past nine o'clock when we had finished; then we came up to the hut, which we were relieved to find in the same position we had left it in October. It had withstood one of the stormiest winters in years. We were all more than ordinarily tired, but I was thrilled when our little friend the snipe rose from the bog before the hut and returned there within a few minutes. Two curlews also got up, and as we went to the loch for water there was a redshank piping at the north end of it. What lovely sounds these were after the interminable weeks of waiting.

Bobbie made us plenty of tea and we drank much with slices of bread and marmalade. The canary had his head under his wing and his feathers fluffed out – fast asleep; I know I envied him at that moment. We let the goats run loose, put the geese into the outlaw's shieling, and then the hens into the box in which the geese had been.

And now we could think about bed, which meant putting up the bell tent first of all on its old site alongside the hut. The circular, drained patch was good and dry, and I felt how simple it was putting up this tent on

this night, compared with that day less than a year before when Iain and I raised it and Scoraig had been getting troubled holding the boat off the rocks in the west landing. Dougal and I slept in the tent that night and did not talk before going to sleep.

I was up at seven o'clock in the morning after a rather cold night and made tea for the company. It was very cold now, with a strong and penetrating east wind, but I was bursting with eagerness to get doing, and surely there was enough to do this day. What a day of hard work! That carrying of boxes of provisions and all the other stuff from the rock is almost heart-breaking as well as back-breaking. There were also the six panes of glass to put into the window of the hut, for we had not had time to do the glazing when the hut was erected the previous October. It was quite a long time before we could find the putty, despite our careful labelling of boxes. I felt it incumbent on me to do the hardest work, so I set Dougal down to the glazing. There was I sweating hard at carrying cases over from the pier rock, and here was Dougal at the hut in the teeth of the wind getting colder and colder and almost blue. So I took over the glazing for the last pane or two and Dougal carried stores from the rock to get himself warm before lunch. We finished all the carrying by half-past three; whereupon a raw-backed party enjoyed a reflective cup of tea, the universal panacea for all ills in this countryside. While we had still been carrying I had worn my binoculars and had seen purple sandpipers on the rocks, some young and old tysties in the west landing, and the winter remoteness of the island was heightened for me when, in broad daylight, I had seen a mother otter and her half-grown young one running from Lochan Iar to the sea on the western side. Now I must have a quick run round the island before nightfall.

There is something attractive entirely in its own way about this winter remoteness. The herbage is bleached to a pale buff colour and the rocks stand out stark. The winter birds, to one who knows them, have a direct effect on the mind. There is a feeling of everything being closed down to the lowest level of activity. It was but a short round I made that afternoon, for I was too tired to go far and carefully.

We had been interested to see what the animals did with themselves on this first day back on the island. The goats, Morag and Blanquette, hung about the hut and tent just as they did last year and were constantly in mischief. The hens stayed about their new house, the goose crate, at the foot of the burn where it disappears into the ramp of the storm beach, all except Troggie (it was in 1939 that Troggie, short for Troglodyte, realised the dream of her life by creeping into a crack of the earth's surface without being seen and hatching out a brood of chicks).

The Chinese geese made their way to the foot of the burn and found it very much to their liking. Soft bog, shallow water and a bite of green made a fine place. Lily looked about her for a few minutes when I let her out of her basket. Then she took a short fly to the burn; after breakfast she held her head high and talked for several minutes – a sure sign that she was going to fly. And so she did; high and far over Lochan na h'Airidh to the north-west, round again, out to sea from the west landing, back and down by the Chinese geese by the burn. She knew quite well where she was. But Lily had become too human to stay with the other fowl and she soon returned to the hut, hardly ever leaving its vicinity afterwards. The call of her own wild kind flying overhead aroused no interest in her, nor would she associate with the Chinese geese.

We had made the hut a homely place within two days. Now there were books on the shelves, a shelf for the canary, hooks upon which hung telescopes, cameras and binoculars, the tools of our craft, and there was even a tablecloth on the table. At that moment I had reached the ideal kept in my mind since childhood, a tiny house with presses and shelves for everything, set down in your own fairy country beyond the reach of an external world. I had played and pretended this bit of escapism all my life, and here it was, as good as the pretending and perhaps a little better, for I had with me those I loved. This moment reached its apogee when a flock of barnacle geese came low in front of the window and landed a hundred yards away to graze at the foot of the burn.

Alasdair delighted in these days, and if he had gone to school he would have missed March on the island. He seemed to grasp this joy with the fervour of a man trying to keep time still. I took him stalking the barnacle geese, creeping within a few yards of them so that he could see their faces and the barred plumage of black and grey and white; and by himself he went round his own little haunts of last year, remembering his way among the maze of lochans and little hills.

We had been back about a week when there dawned one of those perfect West Highland days; the sky cloudless, the water a deep blue, and you could see just as far as it was possible to see. The hills of the Forest of Harris in the Outer Hebrides showed up in their snowcaps, and the deep snow on the mainland hills made them sharply outlined in the sunlight. Dougal and Alasdair and I went to the big herring gullery in the morning to begin building a hide there, the still, warm air tempting us to take off our shirts while we were carrying stone. When this kind of weather comes in early spring its exhilarating power is remarkable; no work is too hard or too long, and mealtimes become the crowning joy of the day.

Dougal suggested we should start summer time henceforth, so we put the hour on during the afternoon. Alasdair asked if he might have the kayak launched on Lochan na h'Airidh, and there he had a grand hour coasting about and running the model motorboat which Donnie and Alasdair Fraser had given him at Christmas. Bobbie and I carried driftwood to the gullery for roofing the hide. Lying there in the sun at the cliff edge we felt this was a day of days and all that wretched month of waiting was shed from us.

The work on the life history and social behaviour of the grey seal was now firmly in our minds and we were busily planning ahead. For this reason we had brought an Arctic Dome tent to Chlèirich to test its reaction to big gales; the seal work would be a wintertime job requiring sound equipment. Messrs Thomas Black and Sons of Greenock had lent this tent to us, a secondhand one which had been with the Oxford University Arctic Expedition to Ellesmere Land. The tent was like a half-sphere with a little ventilation pipe coming from the top, where eight curved ash poles converged and were clamped. There was an inner wall as well, six inches away from the outer one, and this insulating layer retains heat within the tent. Dougal took up his abode within it, crawling in and out each time through a canvas funnel. Alasdair shrieked with laughter and had to be gently dissuaded from constantly going in and out himself.

But next day he was gone from us. Launches and men came to take away the hoggs which had wintered on the island, and to put ashore a few weakly

ewes that would have a better chance of lambing six weeks hence than they would on the mainland where the hard winter had bared the lower hills and the grass parks as well. There was great commotion, for Chlèirich is a difficult island to gather, and once the sheep are together it is not easy folding them near the sea's edge while they are severally picked up and thrown to a man in the stern of a dinghy. All were aboard at last, and Alasdair went away with them in high spirits, for which we were duly grateful. He was going to stay with Donnie Fraser and his mother at Raon Mor. I think it was Bobbie who had the fears and heartburnings, but she took comfort in thinking he would be back in a month or so for his Easter holiday.

We had some cold weather about this time, and we saw the unusual phenomenon of the lochans being frozen over after the thermometer had been down to 25°F in the night. But it was pleasant weather, warm in the sun when you got out of the north wind. That evening we heard of the blizzards on the mainland and heavy falls of snow. A Peeblesshire sheep farmer spoke on the wireless of the trouble they were having with sheep buried in drifts and the country impassable. He had a rich deep voice, and his little talk in a clear, cultured Doric as part of the news was one of the finest performances I have ever heard over the air. How strong and real it seemed after the attenuated southern English of the announcer. Not that I am crabbing the announcer, but to us in the far North, where we speak English and not the Doric of the Lowlands, the speech of the southern Englishman sounds indescribably thin.

March 16th dawned another magnificent day, but the wireless forecast a south-easterly gale, against which we made due provision. This, perhaps, would be a good test for the Arctic tent. We worked on the little flat bog in front of the hut on this day, burning the old foggage from it, digging another drain through to the burn and building the turves into a dyke round the hut and tent. Then we raked moss from the grass after burning and spread some shell sand which we carried up from the little patch at half-tide level at the west landing. It was good and happy work, made happier for me because Lily sat on my coat all the time and chewed at the buttons just as if she had been a puppy.

It was blowing hard by dark that night, so hard that there was no hope of sleep. I went out at one o'clock in the morning to look at the bell tent, which was up all right, but every guy slackened completely. A dry gale means that the guys will not bind, and one with heavy rain means the

ground gets sodden and will not hold the pegs well. If there must be a
gale I like a few drops of rain periodically to keep fabric and ropes tight.
This gale was very dry from the east, but when I went out at two o'clock
again to see how things were the rain began, and I knew she would hold
thereafter. Knowing Dougal's capacity for sleeping, I thought I had better
have a look at the Dome tent, St Paul's Cathedral as Alasdair had dubbed
it, and find out if Dougal could sleep through this screaming turmoil.

The tent was nearly down, and two of the curved ash poles were sticking
through a rent in the roof. It was also tearing round the bottom flap where
stones are laid to anchor it. I thought it best to let her down altogether and
put stones over the whole thing to keep her flat. But where was Dougal?
I dared not open the funnel entrance to the tent because it was on the
windward side, but thought it wiser to crawl underneath from the lee. And
believe me or not, there was Dougal fast asleep, the inner envelope of the
tent draped over him, which was kept clear by a sack of potatoes standing
there by his bed. The man can't be human, I thought, and Dougal himself,
waking so slowly, thought I must be a fussy fellow to be capering about at
such a time. He changed his tune when he switched on a torch and saw the
front half of me on the ground at the opposite side from the door, and the
roof close in on him.

We had everything safe within the hour, and Dougal came back to the hut
to drink tea and spend the rest of the night. Next day we let the east wind
have its own way, keeping ourselves warm by fetching some sacks of guano
from the south cave, taking the turf from a piece of garden and forking
over the tough ground beneath. We spread the guano and some shell sand.
It was back-breaking labour, but gladly undertaken because we wanted so
much to see how new potatoes would do there. It was several days before
we had got the peaty soil broken down and dressed with seaweed, and not
until 29th March, Easter Monday, did we get the potatoes planted.

The sea was calm and had only a deep swell by 20th March, but two
days later we woke to a great northerly gale which shook the very island.
We could hear and feel the boom of the waves in the Cauldron as we lay in
bed. Dougal and I went there after breakfast to enjoy the spectacle of flying

water; spray from each great wave came down into Lochan na h'Airidh (our drinking water), which is itself about thirty feet above sea level. Gulls and fulmars were enjoying themselves in the updraught against the north cliff, on top of which we lay ourselves. A wild sea of green and white, a great sound of water and of crying gulls and the blessed sunlight withal. Dougal and I could not have heard each other speak, but when we smiled across at each other we knew how good it was to be alive. It was on that day we picked up an exhausted barnacle goose and brought it back to camp in the hope of it recovering. But it was so tame I knew it was done.

Easter was early in 1937, and as the weekend came near Bobbie was eagerly looking forward to Alasdair's homecoming. But he did not come, and though Easter Day itself was one of brightness, made the better by the good Easter hymns which came over the wireless, I knew Bobbie was a worried girl. I took Dougal into the great east cave in the kayak, but there was far too much surf to allow of a landing. As it was, we got pooped by a wave as we came ashore on the east side. I happened to be in the stern and got the lot round my ears. Dougal, being forrard, got only his seat wet, and his laughter was quite immoderate as we carried the kayak up the shingle on to Lochan Fada for the short cut home.

The good days came and went, and bad days followed and still neither Alasdair nor the boat came. We were short of paraffin and butter, and yet our appetites seemed to increase. Dougal and I built a little tin oven into the bank, using all our cunning to make it conserve and concentrate the heat; and once we had got the fire hot, Bobbie cooked some currrant scones which were pronounced successful at teatime. But she did not seem much cheered.

We were getting rather desperate, we saw the Altandhu boat shooting lobster creels on the east side. We hurried back for our large packet of outgoing mail and then hailed the boat, which was manned by four old men. One of them rowed over to the Exchange rock to take the letters, and looking round, he saw there was not a dry spot in the dinghy, which was leaking visibly. So the old man continued to hold the letters in one hand and rowed the boat with the other, using the oars alternately. Then another great hand reached down from the big boat and stowed the mail carefully along with the lobsters. These four old men with their worn tackle seemed to me to epitomise the social conditions of the West Highlands at the present time. Old men were carrying on a job here as best they may – the young ones go away to earn money.

Alasdair came home on 3rd April, bursting with high spirits, trying to tell us everything at once and coming out with his Gaelic now and again. The school had not broken up till last night; that was why he had not come at Easter. Also, my eagle eye noticed he had a sniffle – oh yes, he had had a bit of a cold, he said. Thereupon, glad as I was to see him and to dig into a sackful of mail, I expected the worst.

This was the sort of occasion when we pay the price for our isolation. Exactly forty-eight hours after Alasdair's return, Bobbie, Dougal and I went down with colds, such colds as townsfolk never know, for to isolated communities the common cold can be a major illness. I have also noticed that a cold caught from a child is far worse than one taken from an adult. We were simply wretched by the following morning, staggering about with such sore throats as we had rarely known. How much we sympathised with the old St Kildans who did not welcome calls by strange boats because of the round of colds which inevitably followed. We had a feverish day or two, made worse by a south-easterly wind, which we find is always bad for any infection of the nose and throat. Then on the following day the wind had swung round to the south-west, driving away all the dull haze characteristic of south-easterly wind and having an immediate effect on clearing up our colds.

Spring seemed to come suddenly about the middle of April. A softness which had not been there before came into the air, the grass shot forward, willows showed their flowers, scurvygrass began to flower on the cliffs, and the foliage of the sea campion came thick and tender also. The geese were getting stronger on the wing, and the ewes looked better than they did a month before.

One afternoon early in May, Dougal and I were on a knob of rock near the north-west corner of the island. The impression when you were there was that the cliff went sheer to the sea, but Dougal is a climber, and letting himself down over the edge he found a good ledge of rock leading downwards to sea level. He went down and came up again quickly, all smiles. 'There's a big cave down there, more than I could see; let's go and fetch the rope.'

So home we went to tea, and Bobbie came back with us to explore the cave. The climb down was much easier than it looked, because hand and footholds were excellent all the way; there is no danger whatever in climbing a precipice if the rock is sound and the holds good and plentiful. In fact, when I think of myself at the moment of writing these lines, laid up in bed with a broken leg sustained on such an innocent errand as walking down the field to milk the cow, I know that I could not possibly have sustained such an accident going down that fine sound cliff in bare feet unless I had had a brain seizure and fallen off. So are the mighty fallen; safety and danger should never be considered as clear-cut states of being, when your very danger may be in the illusion of safety.

We found ourselves in a narrow cave about fifty feet high, the floor of which was strewn with immense sea-worn boulders. Here there was some danger stepping on these shiny surfaces in the dim light. As it was, Bobbie slipped and found herself up to the waist in a pool. We proceeded slowly, finding this high corridor splitting into two passages and light filtering in from somewhere ahead. The north-west corner of the island is, therefore, completely tunnelled through, and the sea passes from end to end, a distance of nearly two hundred yards, at high tides. This cave of Gothic dignity was one of the best thrills of the island.

Dougal was always doing things which added to the general comfort of our island home. He made a lobster creel one day of driftwood and wire netting, a prism-shaped affair it was, with a beautifully incurved hole in one end. It so happened that some of the Achiltibuie folk came in the afternoon to mark the lambs of the few ewes on the island. One old fisherman among them said, 'Well now, I wass neffer seeing a creel like that one pefore. She will not pe haffing much headroom whateffer.'

Never have I heard anything so artlessly damned as that creel of Dougal's, and Bobbie and I rolled on the shingle with laughter. But Dougal merely

grinned and said he was content to judge it by results. Calum Macleod said
wire netting did not seem to catch lobsters very well, but that we should
get crabs; he proved to be right. Devil a lobster did we see, but crabs were
plentiful enough.

Dougal used the timber which I had brought from the great east cave
to make a fine lean-to about four feet high along the back and one side of
the hut, where we were able to store peat, driftwood and such things as
did not need to be inside. He fitted a table and shelves against the hut just
outside the door so that we could wash up there on fine days and keep
her saucepans outside. It was Dougal who finished the turf dyke I had
begun round the huts, and he hung a gate, built a piece of wall and planted
stonecrop, scurvygrass and other little flowers on the top of it. Indeed we
began to wonder why anyone should ask for a house with more than a
couple of rooms. Ours seemed so easily run and demanded little of the time
one would have preferred to spend out of doors.

It is remarkable how much more work is made as soon as you have a house
of stone and lime with doorsteps and fireplaces and several windows, and
when you have begun to collect furniture. We have reached the conclusion
that the cure for the chronic state of monetary poverty in which we find
ourselves while we insist on doing research which it pleases us to do and
which cannot be conducted in a laboratory in the shelter of a university, is
to simplify needs. Face up to the fact that much of the furniture and fittings,
and therefore of indoor space, is quite unnecessary for comfort. Pare down
continuously and avoid junk like the plague; be careful to see that such
labour-saving devices as you install are not in fact labour-makers. We have
never been more happy than in these wooden-hut days; if there is one fruitless
consumer of good energy above another it is the eternal scramble to maintain
or reach some false standard of comfort, social position or respectability. If
you become suddenly poor, cut your losses and climb down, and if you are
chronically poor but doing what you most wish to do, then I repeat, simplify
your needs with a bold, clear mind. The extra time given you by this means
you can continue doing the things you wish.

Just think for one short moment what was behind our turning a knob on the morning of Coronation Day and having Westminster Abbey brought inside our little wooden hut. There was all the work and organisation behind making the set itself. There was the intricate organisation emanating from the hot and fevered atmosphere of Broadcasting House (I have been there myself and wonder how they manage to keep it up), and there were the King and Queen themselves going through an ordeal, while we, a party of comfort-loving islanders (living the simple life and all that), lay in the sun and heard perfectly that wonderful service and procession. It was magnificent and inspiring. We were enjoying the fruits of an immense labour to which we could hardly think we had contributed. No: if you are going to crab civilisation and extol your own simple life, you must go back to scratch.

We were enjoying a lovely spell of weather at the time of the Coronation, so warm, sunny and calm that it seemed strange to listen to the accounts of rain during the Procession, increasing to a downpour in the evening. Chlèirich was Arcady that day until late at night when a curious set of local conditions somewhat spoilt our fun. The summit cairn of the island seemed an unusually good place to have a Coronation bonfire, and during odd hours of earlier days we had carried up to the cairn large bundles of driftwood and dead heather shaws. It is extraordinary that when we get such a good spell of weather as this had been there is often a wind off the land at night which reaches Chlèirich as a half-gale. Sometimes you see it happening even in the day, and there is a strip of rough water between Ben More Coigeach and Chlèirich, a strip perhaps two miles wide, outside which the sea is quite calm. Why there should be this extremely local disturbance I do not know, but the nearer you may be in a boat to Ben More at such times, the greater your danger. The sea piles up short and steep incredibly quickly, and the velocity of the wind is very great. A roar of waters greeted us when we three came to the summit cairn that night. We knew there could be no bonfire for us, because had we lit a fire it would have spread immediately into the peat, which lies thin on the ridge where the bare red rock is constantly peeping through. And with this good dry weather the peat was parched and cracked; the momentary sport of a Coronation bonfire was no excuse for burning half the island and damaging it permanently.

So we had to content ourselves watching the blazes at Achiltibuie, Ullapool, Dundonnell, Gruinard and at Laide. We could even see a light in the Outer Hebrides. People at all those places, including Alasdair at Achiltibuie, were looking for our fire and we had to disappoint them. Unfortunately, they were not aware of the conditions which prevented our having it, so that, contrary to all our normal arrangements, some of them were a little troubled on this night because there was no fire on the summit cairn of Chlèirich. The heather and the driftwood is up there yet.

We were getting fish regularly all through the second year, fine fat cuddies, occasional large lythe and some mackerel. The offal was boiled for the hens, and Bobbie cooked the fish in a variety of ways so that we never got tired of them. Sometimes she would fry them, sometimes steam them with milk, and one favourite way we liked cuddies was to roll the fillets with mixed herbs and bake them. It was amazing the amount of fish we could put away.

Dougal was fisherman more often than I was now, for I was almost constantly busy with my birds. He thoroughly enjoyed the job, amusing himself now and again by stalking whales and basking sharks. I well remember one evening seeing him streaking down the west coast of Chlèirich in the kayak after a school of four whales. He was quite unaware that a fifth whale was less than fifty yards behind him and following. Then one of the school jumped from the water and there were signs of the whole school becoming playful. Brother McDougall knew when discretion was the better part of valour and left the arena.

June 8th, 1937, was not a very happy day for Bobbie and me because Dougal went away to help his people pack up house in England. We should not see him until the latter end of August, when he would be joining us for the grey seal work on the Treshnish Isles, a job on which we had now set our hearts. James Macleod had brought three cases of stores, two cans of paraffin and two bags of mail, so after despondently watching the launch go away from the Exchange rock we worked off our low spirits humping all this stuff over to the camp.

Four days later the weather was magnificently hot and calm, and I spent a good time finding shady and grassy places in which to tether the goats and the ewe with Fortescue. When I had got them all settled happily I tempted Bobbie to come out on the sea. We paddled towards the south-west point, Àird Beag, but a school of finback whales came by a few yards ahead of us, frequently breaking the water and blowing. Bobbie does not like whales in such close proximity and I was instructed to turn northwards. I obeyed dutifully, but imagine how I was tickled when less than fifty yards directly ahead of us there appeared the great dorsal fin of a basking shark. Bobbie does not like rubbing shoulders with these people either, so I had to take another point eastwards and landwards. And there another basking shark appeared. I turned sadly and with resignation to the west landing, but at this point Bobbie said she would be damned if she was going in if all the marine fauna of the Minch came sailing by.

If we did work at all it seemed play, and now only the good weather is remembered. The longest day was magnificent, and the sun recorder showed sixteen and three-quarter hours of bright sunshine. We built our peat stack that day and fetched in loads of driftwood from the little bays. Blue butterflies appeared for the first time this year, helping the illusion that summer was eternal. That illusion was soon broken, for I, sleeping that night in the heather near the north loch, was woken at four o'clock in the morning to find a smirr of rain and a cold north-east wind. I got up and ran back to the hut to get warm and drink some tea. Next day, the 23rd, was my thirty-fourth birthday, and the weather not much better. But I had work to do indoors, and there were surprise parcels to open and good things to eat, including a fine birthday cake from my mother. To be born on Midsummer's Eve is probably why I carry something of an elfish nature in an elephantine frame. It is my habit on this night to go forth and meet what may come; always it is something of interest. Year after year on the mainland I would pick up a hedgehog on the night of my birthday, but here on Chlèirich I saw the otters, and later the flight of the storm petrels about my head.

That last week of June was a dreadful time of south-westerly gales, reaching hurricane force at times. I went out on the afternoon of the 28th to find sheltered places for the goats, and my hands were blue with the cold. Torrential rain was driving horizontally from the sea. Then, when I came in again, Bobbie was listening to the Wimbledon tennis, and the commentator was remarking that it was a sultry day and the players were obviously feeling the heat. There seemed something exotic about cotton frocks as we looked forth from our window and listened to the blast.

The wind veered to north-west and then north in the night and blew a gale. I went to the Cauldron to see the seas and the big gullery the following morning. What tragedies were there! Many chicks were lying dead, and nearer the edge it was obvious many chicks and nests had been washed into the sea. A big grey battleship passed close under the island that morning, apparently steady as a rock in those great seas; and yet, as I watched her bows carefully through my glass I saw them dip under and the waves break over her decks.

We were utterly sick of this wind and our nerves were on edge. I know that I was getting in a bad temper by 3rd July when there was a fine calm afternoon and the mail launch did not come. I chafed and grumbled, so Bobbie and I took the kayak round to the east bay in the afternoon and thought to fish from there in the evening. We went through the island to the kayak just after nine o'clock, and my temper was not improved by the fact that a fresh north wind had sprung up. I could see a wicked jabble of sea off Àird Glas where wind and tide and rock face were playing tricks with the water, but I thought we could get round it into straight water. Not so. The north wind catching us broadside drove us nearer the cliff round which the peregrines were screaming wildly, and into the choppy water which was of that unmanageable type where the sea comes up in pyramids and a plume of white shoots off the top. There is no rhyme or reason in this kind of sea, and as we were getting too much of it breaking over us for safety, I headed north into the wind and came back into the landing under the lee of the north shore of the bay.

This episode added further to my sense of frustration, for I had nearly gone forward in anger. We carried the boat through to Lochan Fada and paddled about under the aspens and royal ferns which grow there. How calm was this water, sheltered as it is from the north, after the noisy sea in which we had just been! The bit of wind in the leaves of the trees was a lovely sound, and seen from the water these little aspens looked bigger than they were, and very comforting. The honeysuckle tumbled over the rocks to the water's edge, scenting the air so that I was momentarily intoxicated by its sweetness. How lush this bank on a bare island! To hear the wind in these tiny trees, to smell the honeysuckle, to see the noble fronds of the great royal fern and to feel the water of the lochan lapping against my leg through the skin of the kayak – all these after the stark red cliffs, the rasping cry of the peregrines and the angry sea – assailed me with a sudden wave of nostalgia for the kindlier country where the big trees grow, and undergrowth and a wealth of foliage. But is not this nostalgia part of the very joy this life gives? It is part of that succession of contrasts, physical and intellectual, which is the salt of life. On this north-western fringe of an old world I reach an internal peace and occasionally experience these sweet yearnings for trees and deep grass. If I go south, the trees take on a heightened beauty and have a new fascination for me; but within a day or two comes the longing for the islands and indomitable coasts of this country; and this is no sweet nostalgia but a painful longing which does not pass. There is a measure of asceticism in living here, though I believe it is Epicurean. If it is, perhaps my Stoic philosophy is not quite good enough.

The weather improved after this; meadow brown and blue butterflies became active, and the island flowers came forth with a new sweetness to make our world a gay one. The wild thyme made purple whole patches of ground except for the golden heads of horseshoe vetch. The asphodel was flowering in the bogs now, brilliant spikelets of golden flowers, each one like a star. The heather was in flower also and some of the bell heather. Sometimes we wondered if we had ever seen the tormentil flowers so profuse or the golden suns of the hawkbit so abundant as this year. The purple orchis was still flowering and the sea pink had not yet gone from the west side. That darling flower, the ragged robin, showed an occasional bloom here and there, on which we lighted unexpectedly, and the rock faces sparkled with the pink stars of the stonecrop.

Treshnish Isles

Cairn
a' Burgh

Sgeir na h'
Iolaire

Fladda

Sgeir an
t'Eirionneach

Sgeir a'
Caisteal

Dùn
Cruit

Sgeirean
Mòr

Lunga

The Dorlinn

Dutchman's
Cap

Little
Dutchman

N

0   1   MILES   2   3

THE TRESHNISH ISLES

TRESHNISH

WE LEFT CHLÈIRICH in 1937 exactly a fortnight before we found ourselves on Lunga, or Lungaigh, the largest of the Treshnish group which lies a few miles west of that large Inner Hebridean island of Mull. It was little enough time to do all we had to do of final organisation, but we were loth to leave Chlèirich before it was absolutely necessary.

By Sunday, 22nd August, I felt I had done all I could towards having new gear and stores waiting at Oban, cared for by the Stationmaster and Harbourmaster. These gentlemen had both entered into the spirit of the expedition and had given personal attention to our stuff, collecting it in a locked shed near the harbour steps. Our good friends, Messrs Thomas Black and Sons of Greenock, had done their best for us at the harbour there, which was the base of the ship which took us to the islands. We were receiving Government assistance in the matter of transport, for it was realised that our projected work on the seals had a practical bearing on fisheries problems. We were to go in one of the coastal patrol cruisers. I felt satisfied about arrangements ahead, but on this Sunday we were still at Dundonnell with the car to pack and three of us to get to Oban before nine o'clock the following morning.

It was a day of sweltering heat which we felt badly in the relaxing air of the glen after our many months on Chlèirich. More and more gear accumulated, so that I began to be a little anxious not only about its bulk but the total weight. Still, there was no alternative but to carry on, and by five o'clock we were ready to start, all the gear well tied and the last cup of tea inside us. Bobbie, Alasdair and myself were in the front seat of the Ford, and being well packed in we did not get out at Corriehallie where our friends the Morrisons came out to wish us Godspeed. That send-off did help, because we began our journey in a tired state.

The car was so definitely overloaded that I had to be very careful on any considerable bend in the road. Driving was undoubtedly a strain that day, made no less unpleasant by the large amount of holiday traffic on the roads. I never exceeded fifteen miles an hour over the terrible road of the Feighan, and rarely over twenty on the Dirie Mor. Things were a little easier from Garve to the Kiltarlity turn just south of Beauly, which we took in order to bypass Inverness and save fifteen miles. It is a bit of road of which I am very fond, from Beauly to Drumnadrochit, because the crofts look prosperous and there are plenty of trees. We got down the terrific hill into the village of Drumnadrochit by using the low gear only and the brakes not at all. That hill was a milestone past, I felt, and it was with relief we came on to the wonderful new road through the Great Glen of Scotland. It was possible for us to do thirty-five to forty miles an hour in safety.

We were immediately struck by the casual fashion in which youths strewed themselves across the road and would not move out of the way, and when we got down to Fort William we found them playing football in the streets. So much for the big new road, the manners of those living alongside and the decline of Sabbath observance. Once you are off these big arteries you find the people retain traditional Highland good manners.

It was dark when we stopped at half-past ten on the north shore of Loch Leven. The night was utterly still, with low mist, very heavy dew and swarms of midges. None of us slept well, and I know that Bobbie and I were a little afraid of sleeping-in. Bobbie was up first before five and soon had tea on the go while Alasdair and I broke camp and reloaded the car, so that we were on the road again before six o'clock. The sun came out as we rounded Loch Creggan, where the country has none of the starkness of the Northern Highlands. There are low hills, green parks and plenty of trees round wide stretches of sheltered water, and back of all the high, blue hills. We stopped for a quarter of an hour to have a wash, comb our hair and become human again. It was half-past eight as we came into Oban, which time gave us five minutes to spare after we had garaged the car and stepped aboard SS *King George V* bound for Iona. We dived below to eat as big a breakfast as we could get; anxiety was past now and we were going to relax as much as we could for the next two days.

Alasdair went over much of the ship, finding her speed, tonnage, draught and other details which hardly bothered us. Bobbie and I were looking towards Mull where we have spent so many happy days. We picked out the places we know and love well – Lochbuie, Carsaig, and a big rock, almost an island, where we camped for a night years ago. Nevertheless, we could not help feeling this country lacked some of that impersonal grandeur which belongs to that we have now come to call our own. I felt this and was pleased when Bobbie said, 'I'm wanting back to Lochbroom already.'

There is no doubt that Bobbie and I found ourselves shy of all the people and felt awkward in a holiday crowd. I was also nervous about going ashore with a mob at Iona. But our minds were taken from dwelling on ourselves by the sight of a large flock of Manx shearwaters skimming along the water – hundreds of them weaving in and out with the gliding, straight-winged flight. The ship dropped to half-speed as we passed through the Torran rocks off the south-west corner of Mull. How red the granite showed, even at sea level! And then there was the sudden change of seeing the greenness of Iona and its grey, gneiss hill of Dun-I, an ever-beautiful island.

Big longboats came out to meet us, and the ship spewed forth its mob, ourselves included. I was not happy just then – still less so when we got ashore and saw a fat blonde woman in beach pyjamas. This was Iona of the soul's rest vulgarised in a holiday August by fast transport. Last time I had come here I had taken a pilgrim's way, walking through the hill and then down the gruelling road of the Ross of Mull. I had rung a bell at Fionnphort and a boat had put across the mile of Sound, its crew a great Viking of a man and a dark woman whose raven hair streamed in the wind and rain. That was the way to approach Iona, and in the spring of the year, when the only people visiting the island were doing so in a spirit of pilgrimage and quietness.

Well, I had come to meet Ian Mackenzie, who rented the grazing of the Treshnish Isles and who would be bringing us mail from time to time. He was there on the concrete slip and came directly to us, picking us out from the crowd though we were previously unknown to us. Happily, the hotel was full, and he took us to stay in a tiny cottage which had no garden, but rested on the grass near where a burn ran down to the sea.

We put Alasdair to bed after lunch, for he was dog-tired and had a hard time ahead of him yet before he would be on Lunga. We ourselves went into the island, lay down in the sun and went fast asleep for a couple of hours. Thus, we found ourselves refreshed and eager again after tea, and ready to visit the Abbey. It seemed quite untouched somehow by the number of visitors who must pass through in the year: even now, it was empty but for ourselves.

When we came out of the Abbey, Iona was Iona again to me, and later in the cool of the evening all its charm and beauty came back. We went to the white sands at the north end of the island to augment my store of pebbles of green marble and to bathe our feet. And lastly, before a welcome bedtime, we talked with Ian Mackenzie, who told us details of the landings on Lunga, the best place to camp, and where the water was – all good information which saved a lot of time two days later.

Next day after lunch we boarded the *King George V* again. The ship was lying off a quarter of a mile because there was a fresh southerly wind and a fair sea running. The longboats got rather knocked about against the side of the ship, and some of the passengers were drenched. Once aboard, we had half an hour to wait while further relays of people came in the longboats, so I amused myself taking flight photographs of young greater black-backed gulls which were hovering about the porthole by the galley. They were in a grand position below me, heedless of my attempts to photograph them. The results were good, and one of them I look upon as one of the six best photographs I have ever taken. Two of the birds with wings outstretched came parallel with each other and diagonally across the field of the lens; every mark of the intricate pattern of the young gulls' wings is apparent, and below is the glinting, summer sea.

When we turned into the Firth of Lome Bobbie and I began to get more and more excited and impatient to be ashore, for if everything were as it should be, Dougal would be meeting us off the boat and there should be signs of the cruiser. It was a lovely evening as we turned into the harbour at Oban, and there she was lying at anchor and looking rather remote in her battleship grey. Lying near was the well-known ocean-going yacht *Norseman*, and the masts of smaller craft reached skywards beyond these two ships. I cannot describe the kick we felt when we saw Dougal's grinning face in the crowd as the *King George* came alongside the quay. It was one of the great moments – a lot of fikey work now in the background, a rosy future ahead and this present meeting of good friends. Dougal had been aboard the cruiser and talked things over with the Captain and First Officer, who, he said, were rather looking forward to this little trip with us, but that they wondered what like of folk we were.

An officer was on the steps above a grey launch full of men. He stepped forward and shook hands. 'Dr Fraser Darling? My name is C—, Second Officer of F.C. —. You are right on the dot for time.' I heaved a sigh of relief; for weeks and weeks there had been on my mind the responsibility of this zero hour. You start badly if you start late. I moved towards the car again to start unpacking. 'No no no,' said Mr C— in a shocked voice, 'just leave that to the boys.'

The half-dozen boys ranged from about twenty to sixty years of age, but they were all equally proficient in stripping my car of gear, and would have taken seats, tool pack and all if I had not watched them. A lorry came along with our stock of paraffin loaded into petrol tins, and almost at the same moment I saw Dougal and a porter coming from the little station lock-up shed, with our gear on a platform truck. Everything going like clockwork. I deposited the car in a garage for four months' rest and got back in time to go aboard the cruiser with the first load. Captain M—r said he would like to wait for the post at 10.15 a.m. so Bobbie and I went ashore again to do one or two oddments of shopping.

There was a freshening north-westerly breeze as we crossed that choppy stretch of water at the south-west corner of Lismore and near the Lady Rock, but we felt nothing of it once we were into the Sound of Mull. At noon Captain M—r asked me on to the bridge, where we looked at charts of the Treshnish Isles and one of the Summer Isles which showed the anchorage of Tanera. 'I have always promised myself a night in there,' he said.

As we had not emerged from the north-west end of the Sound of Mull by one o'clock, I thoroughly enjoyed my lunch. In fact, I enjoyed life for a while longer sitting in a deckchair and watching the scene about the mouth of Loch Sunart and the south shore of Ardnamurchan (Àird nam Murchan). It was rather different when we got out beyond the north end of Mull and my beautiful lunch became a libation to Neptune. The swell was strikingly deep and a big surf was breaking on the west shore of Mull. I managed to stagger around in between times, pointing out the approach to Lunga and the landing place at the Captain's request. Nobody else felt the slightest bit squeamish, of course, and I cursed my misfortune. But it could not utterly take away the thrill I felt in the fine day and the sight of these plateaued islands which were now so near us. I remembered the first time I had ever seen them, long years ago on a May evening, from the top of Ben More on Mull. How deeply I longed to visit them then, and how near I was now!

We anchored off the eastern shoulder of Lunga after the sailor who had been swinging the lead from the starboard bow had called 'Mark thirteen, sir,' which, from looking at the chart, I took to mean 6 fathoms. The anchor settled snug, the launch was lowered from the davits, and we passengers went aboard her with Mr O— and six men and a light load of gear.

The idea was that we should find the channel between Sgeir a' Caisteal and Lunga and nose about for the landing which Ian Mackenzie had explained to me. Well, there was no channel to be seen and we had to land ourselves and the gear on a skerry by Sgeir a' Caisteal. A very light-coloured grey seal cow came alongside and looked at us calmly while the sailors made remarks of various kinds, cajoling, complimentary and otherwise. Mr O— and I went to spy out the ground, for we could not understand this dry crossing to Lunga. According to information, the channel did not dry out. What had really happened was that we had arrived at the dead low of a new moon spring tide, the only time when the channel is dry. It was not pleasant going over those weed-covered boulders, but we thought we could just carry over this small lot of gear before the tide came in. We did not know that sound of water as we do now.

We picked up loads and started for the channel, but there was water among the stones already and it could be seen rising. Dougal waded through with a case and a young sailor in sea boots followed. They found it bad going; Dougal ran back after dumping his case, and Seaboots came over a minute later and rather slower because of his rubbers. The water was up to the top of those boots before he got back on to the rock. All we could do was to wait for the tide, so we lay on the skerry in the sun, enjoying our ease; the work would come soon enough.

The cruiser's launch came back with the steward aboard, who with professional slickness produced an immense teapot full of tea and a small mountain of tomato sandwiches. This was truly a marvel, for my mouth was on fire and I was famished after that round of sickness. It was one of the high spots of this memorable day.

There was now more water and we left the skerry and Sgeir a' Caisteal, ran slowly through the channel and landed on a small spit of shingle, the only bit of its kind on all the island. Then began that gruelling task with which we were now familiar – carrying the gear from the shore to the camp. Here we had to camp about ninety feet above the sea and a quarter of a mile from where the stuff was put ashore. Bobbie and I ran ahead as fast as we could and found a sheltered hollow near the old houses which we thought suitable for the tents. By the time we were in full swing carrying, there were eleven men crawling up and down the steep path from the shore, just like a lot of pirates or smugglers with contraband. Those men were great and remained entirely cheerful under a succession of loaded Tate sugar boxes.

From the shelf on which we were to camp we watched the launch return to the cruiser, being hoisted aboard and the ship's anchor drawn. We saw white handkerchiefs waving as she steamed away, and then, when well out of the skerries and going northwards, she gave us a few notes of farewell on her siren.

Lunga is a lump of an island and we could not get inside it to pitch our camp in a sheltered place as we could on Chlèirich, so we naturally pitched on the north-east corner near the water and near the remains of the old houses. A few yards east of us was the cliff edge, a ninety-foot sheer drop to the big boulders at the foot, and then the sea; a few yards the other way rose the steep, rocky slope of the hill of Lunga which reaches 337 feet and is known as the Cruachan, meaning haunch. Sgeir a' Caisteal was out of sight of the tents, but we could see reefs to the north-east of it. Then to the north we could see Fladda and the tops of Cairn a' Burg beyond. Along the whole eastern horizon was Mull, a fine skyline indeed, topped by the shapely cone of Ben More. Between us and Mull were Gometra and Ulva and Little Colonsay, and as we gazed we were impressed once more with the characteristic features of this country. The cliffs are sheer, then there is a little flat; then another steep slope and cliff and another flat on top of that. Lunga itself is like that, and so is the Dutchman or Bac Mor, two or three miles south-west of Lunga. But the other Treshnish Isles have only the sheer cliffs rising from the sea, and flat tops on which you could play cricket. The formation is volcanic, and the Treshnish cliffs themselves are of a grey amorphous rock lying on a platform of lava near the sea level. This laval erosion platform runs out into the sea at certain points and forms suitable breeding grounds for the seals.

At the Cruachan of Lunga we see the white sands of Iona to the south and the little hill of that island, Dun-I. Westwards lies Tiree, once the 'Granary of the Isles' because of the good corn which could be grown there, and the island which, in the language of the Gael, 'lies below the waves'. It is indeed a low island for the most part, and many were the queer effects of the mirage; sometimes the island would seem to be cut in two and the houses would stand like skyscrapers with their feet in the sea. Between Iona and Tiree were the two isolated lighthouses of Dhu Artach and Skerryvore. A little north of Tiree begins the long, low, rocky coastline of Coll, over the top of which we could see the Outer Hebrides on a good day. North again was the spectacular outline of Rhum with its mountain cones rising over 2600 feet. Beyond Rhum we were able to see the Black Cuillin of Skye, and Blaven, and also the Red Hills of Skye. We could see Muck and the prominent Sgurr of the Island of Eigg. East again was the tall columnar lighthouse on the point of Ardnamurchan, the most westerly point of the mainland of Great Britain. We could see the high mountains of Ardgour over the top of the peninsula of Ardnamurchan.

That evening I thought I owed it to Alasdair as well as myself to take a look round a bit of the island, and we set off westwards. We found that the Sanctuary Rock, or more correctly Dùn Cruit or the Harp Rock, was actually an island, cut off from Lunga by a narrow channel and sheer cliffs. The upper eastern face of the rock is riddled with puffin holes, and even now there were a few kittiwakes and fulmars still at their nests.

The buzzards were busy overhead engaged on their evening rabbiting. We also saw flocks of curlews and peewits and a couple of shelduck in a little inlet at the north-west of the island where the water collects an immense quantity of marine detritus. Later we came to call this place the Dirty Inlet, from the mess and stink which was set up as the weed and rubbish rotted. There were shags in hundreds, but few cormorants.

We found the west coast of Lunga an imposing place. The cliffs are rugged and sheer, and their foot is washed by the open Atlantic. The erosion platform, running out there just below tide level, caused the waves to break in a fine roll as they never did about the cliffs of Chlèirich where the water is deep close in to the face. Halfway down the length of Lunga the island nips in suddenly to a narrow, low neck only a few feet above the sea. The place is called the Dorlinn. Beyond the Dorlinn is a long, low plateau with sheer cliffs almost all the way round, sixty to seventy feet high. Apart from the Cruachan itself, on which the soil is necessarily thin, the island is covered with rich grass, and in the frequent hollows the brown volcanic earth reaches a depth of two or three feet. If you could make shelter here you could grow anything on such soil.

We had already become acquainted with the nocturnal habits of the Manx shearwaters. These birds make an indescribable shrieking cry which is enough to frighten anyone. It is a cracked, half-choked scream, and you do not hear the beat of wings as the birds come nearer and recede again. There is the story in the West that a mainland shepherd took service on the island of Eigg many years ago; the shearwaters were nesting in burrows near his house, he being unaware of their existence because they are not obvious about their breeding haunts during the day. He had not been in the house a week from the May Term when the shearwaters began shrieking, and then nothing would induce him to stay another night.

Two days after taking up our abode on Lunga we had a visit from the Robertsons, the family which has fished lobsters about these islands for three generations. They have a little hut on Fladda where they spend the summer fishing, and they return to Tobermory for the winter to make good their creel stock and equipment for the following year. Our visitors today were the old gentleman of eighty years and his son Donald. Donald was one of the biggest men I have ever seen, with an immensely strong face and a voice as soft as new milk. It was for me one of the greatest disappointments of our expedition that we saw him only once more before he went back to Mull. Our hope had been that we should have made a deeper acquaintance and got about the islands with them. But an extremely rough spell of weather and an illness of the old gentleman prevented contact between us and caused them to leave Fladda earlier than usual.

They brought us lobsters and crabs this day, told us the news they had heard on the wireless, and then a lot of useful stuff about the seals. The animals did not mind them and would allow them quite near, but they were frightened of strange boats and tended to go out westwards into deep water. The Robertsons' work about the islands had made the seals their friends, and I could tell how proud they were of the seals and how anxious to take care of them. These men were also good observers of bird life and had kept records for several years of the spring arrivals of the nesting species on the Treshnish Isles. In this intelligent interest in the wildlife of their territory the Robertsons reminded me of Shetland folk, many of whom are first-rate observers and recorders, but our West Highland people as a whole have an extraordinary ignorance of any animal life that does not directly concern them. It is a difference of outlook between the two areas for which I cannot account. There is a lot of Norse blood in the West after all, though the social traditions have remained very distinct.

The good weather went out with August, for we woke to high wind and showers from the south-west on 1st September, the first day of what proved to be a trying fortnight. But we had come to watch seals and were full of eagerness and joy when the great beasts began to collect about the place in increasing numbers. There was one bull of tremendous size, probably nearly ten feet long and weighing, perhaps, seven hundred pounds, who came to lie out at a particular place in the sound between Lunga and Sgeir a' Caisteal. His personality soon became evident to us, and I think it was Dougal who christened him Old Tawny. What a magnificent head and proud bearing he had! Never since, either on the Treshnish or on North Rona, have I seen a bull seal to equal him in size or majesty.

His movements ashore were delightful to watch – the way he would make himself comfortable on the rock and then the expressive movements of his forelimbs, which I prefer to call hands because they can be used in ways so like the human hand, fingers and knuckles as well, rather than as some awkward mittened limb of whale or manatee. You would see Old Tawny scratch his belly delicately with his fingernails, waft a fly from his nose, and then, half closing the hand, draw it down over his face and nose just as men often do. Then he would smooth his whiskers with the back of

his hand, this side and that. His hands would be at rest over the expanse
of his chest for a while, and then you might see him scratch one palm with
the fingers of the other hand, or close his fist and scratch the back of it.
A seal's movements are often a most laughable travesty of humanity, but
considered more carefully as seal movements they have great beauty.

The wind increased to a gale from the south-west and we saw waves
breaking three-quarters of the way up the face of Dùn Cruit or the Sanctuary
Rock, which is one hundred and fifty feet high. Between there and Sgeir
a' Caisteal great rollers were coming in and breaking long before they
reached the shore. The seals were out there obviously enjoying themselves.
I saw Old Tawny letting the waves break on him and coming up again in
the trough to wait for the next one. None of them was fishing; it was just
the fun they were having.

The gale and rain seemed to reach a climax on the night of 4th September,
and we had no sleep before 3 a.m. Then we went off oblivious to everything
until six o'clock, when the wind had dropped and the rain stopped. Blessed
peace. We turned over again, and the next thing we knew it was a quarter
past nine. The seals were calling loudly in their high falsetto while we had
breakfast, and I was thinking to myself that the tide should be low enough
about noon to let us across to Sgeir a' Caisteal. I looked over the cliff to see
twelve cow seals lying out at Old Tawny's place. Soon there were sixteen,
and then Old Tawny himself came out of the water and lay by them.

I had much to learn about the Atlantic grey seal at that time. This was
the first time I had spent any considerable spell at one of their breeding
grounds at the breeding season, and I was much afraid of being too eager
to stalk them and of frightening them away. Money from scientific bodies
and much goodwill from individual people had put me in this favoured
position in which I could do a self-chosen job of work. It was not for me
to amuse myself with a very close stalk, if by that act I imperilled later
research. My previous attempts at stalking seals at home and elsewhere
had shown me that they were extremely wary. But as I looked at that mob
of seals and at Old Tawny, then at every inch of the ground between me and
them, and felt the wind coming in from the west, I thought the job could be

done. Surely a photograph of Old Tawny would justify my going.

Dougal and Alasdair wanted to explore part of Sgeir a' Caisteal, so we three started together on condition they left the group of seals to me and kept well out of their sight and wind. We crawled over the floor of the sound on our bellies in full view of the seals two hundred and fifty yards away. But wind and sun were in our favour and we went extremely slowly over that expanse of tangle and wrack, myself encumbered with camera, lenses and binoculars – nearly a hundred pounds worth of stuff about my neck. It was agonising but exciting, and we got over and out of sight without arousing the suspicion of the seals.

Now I went on alone, a big stalk ahead of me and all over seaweed, or so I thought until I came to a place where I realised it would be better tactics to be in the water than to be in full view on top of a rock. I left my boots, stockings, binoculars and some of my camera gear, and waded in slowly until the water was nearly up to my middle. The bottom was so slippy and my tackle so precious. Then a cow seal came near to me in the water and was most interested in my slow and laboured progression. She was not frightened, just curious, and I changed the lens of my camera without mishap, took careful aim and got the photograph which later turned out to be a favourite. She was kind to me and went away quietly. Metaphorically, I raised my Sunday morning hat to the lady, for indeed it was the Sabbath, and then carried on.

I was over at last and crawling up a sunken skerry, along the top of it and in full view of the seals at less than fifty yards range. By this time I was sweating and excited but had managed to keep my large red face to the ground. I took advantage of cover to shed more clothes and go forward with only the bare camera; then down the rock into some shallow water, moving so that it did not splash, crawling on again, and then a peep to see where I was. Only twenty yards, but a rotten position for a photograph. On again with my face to the rock; foot after foot.

And now I was lying alongside Old Tawny, near enough to tickle him, and he was still dozing. I looked at the great furred belly of the seal, at his powerful hand with its five black claws. He rumbled inside and the very rock seemed to shake; never have I felt more insignificant. There is six feet three of me, but I was a dwarf beside him and he was twice as high through the shoulder as I was, lying there beside him. I do not know how long I lay there in wonder at the beauty of the seal, but at last I brought myself to the serious and technical job of photography. The focussing, the exposure, the stops – and him. Was he in a good position? No, I was too near, his head was down and eyes closed. I edged backwards, using only my body muscles, then I whistled gently and he raised his head to look about him. My chance had come – and it was the last exposure in the film of thirty-six!

Old Tawny looked round, lay his head again for a moment and then up again. He looked calmly at the recumbent figure beside him. It was strange; he had better get away from it, but he moved leisurely and without fright. If a human being can get close enough to a large animal, I find it will not take precipitate flight as it would if it saw him several yards away. I had got through the barrier of this beast's watchfulness. Luck was with me that day, the twelfth anniversary of my getting married, I noticed, and the portrait of Old Tawny is in my house, while Old Tawny himself, I hope, is still swimming the seas of the Treshnish Isles with his usual joy and serenity.

TROUBLES AND SUNSHINE

O N MONDAY, 13th September, the time had come for Alasdair to go to school, not to Achiltibuie, but to Gordonstoun in Moray. This meant that one of us must go with him, and after much discussion it was decided that Bobbie should go. Had I gone myself I could have taken him in the car and got back to Iona in quick time. But the question was whether the weather would hold for me to get back to Lunga. This was a highly important time in the work, and I could not afford to be away more than a day or two. Ian Mackenzie happened to come that afternoon, and with much sorrow I saw Bobbie and Alasdair go away with him. What a journey it would be! Back to Iona that night, to Oban the next day by steamer, and then a God-forsaken journey of changes across Scotland to Aberdeen and out to our friends at Williamston where Alasdair was to stay until school began. Then the nightmare journey back again to Oban and Iona – and back to Lunga when the sea allowed.

Dougal and I were busy while she was away and managed quite well for ourselves except that I put too much Holbrook's Sauce in a rabbit stew one day and nearly took the skin off our throats.

We explored a cave on the south-west coast of the island and found that the cave came in from the sea's edge to a great hole in the middle of the southern half of Lunga. The floor was thick with pigeon droppings accumulated during countless years, and even now there were two young rock doves on a ledge, not quite fledged. We could not resist taking these home to see how they shaped as pets, but we paid dearly enough for succumbing to this temptation. They would not feed themselves yet, of course, nor did they much like pellets being thrust into their crops with a little stick we smoothed for the job. Eagerness to be fed made them no easier to feed, and we never gave up until their crops bulged with oatmeal and tinned milk. Nevertheless, the pigeons throve and fledged and ultimately flew, but they would not feed on the pellets we threw down for them; instead they would fly into the tent, sit on our knees and beg, and then be awkward when we put food in their mouths. They began to peck about outside in the grass as the days went by, studiously avoiding anything thrown there by us. Each night they came to a box we put for them near the store tent, but when we had drained a hollow a few yards away and moved the tents down there, the pigeons were quite upset and would not come to the new place though tents and box fulfilled the earlier conditions. It showed once more how significant in a bird's view of things is a particular point in space, and the irrelevance of previously relevant objects moved but a short distance from their former positions. This change seemed to snap the personal link between the pigeons and ourselves, for they came no more for food and were much wilder. Thus, our rock doves returned to their natural habitat good and strong on the wing and less likely to be snapped up by the peregrine falcon than if they had emerged naturally from their cave so late in the year.

We were surprised to hear a launch below us just after lunch on Friday, 17th September, and running to the edge of the cliff we saw Bobbie in Ian Mackenzie's big launch. By Jove, I was glad; fancy getting back here in four days; it was a grand performance. Dougal and I ran down to meet her and listened to a long story of an awkward journey. What struck me most was that she had received much kindness from individuals of the railway staff.

Exactly two days after her return Bobbie felt ill – really ill, because she went to bed. Next day she was worse and very feverish. She had brought back scarlet fever. This ran a flaming course for nearly a week, during which time she grew very thin. We had no invalid diet for her, and on this expedition we were making soda bread because we had not yet learnt of the dried flaked yeast which we were later able to obtain from the Distillers' Company. We were also using tinned margarine, which keeps better than butter, but is not so appetising. The poor girl could eat little or nothing.

All this time the wind was blowing hard from the south-east and south, directly on the tents. These two winds are always unpleasant ones in this part of the world, and at this time they were more nerve-wearing than ever. Oh how I wished it to be calm to give Bobbie a bit of peace, but no, it just kept on blowing hard. I was very troubled. Ought I to put up a flare and get help, supposing a launch would come in these high seas? What was the good anyway? Bobbie was at least in a natural isolation hospital, and as for her as an individual she was better where she was than being carried away. What does the treatment for this kind of disease boil down to in the end? Waiting till the fever has run its course and keeping the patient open and warm. So Bobbie endured her adversity and said she felt much better a week later; then she began the characteristic peeling of the skin, but she got none of the pumice-stoning of the soles of her feet which is my chief remembrance of convalescence in childhood. I was much relieved when she stood on her feet once more.

The danger of scarlet fever is in its sequelae: no sooner had Bobbie begun to feel a little better than I came in one morning to find her in great pain in her ear. This troubled me far more than the scarlet fever, because this might mean a complication we could not relieve. That afternoon I put her to bed again with nearly a quarter of a pint of rum inside her. She has told me since of the blessed feeling of disassociation it brought her, and I crept about quieter than a mouse for the three hours she was asleep as a result of my dose. Then, of course, the pain came back when she awoke, but I did not wish to use more rum until last thing at night, because its effects would obviously lessen and a system full of alcohol is being handicapped in setting its house in order. But severe pain is also dangerous, so I immobilised poor Bobbie with rum for those dreadful hours of the early morning when pain is at its worst and hope its lowest. Dougal is a veterinary surgeon, and in advising against any interference with the ear in the way of pouring in olive oil or hydrogen peroxide, held out the hope that if it was an abscess of the external ear it should burst soon. We gave Bobbie hot bottles to put to her head and these helped a little.

Then suddenly at ten o'clock the next night she felt a quick relief from pain and pus began to flow from her ear. It was as if pressure had been lifted from the whole camp. Now at least we knew that the trouble was not in the inner ear, Bobbie was out of pain and time should put her right. And so it did. Gradually, very gradually, she grew strong again, and seemed completely herself by the end of October. Good air, fresh fish and rabbits and winkles must have helped her. I still think I did right to keep her on the island (and she herself refused to leave it), but there are some people who think me a callous devil.

Whenever the wind let us, Dougal and I would make little expeditions about the islands. There was Sgeir an t'Eirionneach and Sgeir na Giuthas, between which ran a shallow channel where the water showed green above the white sand. Dougal thought he could get flat fish there, but the current ran at about three knots and he was no sooner set for fishing than he was carried out at the south end.

This continual and rapid current must have been the reason why no seals bred on Sgeir an t'Eirionneach, a point which always puzzled me until I knew the rate of drift, for the shoreline was perfect for the young seals and the water appeared calm in every wind. It was while we were poking around those skerries one day that we saw a score or more of common seals lying out on a rock. This was their chosen territory, and we never saw them in the waters round Lunga. They looked very small now that we had become accustomed to the Atlantic grey seals.

There was another day when we thought Bobbie fit to leave for the time it would take us to get to Fladda and back. It was beautifully calm when we pulled into the southern anchorage of that queer little island. Apart from that low-lying neck between the north and south anchorages, Fladda is a plateau about forty feet above the sea, bounded by small sheer cliffs, and, unlike the rest of the Treshnish Isles, has a poor herbage containing more sedge and rinze heather than grass. We explored the island clockwise, and it was for that reason we did not come upon a little bay on the south side until last. There we found great quantities of brambles and Dougal and I stayed much longer than we ought to have done, picking them as hard as we could, filling handkerchiefs and scarves with the welcome fruit. We took back nearly half a stone for our trouble, but the sea was whipping up white with a north wind so that we had rather an anxious journey with the Water Beetle. Bobbie was also anxious, wondering why we did not come when the wind freshened. The sight of the fresh fruit happily eased our path towards a lunch kept waiting.

The year was changing, and that more obviously when we had a respite from the wind. October 4th was a lovely autumn day of sunshine, marvellously peaceful to us who were ridden by wind and rain. It was the high spring tide at the new moon of the autumn equinox, and it drew me to the south end that evening, to see how the young seals would be faring on the erosion platform. The year was dying, and comfortable as the sunshine had been, there had been that golden quality in it which spoke of the failing light. As I walked down that flat plateau the sun was setting behind the southernmost point of Tiree. Where there are trees, I thought, the leaves will be browning, but still the year will have a graciousness of summer. Here there were no leaves to brown and the signs of coming winter were of harder kind. Already the grass was withering and the stems bleaching, so that on a dry day the landscape was turning from green to light buff and many shades of brown. There is a cold dignity in the way the little islands accept the coming of winter. This night it surged through me in the half-light. A flock of peewits rose, calling ahead of me, and here and there snipe flew from the edge of little pools and zigzagged into the gloaming. The grass was dark as I came back and those irregular pools of rainwater threw back the fine light of evening, and I was reminded of those lines in my favourite hymn of 'Lead, kindly light'; this scene was ever in my child's eye as I sang:

> 'O'er moor and fen, o'er crag and torrent, till
> The night is gone.'

Down there at the seal nursery on the south end of Lunga the surf was tremendous. Two well-grown calves were washed off their ledges into the surf and were dashed unmercifully among the boulders. Then a great wave lifted them high to the foot of the cliff; they held on desperately while the swirl receded, and as soon as the pull of the water released, made their way out of reach of the next wave as quickly as they could move. A cow was lying below her young calf, taking the force of the waves and preventing the little one being taken down in the backwash. A bull came out near her; for a moment I could see the indecision in her face before she chose the wrong thing to do! While she went to drive the bull away a wave took the calf far out, but happily the next one brought it back to almost the same place and the mother came back to her task of sheltering the calf. The encroaching sea had driven the seals on to a much smaller space than was their usual nursery ground, and it was a wild, troubled scene. The mighty sea.

I remember that the day after that was one of bright sunshine and strong south-east wind, a bad day for seal watching here. If I went to the south end of the island I should have to approach from the west side and have the sun in my face all the time. The seals, on the other hand, would detect my slightest movement. If I stayed on the cliff and looked over, there would be a vertical blast of air which would soon make my eyes run and further watching would be most unpleasant. It was also impossible with this wind to watch the seals on the west side in the tiny bays; they were all very wary there and the slightest puff of my scent would drive them into the sea in a panic. And at the north end I could not go to the edge of the sound because my scent was carried over directly to the seals on Sgeir a' Caisteal. So I took up a position on the cliffs between Dùn Cruit and the Dirty Inlet, where I was out of the wind, in the sun and in sight of many seals.

This day I was lucky in seeing one thing I had never seen before. The mother of a calf in the Dirty Inlet went into the sea about half-past three, and when she was but a few yards from the shore I saw a quick movement by her on the floor of the sea. She came to the surface with a good-sized flat fish in her mouth. She rolled over and over in the water, and by the way the fish's tail kept flapping it seemed she had not yet bitten it hard, but was playing with it as a cat does with a mouse. In a minute or two she took the fish from her mouth with her right hand and held it horizontally, fingers upwards and knuckles outwards. Then she took a good bite out of the fish just as you or I (or perhaps only I) might from a large jam tart. Two bites more, still standing upright in the water, and then she took the fish in both hands, pushed it into her mouth and held her muzzle high until the tail gradually disappeared.

We had made an arrangement with Ian Mackenzie that we would go in his big launch to the Dutchman one day if the weather was fit. But that day which opened so full of promise for me ended miserably. Ian Mackenzie did not come because, as we found later, he was asked to move some cattle; but I, looking through my glass over that calm sea, saw another boat come from Iona and anchor off the Dutchman. The distance was 3¾ miles from where the boat lay to where I was on the Cruachan, the sun was in my eyes and there was a slight haze. But my glass is a good one and I can use it; I saw a dinghy pulled up on the flat rocks of the erosion platform at the south end of the Little Dutchman and figures of men coming towards it and going away again. Then I knew it must be a raid on the seals there. I saw the dinghy rowed to the launch, and then a heavy mass which caught the glint of the sun pulled aboard. A figure carrying a gun walked along the skyline and came down to the platform between the Little Dutchman and Dutchman's Cap. Later I saw two men bending low for a long time, and they held something up at last and threw it down again. It was a sealskin. They were there altogether for five hours, and here was I on Lunga, helpless to stop this shameful thing.

Ian Mackenzie came next day to take us to the Dutchman, and as he wished to take some sheep from Cairn a' Burg we went there with him also. Cairn a' Burg Mor is an island of high cliffs all round, and on top are the remains of an old fortress where a MacLean chieftain used to retire in troubled times. One of them held out for three years against the Hanoverians after the Rebellion of 1715. Cairn a' Burg was considered as impregnable as Dumbarton Rock, and I suppose it was until heavy artillery changed the whole notion of impregnability. There is some fine masonry built into the cliff to make it impossible to climb, and we were amused to see the several dykes and wall built to hinder attack. The island feels a romantic place and full of history. The remains of the living-quarters of the fortress are on the flat top of the island, and there is also left the form of the old chapel and its altar stone. What a place this must have been in a battle! Imagine bearded gentlemen rolling rocks and pouring boiling water on to the invaders!

The grass is short and good, and the seven grey-face lambs we took from the Blackface ewes were bigger than their mothers and very heavy. We found seven seal calves round the shores of Cairn a' Burg, and on the way over we noticed two calves on Sgeir an Fheoir, east of Sgeir an t'Eirionneach. These small nurseries all contain very young calves, or in other words, the larger nurseries begin breeding earlier.

We joined the launch again and landed a little farther north on the Dutchman's Cap. There were no seal calves here, nor did we expect to find any, for the sea washes the base of the cliffs. There is one way up the cliffs at the south end of the island and another at the north – ways good enough up which to get cattle on a calm day, but there are more days when you cannot land on this island than when you can.

The light north wind persisted for a few days, and that meant good, fine weather. We woke on the following Sunday morning after having felt it cold in the night, though the temperature had not been lower than 44°F. I felt brimful of energy in this northerly breeze and sunshine, so promised myself a morning's close stalking down the west side, where the wind was just perfect for the job. I went down the cave from the top of the south end of the island, came out on the west shore and worked up to my seals. A day-old calf was on a rock ten feet beyond and slightly below me, and the mother was idling in the water. I just lay there waiting, the wind in my face and bright sun behind – the stalker's idea of heaven. The mother came out of the water on to the rock and arranged herself to feed the calf. I got a lovely series of photos, but was waiting particularly for a photograph of that scratching and fondling behaviour which almost invariably follows suckling.

The wind was cold; being so near, I could not move an inch, the rock seemed like a spike harrow and I got more and more uncomfortable. That calf was really lazy, for he went on feeding in a desultory way for three-quarters of an hour, and at the end of that the cow just slid into the sea.

A week later we had one of the loveliest days of the year after an intervening bad spell. The wind fell in the early hours of the morning and I rose before the sun appeared from behind Ben More Mull. The last clouds dispersed and the sun shone its full round. We sat on the summit of the Cruachan and examined afresh and in detail that great view. Applecross showed beyond the Ardnamurchan peninsula, and Ben Resipol in Moidart was deeply capped with a glinting snow. The lighthouse on Bernera at the extreme south of the Outer Hebrides was visible with the naked eye. Think of the pale blue of the sky, the general blue tint of the ring of land, and the deep blue of the sea; all seems blue, with a touch of green, white or brown here and there. And that night the sky was a dome of stars. Each one of the seven Pleiades was distinct, the Eagle shone in the south-west, and in the light of the Milky Way was the beautiful cruciform constellation of the Wild Swan. The grass beneath our feet was a silver carpet; the air, being so still, brought the crying of the seals to us undistorted, a more pleasing sound since the anxious maternal jealousy went out of it. We lived in a beautiful world and were thankful for it.

The seal nurseries were almost empty now and very few new calves were being born. As soon as the calves change coat from the white fluffy one of the first fortnight to the blue, seagoing coat, the cows cease to take interest in them, and the babies, now extremely fat, remain about the nurseries for another week or two, sleeping much and playing by themselves in the pools. Hunger must eventually call them to the sea. That afternoon I had gone down to the Dorlinn and sat beside a baby cow seal just over a month old, pale-blue coated and ready for the sea. She was lying on her back fast asleep with her hands lying open; hard places were forming on her palms where she pulled herself over the rocks. I looked at her a long time, gently stroking her silvery-white belly; it was cool, being insulated by the thick layer of fat; then I stroked the back of her hand and found it warm, for no layer of blubber covers that. Soon all my children would be gone. This little cow who now looked so fat and happy would not have been alive today had I not run into the surf of a westerly gale here on the day she was born. She was getting a terrible battering and would have been carried far out on the ebbing tide. How she had wriggled in my arms as I lifted her and ran for a safe place above the high-tide mark; and yet she had made no attempt to bite my ear, because she was only a few hours old and had not acquired the power of discriminating between big living things.

There had been a great immigration of thrushes and blackbirds to the island about this time, not dozens but hundreds of birds. Every patch of cow dung was well spread by them as soon as it was stale enough to have gathered below it the insect fauna characteristic of such an environment. A ring ouzel or mountain blackbird was among them one day at the end of October, and I was caused to pick him out by the loud 'chacking' which I recognised to be his note and not his cousins'.

Dougal was counting the number of flowers in bloom on 1st November. There were primroses, violets, buttercups, daisies, ragwort, duckweed, sowthistle, wild sage, mayweed, stonecrop, sea pink, storksbill, bell heather, prunella, scabious, a geranium-like flower I did not know, another little low, pink flower and the rich blue flower with dull, blue-green leaves which grows in the volcanic gravel almost down at sea level – eighteen in all. Summer lingers into winter in this West if you will but seek her in tiny, hidden places.

And yet by the next night there was a full gale blowing from the south-east. It was a bad dry gale which gave us the worst night we had had since we had moved camp into the brackeny hollow which Dougal had drained. The rain fell in torrents with no slackening of the gale all day. It was a spring tide this evening and we had pulled the boat high because of it, but the surf was tremendous and caused me a little anxiety. There had been a new calf born the day before on the east side of the spit of shingle at the north end of the island, a place which was getting the full force of this gale. I saw the mother patiently engaged keeping on the low side of the calf to prevent its being washed away. This is the time when you see the cow seals at their best – all care for the babies, and their eyes soft with concern.

If it was a gale when we went to bed, it was a hurricane later. I slept for an hour as soon as I got into bed, for I was dog-tired, but then no more at all. The rain stopped at three o'clock in the morning and I was sorry, because I knew the tent would soon dry and I should have trouble getting the guys tight again in this inferno. Trouble began at four o'clock when the eave ripped from part of the windward side of the tent. In half an hour another stretch of canvas had gone, and the increased wind resistance which the tent now offered was causing us concern. I felt, also, that I ought to go down to the boat, because a spring tide on her shore with such a gale might reach her. It was then approaching high tide, and I wished she were well up at the Dorlinn instead of at the north-east point where we had made an alternative slip. I went down the cliff path at the north end of the island, finding sudden breathing space there after having difficulty in keeping my feet on the top. A thrush came up from the ground and hit my electric lantern. I picked it up and placed it in a bield under a rock, but the poor little soul had not wits enough to stay there. It flew into the night, the wind caught it and carried it towards the sound where the sea roared, and I wished then I had kept the thrush in my pocket until morning.

The boat was all right, though the spray was splashing into her and I could see the tide was higher than we had ever seen it before. Then I went back to the tent as fast as I could move, there to find the eave had ripped off completely on the windward side, which was now against the centre pole and cracking about us like a cannon. Dougal now appeared and helped us get essentials from inside while Bobbie went to the store tent and tried to make room in there. Then we loosened the pole and let the tent go before she ripped to ribbons. Both Dougal and I felt it keenly, because this tent had been a good friend these two years. Even now the guying system had worked perfectly and disaster had come through the canvas itself giving way and not by the tent blowing down.

By this time it was after six o'clock, so we made breakfast in the cramped space available in the store tent. Plenty of good porridge and endless tea. The sunrise was the most wonderful I have ever seen – and the most dangerous. The gale was blowing as hard as ever, and when I looked at this riot of green and gold and steel-grey, with patches of bright cobalt blue – a colour I had never seen in the sky before – I knew we could expect no cessation yet. And I was right. All through that day the gale blew, while we built a shelter of driftwood and tarpaulins for the stores in the ruins of one of the old houses. It was killing work carrying the stuff up there in that wind because of the initial labour of keeping upright. Bobbie had arranged things in the little bell tent which would henceforth be our home, and I was immediately struck by the snugness and tidiness.

The gale continued all that night with these terrible gusts which were worse than a fortnight before; it blew all next day as well, though not quite so strong. I wrote in my diary on 19th November: 'I said the wind was slackening as we went to bed last night, and so it was, but hardly had we lain down to sleep than a series of great gusts came, and after an hour or more the rain began. Of course I had to get out to slacken the guys, but with these gusts I could do no more than half-slacken with safety. Then another wait in bed until the tent tightened once more, and out again to slacken fully. A drink of tea at one o'clock and attempts to sleep. End of rain at three o'clock, but continuance of south-east wind which dried up the canvas and guys. Bobbie, the rascal, went out at five o'clock to tighten, I then not being in a sufficiently conscious state to know she had gone. Out again a little later myself to tighten fully, and then some sleep until eight o'clock. Three nights of this sort of thing have made us look a trifle grey about the face, and yet we know how much we have to be thankful for. As I write, lying here in a warm, dry bed, the wind has gone round to north and fallen light, and the tent is in calm. All the cloud had blown away before I came in last thing and the moon had risen into a fine sky. The sea is a sheet of silver tonight, and the old grey rocks of the island are silver too in this light. How bright the lights of the lighthouses gleam! We were up the hill watching them tonight – Ardnamurchan, two flashes every twenty seconds; Dhu Artach, two every thirty seconds; and Skerryvore, one every twenty seconds. Such is the land of change in which we live: last night we could hear only the howl of the wind, its thunder on our tent, and the roar of the sea below. Tonight the sea but murmurs, the wild geese talk as they settle to graze on Sgeir a' Caisteal and Sgeir an t'Eirionneach, and the cheerful note of the snipe reaches us as the birds come down near the tent.'

'The starlight is wonderful and the air is very still. Long swells are booming rhythmically out east of us on Sgeirean Mòr. One or two seals are crying full and clear, and I know what a nostalgic sound this will be for me now. It will go along with those of the barnacle and greylag geese – noises that will stir me for the rest of my life and call me back to the islands. Indeed, this music of living things is becoming symphonic in the halls of my mind, and it moves me ever more deeply.'

I nipped out of the tent the following morning while the others were still sitting over breakfast, and I saw a speck in the sea off the Point of Ardnamurchan. It was a ship, of course, but the interesting thing to me was that we rarely saw a ship in that position and end on. I ran into the tent again and announced that the cruiser was coming for us. Bobbie groaned, oh *no*! and Dougal just grinned, frankly incredulous, how did I know? Well, there was the ship off Ardnamurchan. But that doesn't mean to say it's the cruiser. No, but it is all the same – give me my telescope. With the aid of my glass I could see the ship was coming south and she was battleship grey, though no other distinguishing marks were visible at that distance.

This was terrible, we expected to be here for another fortnight. We washed and shaved and packed and packed as hard as we could go. The ship was under Lunga two hours later and giving us a shout on her siren. I ran down to the launch which came off, and an officer I had not met before asked me how long we should be. Two hours, I said, and suggested he might drop a few men to save time carrying down. Several of our old friends now came ashore and were eager to know how we had fared these months.

When we climbed aboard it was not Captain M—r who greeted us but Captain P. We went down to lunch immediately, lots of fried haddock, and while we were eating Captain P seemed most apologetic about not having come sooner. He said he looked in the log and saw when we had been landed in August and had come immediately.

'Don't worry,' we said; 'we had not expected to leave for at least another fortnight, and, in fact, we were a little disappointed to see you coming down the way today.'

But he still seemed to think it was an awful thing to have been left so long. It was calm going all the way, and once we were into the Sound of Mull we all had magnificent hot baths. What luxury!

We left the ship at Oban at about seven o'clock that evening. There was a drizzle of rain, and to our eyes and noses the town was a filthy place. Captain P insisted on one sailor coming to carry our bag to the hotel where we were going to spend the night, and as he would not take no, we suffered having the little bag carried till we were into the darkness, then we relieved the sailor of it quickly, for we knew he had designs on the cinema that evening. It galls me dreadfully to have anyone carry my bag when I am well able to carry it myself.

The hotel was almost empty, of course; it was centrally heated, and the management evidently aimed at making patrons *comfortable*. Dougal said 'phew' and went to the flicks. Bobbie and I wandered about trying to find a cool place, but for that we had to go out on the streets in the drizzle and they were most depressing. We went to bed early, pushed back all the curtains from the windows and folded back the eiderdown. But the mattress seemed to rise all round us until we were enveloped in a fulsome softness. I finished the night on the floor in moderate comfort. The bacon-and-egg breakfast seemed a heavy meal to us who feed lightly in the morning, the walls and ceilings were suffocating and the furnishings were ponderous after being used to our lighter occasional table by Tate and Lyle. It was good to get outside.

We unloaded our gear from the ship, put some on the rail to be sent home, fetched the car from the garage and once more grossly ill-treated it by overloading. It was just as full, but not quite as heavy, as when we came, but now Dougal was in front with Bobbie and me instead of Alasdair, and there was not much room to spare.

It was about dark when we reached Beauly, and it was after that we all began to feel tired. Would there ever be an end, I wondered, to the Dirie Mor and the home road over Feighan? On and on in the darkness, all of us singing Christmas carols until we were hoarse. Then down that last bit till we saw the lights of Corriehallie. Bobbie had wired the Morrisons from Oban, and those good folk had prepared an enormous meal for us. We seemed to go on eating and talking for hours.

How lovely seemed the trees of Brae next day, and the woodsmoke of the great fires we made to air the house and bedding! We had a fortnight more of Dougal's companionship, and because the Feighan road was blocked with snow we took him over the hill to Ullapool and there we said goodbye for the present. He was going to America.

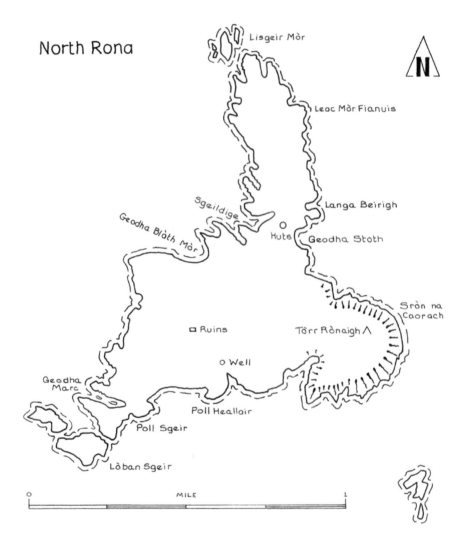

North Rona

Lisgeir Mòr

Leac Mòr Fianuis

Langa Beirigh

Sgeildige

Geodha Blàth Mòr

Huts

Geodha Stoth

Sròn na Caorach

Ruins

Tòrr Rònaigh

Well

Geodha Marc

Poll Heallair

Poll Sgeir

Lòban Sgeir

0   MILE   1

NORTH RONA

NEARING THE GOAL

THE FIRST TIME I EVER SET EYES on North Rona 'afar off in the lap of wild ocean' was from the summit cairn of An Teallach. It was the early morning of a June day. The heat haze was not dancing. I could see through the telescope a small speck in the sea a hundred miles away. Just a speck, there was no detail to be seen, but as it did not move from the absolute direction in which North Rona should be, I felt satisfied I had seen that island, which occupies less than half a square mile, attaining a height of 355 feet and lying in the North Atlantic 47 miles north-west of Cape Wrath and 47 miles north-east of the Butt of Lewis.

I remember thinking that the day would come when I should go ashore, though at that time I had not thought of the grey seals, nor even of going to live on Eilean a' Chlèirich. I was busy observing the life and social affairs of the red deer in the wild country around An Teallach. But as that work developed I naturally began to think of the social life of other gregarious animals, that of the grey seal among them. How was their sociality ordered, and how did it compare with that of these deer?

Thus North Rona took more definite shape in my mind and I gleaned every bit of information I could find. *Ronay*, by Malcom Stewart (Oxford, 1933), was immensely useful, and few of my books are more thumbed than that one, for, contrary to my usual finnicky care of books, I boldly used the wide margins of this for pencilled notes relating to the expedition. Stewart had spent two short periods of a week or more each on North Rona and had scoured the literature. This little book of his not only describes Rona but Sula Sgeir and the Flannan Isles as well. I also met and corresponded with John Ainslie, who, with Robert Atkinson, did a fine piece of research on Leach's fork-tailed petrel during a six weeks' spell on North Rona in the summer of 1937. Stewart and Ainslie, both hard lads, looked at us rather sadly over our projected stay of six months. 'A little fun, Josephine,' they seemed to say, 'but not that.'

It was a blow for both Dougal and us when he had to go to America, for he had been part of the scheme for so long. Several older friends pointedly advised us that we ought to take another man for the trip. But we knew enough of island life not to enter on such folly as taking another party we did not know. There was also the question of the child. What madness! people said. If we did not take him with us, where else was he to go? And both Bobbie and I felt that we were not justified in depriving him of this experience. Alasdair had been on the other trips and had learned a sense of responsibility, so he could come on this and take his chance. It is a decision we have never regretted, and for him Rona is a treasured memory.

The boy's coming, and the fact that we were persuaded against our better judgement to take wireless transmitting and receiving gear, let us in for an awful lot of publicity in the Press. Even one or two of the London dailies printed a lot of nonsense about us. Their great aim, it seemed, was to create a scare about us. One of those so-called national daily newspapers with hotted-up circulations sent two men by car all the way to Dundonnell to 'get the story'. The weather had been consistently against us just then, otherwise those two professional snoopers would have found us gone.

I curbed my initial impulse to refuse to see these fellows. Instead I gave them tea, briefly outlining why I was going to North Rona. One of them was a Yorkshireman, and straight-spoken to the effect that he said they wanted thrills.

'Yes, but I don't,' I said. 'Why not stick to the facts?'

'But the public wants a thrill. You're topical till Christmas, and while we don't wish you any harm, we'd like something or other to happen.'

So when we were well out of the way on Rona they and many other newspapers made up all sorts of cock-and-bull stories. There was one delightful example, when we went to the Treshnish Isles. 'Are you taking a wireless?' asked the reporter. 'No, no wireless,' I replied. 'Not even a receiving set?' 'No, no wireless whatever.' Imagine my feelings, therefore, when I was later sent a page from a newspaper announcing that 'scientist tries radio swing music on seals!'

But this takes me away from Rona.

Cold and rainy as it was that early morning, and wretched as I felt aboard the cruiser, my first *close* glimpse of Rona thrilled me. Here was the speck in the sea at last. A noble shape she was, of rounded hill and sheer cliff on the east, sloping away to sea level at the south-west; how green her mantle, and the band of white surf played along the black foot of her cliffs! I knew little more until I heard the engine bell ring for half speed, dead slow and then stop. We were in the east bay of Rona aboard the cruiser and my spirit rose above seasickness, for it is the wonder of that first view that has remained. My heart was full of sheer joy. But immediately the great practical question leapt into my mind – should we be able to land on this island which is notoriously bad for landing? For the moment that was not my business, and wonder returned as I looked at the hundreds of thousands of seabirds which flew from the cliffs, startled by this most unusual advent of humanity and a ship.

It was awe-inspiring. The swarms of puffins, guillemots and razorbills circled like bees from the hive of the cliff; kittiwakes flashed white from every coign of the rock face which would hold a nest, and fulmar petrels glided silently on motionless wings like small monoplanes. The birds of the sea! The very phrase rouses a naturalist's enthusiasm because they express such a tremendous surge of life. Shags flew hither and thither, black and cumbrous compared with the grace of the smaller birds. The sound of it all was the most thrilling a bird watcher knows – the composite skirl of a million throats. Seabirds express their emotions with great intensity, and the discordant cries blend into a harmony accompanied by the deep voice of the sea. There is nothing else on earth like it; who has lain receptive by a cliff of seabirds has known wonder.

All I could think in that moment of wonder was: and we are going to live here and know every bit of this place as if it were home. After all, it was home. Then I had to become more practical, for I alone knew just where the landing was. Cap'n M said Alasdair and I were to go ashore first trip and take a certain amount of food with us as well as a little tent. This was an island with a sinister history and he was taking no chances. The launch was down now, and soon we were bobbing over to Geodha Stoth on the eastern side of the northern peninsula of Fianuis. There was certainly as much swell as we liked against those low cliffs, but we saw one face where the swell did not break, and being sheer it was almost like a dock. Many are the times I have watched that curious place since then; you can land there in quietness when as little as ten yards away the state of the sea would make it impossible.

We sidled up to that rock carefully and I pushed Alasdair ashore. It was a little gesture it pleased me to make, that the child should be the first of the expedition to land on Rona. I followed him and took the tent and stores thrown up by the launch, which then cast off and went back to the ship.

Forty or fifty grey seals in an excited state came round the boat and maintained a lively interest in us throughout the day. I looked at them as beasts I now knew better. These individuals had never seen me before, but fancy put it into my mind as I looked into their deep eyes that they knew me for a friend and as one who knew their language and civilisation, though imperfectly. Those sleek heads did not show fear.

Once ashore, it was for me to give up fancies and find the right place for the permanent camp in the shortest possible time before the launch came again. I chose the little sheep fank at the narrowest part of the neck of Fianuis. If these dykes have endured, I thought, it would not seem that the sea comes right over, though at that moment the western ocean was pounding the fifty-foot cliffs only forty yards away. Also, these walls could be raised a little and would provide shelter all round the base of the huts. My decision thus rapidly made was one we never had cause to regret.

The weather on this day became kinder and kinder. As the tide fell the little dock-like rock became better for landing and we were able to keep a continuous stream carrying up to the fank; all the stores were ashore and under the truck cover by one o'clock. How glad I was for a rest and a quart of tea! I lay on my back then for a quarter of an hour, all effects of the journey left me and I felt fit for anything.

The huts came ashore in sections after lunch, and a squad of men fell to erecting them. By seven in the evening both huts were ready for occupation, the larger one being lined with half-inch Cellotex for warmth and protection against draughts. Each evening during our first few weeks on the island we carried stone and built up the dyke to the level of the eave, so that when the winter gales came we had a very good shelter from the west and north. With some difficulty we got these kindly men to stop working at nine o'clock that evening. They had helped us more than we could ever repay them, and later I was to learn the depth of their loyalty, after they had returned to ports of call and had been pestered for details of the landing and making camp on Rona by news reporters. They never let out one word. Grand fellows, every one of them.

We slept sound that night, feeling that things had gone better than we could possibly have expected. The job of landing the gear, which had been the biggest problem of the whole expedition in my mind, and which had certainly taken up the largest part of my time in preparation, was now a thing of the past. Getting off an island is always easier than getting on, and we were content to let that matter wait.

Though I do not consciously worry and felt no anxiety during our stay on Rona, there can be little doubt that the responsibility of the expedition, for during our first three months on Rona I often had anxiety dreams. It was curious how these came when the tension of preparation was over. I would dream of our flour whitening the waters of Little Loch Broom as great waves washed it out of the launch. They varied in their incidence and in terror, but always they woke me in the state I used to wake from a nightmare as a child – wanting my mother. Sometimes the cruiser would be waiting for me to embark and I was miles away, unable to move hand or foot; and another time I dreamt I was to have my tonsils out a second time before going to Rona (safer, you know, someone had insisted), and the operation was to be done on a dray standing in a covered station goods yard!

We woke to south-west wind and rain on our first morning on Rona, weather which later became continuous driving mist through which we could see nothing of the island. That did not matter much for there was so much to do indoors, fitting shelves and unpacking boxes. I know of nothing more thrilling than the first day on an uninhabited island.

The cruiser left by eight o'clock, as the wind was freshening and making the anchorage unsafe. The sea floor of the east bay is of rock and does not give a good bite for an anchor – very little wind is needed to make the anchor jump. There are also sunken skerries at about 4½ fathoms off Leac Mòr Fianuis and off the north end of Rona. These break spectacularly in heavy gales, and in such weather we have seen a break about two cables south-east of Leac Mòr. Below this place is a needle of rock at about two or three fathoms, not shown on the Admiralty Chart. It is probably the greatest hazard to shipping round Rona because it is so sudden, inconspicuous and unknown. A south-easterly gale can make the north-west bay a welcome shelter, for the cliffs are high there, but a ship will not lie quiet, for a big swell from the west is nearly always coming in. I once saw a trawler called *City of Leeds* anchored off Rona, but the immense swell gave her no quiet berth. She rolled at incredible angles and I thanked my lucky stars I was not aboard her. How did they manage to keep water in a kettle or tea in a cup? The skipper seemed to spend a lot of his time during those three days in his raised wheelhouse. I could not see his look of surprise at seeing me on Rona, but it was obvious enough in his gestures as he shot head and shoulders out of the window and gave me a wave.

If you are on the hill ridge of Rona when the big gales blow from the southwest, you can see the long lines of the immense swells cartwheeling round the north end of Rona and coming in white against the cliffs of the east side – a very fine sight as long as you are not wishing to leave in a hurry.

Man has such a little interest in North Rona that this island of less than half a square mile has disappeared from many maps of Scotland. Its true position is 59° 7' 16' North Latitude and 5° 49' 44' West Longitude. The island is completely rockbound, the cliffs varying from 355 feet down to a great expanse of rock almost at sea level on Lòban Sgeir.

Rona is a northern outpost of the Hebridean hornblende gneiss, intersected here by several veins of pegmatite. These are more durable than the gneiss and thus influence the scenery of the cliffs, vividly so on the northern face of the west cliff where a sheer column stands 300 feet above the sea. Crystals of quartz and felspar in the pegmatite make these seams a feature of great beauty. Curious foldings are evident in the western cliffs, and when Geodha Marc is reached the strata lie vertical and there are some curiously shaped upthrusts of rock. The idle collector of pretty pieces of rock will come away from Rona heavily laden; some are like coal, others salmon-pink, and the mica glints everywhere in the sunlight.

That peninsula of Sceapull (also called Poll Sgeir) and the island rock of Lòban Sgeir must be one of the barest places in Scotland – a low, serrated expanse of rock ringed by a never-silent sea. We explored it well two days after getting to Rona, and for the first time I felt its remoteness and the wild strength of the place. As I sat on this bare rock I felt acutely what a frail hold a single human family has, living alone on a small island. Times before, I have realised the physical limitations of one family – there are so many things you just cannot do – but here I saw the elemental strength of wind and water, and I was awed. Bobbie was wanting away from the place, but I felt it good to sit around for a while and dwell on my own insignificance. I have noticed it before on the top of a mountain in mist, and I thought of it here, a whole lot of stuffing goes out of you when the ground beneath your feet becomes devoid of any vegetation. That thin green carpet of more simple life is a thing of untold comfort. Our place is above it, and when we are on a great piece of bare rock we are naked and of little consequence.

The main mass of North Rona is a hill ridge running NW-SE, falling steep or sheer on the north-eastern side and more gradually to sea level on the south-west. This main lump of the island holds much of interest, but it would not be Rona, *Ron-y*, seal island, were it not for the northern peninsula of Fianuis. Fianuis means 'witness' or 'looking forth', and from there an observer sees an unbroken ocean.

Although North Rona is geologically the northernmost point of the Outer Hebrides, it differs much from them botanically. The northern end of Lewis is one vast peat bog which grows a characteristic herbage complex dominated by heather. There is no peat at all on Rona. The rock is covered a few inches deep with a sandy soil held together by organic matter and the roots of a good turf of Yorkshire fog, bents and fescue grasses. The sedges which are so commonly found on the gneiss areas of the Hebrides and north-western mainland are more rare on Rona, occurring mostly to the west of the ancient village site where the turf has been cut for fuel hundreds of years ago. Such scars never heal completely in our northern lands, where the soil is originally very thin. The strength of the mat of turf is amazing, and it needs to be strong indeed if it is to withstand those raking gales from the Atlantic. I have seen the turf torn from the rocks by the wind and rolled inland, and even stones as big as a man's head pushed from their bed an inch or two in the turf and rolled two or three yards uphill. The wind on Rona has to be felt to be realised.

The drier rocky places are covered with a wealth of sea pink and a fair amount of buck's-horn plantain; the cliff edges, heavily manured by the summer population of birds, grow luxuriant sprays of scurvygrass, some sheep's sorrel, Scotch lovage and mayweed. The village area with its large number of lazy beds grows wild white clover on the dry banks of conserved soil, and in the immediate vicinity of the houses silverweed almost crowds out everything else. There is no bracken, no fern, no spleenwort, and few of those flowers which make the northern lands gay in summer. The riot of sea pink makes up for the loss, many of the tufts being of a very deep colour and others pure white.

The whole of Rona is washed by salt spray in winter gales, but Fianuis is often impassable under a continuous driven cloud of it. Only plants with high tolerance of salt can grow there, annual poa grass, sea pink, sea-milkwort and chickweed. Nowhere else have I seen such a refulgent growth of chickweed as on the eastern side of Fianuis. There are about twenty acres of it growing to a foot in height.

There are no permanent pools of fresh water on Rona, and the human resident may find this one of the major problems of existence. The cruiser left us with about five gallons of water that first night, and in the afternoon of the next day, when we went for our first prowl in the heavy mist, almost our first thought was to look at the wells marked in such profusion on the map. They were disappointing, being very shallow, stagnant and full of ooze. There is a fair drain of water from the area west of the village down to Leac na Sgrob, but the birds use the temporary pools for bathing and make the water taste musky. We dug one or two of these pools deeper, but that was not a good thing to do because we had destroyed the waterproof surface of the pool and next time we went to them they had gone dry.

Bobbie objected strongly to this water, and I admit myself the tea was spoilt, and I did not look forward to six months of poor tea to drink.

On the night of our arrival, the Chief and the Second Officer had dug a well about forty yards south of the huts, and the following morning the water looked clear and good. Unfortunately it was very brackish and soon dried out – or perhaps it was fortunate, because all that area in the wintertime is an indescribable mess of living and dead seals. Any water from north of the hill ridge is unfit to drink. Bobbie went hunting for a better well and found it at the head of Poll Heallair on the southern coast of the island. The true well is nearer the edge of the cliff than the one marked on the map. It has obviously been chiselled in the solid rock and then topped with stone. The water which drips constantly into this well, even in dry weather, makes a store of about ten gallons. It is only seepage from the slope above, but is always sweet and cool. We used to make a journey over every day from the huts to fill a white-painted petrol can, marked with a brass label – WATER – which we found washed up on Lunga the year before. A journey of a mile to fetch the daily supply of drinking water – and yet I do not remember it as an irksome task at all.

Rainfall is fairly heavy on Rona, though we have known a whole fortnight without rain, and despite what I have said about there being no permanent pools of fresh water on the island and a lack of boggy places, it is surprising to find that the island is continually wet, wet in the sense that you could not sit on the grass in a pair of grey flannels without getting a wet seat. The steep northern face of the island runs a thin film of water all the time in winter, and passage up and down there without slipping a few yards now and again is almost impossible.

I wish I could say more of the underground world of Rona, which has never been explored. But this would be most difficult, because all the caves are sea caves running in from the west coast, and the sea is hardly ever calm enough to allow entry with a boat. We took our old kayak with us, but launching was always a difficulty because of the swell, even in Geodha Stoth, and I never felt justified in getting her down on the west side to go exploring. The responsibility of wife and child left above was too great.

The best-known cave on Rona is the Tunnel Cave running up from Sgeildige. From the head of the cave there runs a blowhole over thirty yards long, coming out to the surface in the middle of the neck of Fianuis.

The hole is about three feet high at the top, but broadens out farther down, and at the foot you can stand upright. The first few yards of the journey down are extraordinarily slippy because of a growth of algae, so it is best to go down the whole length on a rope. Once down, the play of light on water and rock make a scene of great beauty. But the days are few when you can get to the foot of the hole, and in a big gale I have seen a plume of spray coming from the top. The head of the cave must fill with water as the immense swells come in, and the pressure up that thirty-yard passage to the top of Fianuis is great.

Two more caves go under the island from Sgeildige Geo and reach to just below the sheep fank. As we lay in bed with our ears near the floor of the hut we could hear the rustle of water in the caves below. That was a pleasant sound, but it became awe-inspiring when a deep swell caused great breakers at the head of the caves. These two caves were much haunted by an exceedingly vocal crowd of seals. They cried day and night in their rich falsetto voices, bulls and cows in different keys, and the sound was mixed by the acoustic qualities of the caves and given forth as a wonderful harmony, comparable in effect with that which reaches the listener at the foot of the nave of St Paul's Cathedral after the singing of the choir has been mixed under the dome.

The finest scenery on Rona is Geodha Blàtha Mòr. It is possible to climb a little way down the cliff to the north and to look part way into the immense cave which runs inland from the geo. Three hundred feet of cliff face you, and the great mouth of the cave to the east and left. Every conceivable niche is occupied by kittiwakes and guillemots, even far into the cave. Thousands and thousands of birds, all crying; the sound is amplified in the yawning mouth of the cave and accompanied by the boom of the swell and the crying of seals within. I was so impressed with this place that I took Bobbie and Alasdair there the same evening when the sun shone into the cave. First they exclaimed, then were silent for a long time. It is one of those places that are wonderful as a whole but which repay examination in detail.

Such, then, is the face of Rona, a mere speck in the northern ocean; but such an island is much more than that biologically. Rather is it a metropolis for widely different animals through the seasons of the year, and a most important halting place for many others. The one occupation influences the other, and to the resident observer the island takes on a quality of wholeness in the mind which is denied the casual visitor.

GOOD DAYS AND BAD

THE WIND WHICH DROVE the cruiser out on the early morning after we landed blew all day long and fell light on the following morning. Then the sun came out for a magnificent day and we spent a good deal of time on that grim west coast of Fianuis watching the surf and the seals. Enormous waves broke against these cliffs and the water was churned to white foam for seventy-five yards from their foot. The scene and the sound filled us with wonder. It was the sort of sea of which people sometimes say, 'Nothing could live in this terrible surf'. So you would think, but close in to the rocks and where the waves broke most fiercely were our friends the great seals. They were not battling against the seas but taking advantage of them for play. It was nothing but play and joy of life which was keeping them there, for they were not sounding as they do when fishing. They were keeping to the surface, nearly a hundred of them, enjoying the deep rise and fall of the sea and the spray of the shattered waves. They were living joyfully, and I in my own way rejoiced with them. The sky was a shining vault of blue, the sea was a deeper blue, and as we watched the surf grew even bigger. The whiteness of it shone in the sunlight and the movement and sound of it all were glorious. In those days I think we were lifted out of our earth-bound humanity for a space.

The firm which supplied us with the wireless gear had made out a series of charts and instructions. I began with the aerial masts, two of them, tubular steel, twenty-five feet high. Each mast was to carry twelve stranded wire guys, and we fastened these to the masts with a 'Post Office splice' explained to us by Cap'n M earlier in the month. We got these up by teatime and the aerial strung between them. The job looked quite professional. I fixed another wire called the counterpoise after tea, took the leads through the walls of the huts, earthed the generator, brought a lead-covered cable from the engine to the hut and set up the main switch. Then there were all the connections and junctions to make inside the hut, but there was still a bit more to do when we stopped at half-past eleven from sheer tiredness.

We were at it again first thing the following morning and had everything ready for the premiere at 10.45 a.m. The engine started with a flourish, I drew down the switch, and lo, there came a little red light where a little red light should be. Marvellous! Then we turned on the receiver switch and the dial lit up also, and soon, as we turned the tuner, what do you think? There came the sugary tones of the BBC cinema organ – Bobbie's *bête noire*. What an anticlimax that this should be the first wireless sound heard on this remote isle! We kept on twisting and heard a trawler skipper talking to another one called George. He was a jolly man with a great laugh on him, and he was cursing the weather he had had round about the Faroes.

And now, we thought, we will try the transmitter. How nice it would be to join in that merry talk with the trawler skippers now and again! I changed over the switch and pressed another button. There was a splutter and the little red light disappeared and no pointers waggled as they should have done. Then a smell of heated fat greeted our nostrils and I opened a heavy metal box called a power pack, inside which some rolls of greasy paper were certainly melting. There was another thing in there also, a pretty lamp called a valve. Even as we watched, a lovely violet flame waxed within it, reached an ecstatic zenith, and quite suddenly went out. The smell of hot fat was getting worse, so we rightly assumed we were not transmitting; and that was the end of that. I put wireless at the back of my mind altogether and went out to begin a count of the numbers of bridled guillemots. The wireless did not bother me at all, but back on the mainland the newspapers were screaming and making things unpleasant for relatives and friends. Had we not been badgered into buying these playthings I am convinced they would not have worried about us half as much as they did when they received 'no news from exiles'.

Our three hens took to life on Rona like old campaigners. They came into a surge of egg-laying which surprised us, for within ten weeks the three of them laid 144 eggs, and then stopped suddenly. Bobbie always says cooking holds no fears for her if she has plenty of eggs. These twelve dozen eggs were a help to our store of pickled ones and they cost us nothing, for the hens lived on what they got from the island. The hens were very fond of the chickweed and were not alone in this. There were four greylag geese which lived almost wholly on it; they would spend most of the day on the sea and come in to the chickweed in the evening. The few sheep on Rona lived like wild ones; they used to come down from the ridge during the night to feed on the chickweed, and then with considerable regularity would pass by the huts again on their way back to the main body of the island at about seven o'clock in the morning. It was two or three years since the Ness men had been to Rona, and there were two crops of lambs that had never been docked or castrated. The population of sheep seems to keep fairly constant, the heavy winter losses about balancing the annual increase of lambs. Had a fence prevented the daily trek to the chickweed I am sure the sheep would have felt the deprivation. We ourselves, also, were glad to be nibbling this succulent weed and putting some into sandwiches. I tried some scurvygrass one day, but found it most unpleasant to the taste; perhaps the thick green leaves of the giant form of the plant are not so good as the tiny ones on Chlèirich.

Although these were good summer days we thought it wise to prepare for a possible winter's worst, by building up and cleaning out a beehive shieling

which stood two hundred yards away from the huts on Fianuis. We imagine this place must have been used by the sealers in the eighteenth and nineteenth centuries; it is about fourteen feet long and seven feet broad, and oval inside. The door is approached by a narrow and tortuous passage and you enter on hands and knees. The stones of the walls have been laid in blackhouse style, i.e. they slope downwards and outwards to shed the rain. I added two or three courses on the same principle, and threw up more stone to the ramp of earth and stone all round the outside. I had found a spar of timber some days before on Leac Mòr Fianuis which just rested along the top of the shieling lengthways. Thus, if our huts did blow down in the winter we could bring the tarpaulin up here to lay over the top of the wall and the ridge spar. Earth and stone could have been banked all round and we should have had an emergency lodging which would have kept out the rain. 'Better a wee bush than nae bield', said Burns. Happily, we were not reduced to living in what would have been the most primitive dwelling in Europe.

Bobbie and I went for a walk over the hill together on the afternoon of the last day of July, thinking the end of the month saw us a happier pair of people than did the beginning when we were still in the stages of preparation. We sat for a long time by the chapel saying nothing, for we were enjoying the blue of sky and sea and the green of Rona's hill. The warm breeze turned up the leaves of the silverweed and dipped the heads of the bents, and dappled the hillside with a shimmering pattern. Large white clouds stood out clear against the blue, and the sheep were little less white, dotted about the green hill. This is Rona also, we thought, as well as Rona dark in the sea mist and windswept. Old Muir wrote well eighty years ago:

> O these endless little isles! and
> of all little isles this Ronay!
> Yet, much as hath been seen, not to
> see thee, lying clad with soft
> verdure, and in thine awful solitude,
> afar off in the lap of wild ocean,
> not to see thee with the carnal
> eye, will be to have seen nothing!

That night the sun set at ten minutes past ten, going below the horizon with a green flash.

The first week of August was a giddy social whirl. Bobbie woke me rudely just after six o'clock in the morning on the first day of the month, shouting in my ear, 'There is a boat in the anchorage, what is it?' In a semi-conscious state I leaned up and said it was the cruiser. Then I flopped back again, unable to feel as pleased as I really was when it really dawned upon me.

Oh, how grey-faced you feel, being yanked out of bed! But a Primus does not take long to boil, and a cup of tea soon made me human again.

We sat down to letters immediately, for we knew there would not be much time for writing once the boys came ashore. They came soon after half-past eight to Langa Beirigh. We were met as old friends and they had a good laugh at my beard, which was neither one thing nor the other – I not being one of Esau's kind.

Cap'n M began work on the wireless transmitter and found it was well and truly dead, but he brought us the news that as our wireless was not working, we might get a call from the cruiser now and again on her way to and from the Orkney station. This indeed was better than having the wireless, and I confess to being secretly pleased when the wireless did not work.

Alasdair was delighted to see his friends from the ship and a game of cricket was soon in progress – an empty oil drum for wicket and a batten of wood for a bat. Play continued hilariously until Bobbie made some coffee, when the team came into the pavilion to refresh themselves.

Next morning as I sat at breakfast I saw the smoke of a ship in the light of the sun a little north of east. I could see the hull of the ship after breakfast, and as it was a round speck rather than a long one it was obvious she must be end on to us and coming our way. We soon had no doubt that she was coming to Rona. I could see through my telescope that she was rather more fancy than a trawler, having a large bridge and boats on davits. She also had a cumbersome sort of boat hanging from a derrick forward.

'I don't think we'll wait for them to come ashore,' I said. 'We'll get the kayak down and I'll go out to them.'

I pushed off from the shore when their anchor grounded, and paddled over the quarter-mile to the ship. Several piratical gentlemen of the crew were leaning over the side and a civilian in a windjacket was firing a small cine camera at me. The very worst, I thought – reporters! But just then the Captain and First Officer looked over the side and introduced themselves, and I was completely reassured. The ship was the Research Ship *Explorer* on her way from Orkney to St Kilda.

The Captain pointed to the old flat-bottomed coble which was hanging from the derrick and which had puzzled me earlier as I had looked through my glass. 'We picked this from the sea twenty-five miles east of here. It is a danger to shipping, but rather than sink her we thought it might be useful to you as firewood.'

I gazed with a new interest, for three days before I had seen this thing pass by the island from north-west to south-east, about a mile offshore. It had drifted at the surprising rate of a mile an hour and I had watched it carefully. 'She will do for more than firewood,' I said. 'What about using her as a roof for a store hut?'

This tickled the Captain's fancy, though he did not know just then the difficulties of getting such a hulk on to Rona. I felt that if there were enough of us it could be done. A dozen or more tumbled into the launch and we brought the coble and my kayak in tow. There was a bit of a swell running on the shore and the coble was leaky; when we got her nose on to the rock a wave pooped her and the rope painter broke. We were in danger of losing her, so I, being barefoot, leapt in and tied a long rope of tug-of-war to a ring in the floor of the coble. We got her up three or four feet on the rising swells and baled out the water from the stern. Then began the terrific job of getting this heavy old thing up rocks inclined at 30o to the sea. The Captain took charge and a big fellow called Jock did a lot of shouting by way of encouragement as well as doing a lot of work. This big East Coaster, strong as an ox and kind-hearted withal, gave me a private laugh. I asked him if he was from Aberdeen; his blue eyes looked at me blankly and shocked: 'Good gracious no,' he exclaimed. 'Stonehaven.'

I think I must be slow not to recognise immediately the difference between men from places fourteen miles apart.

The ship's company had been on a station all night and were ready to stretch their legs in a little relaxation ashore, otherwise I doubt whether my quiet rascality would have borne fruit. We gave many concerted pulls getting that coble up the rocks, and when she was on the chickweed at last we used the technique of a winning tug-of-war team, of spinning round and walking the boat up a long way. We were all a lot of lads together that day. The coble came to the sheep fank and we turned her over so that her gunwale rested on the lower part of the dyke; I knocked the stern and thwarts out of her later, and there we had a ready-made store for tinned things, tools and so on.

Some of the ship's company went over the hill to see the chapel, and the Captain asked us aboard for coffee. Big Jock took Alasdair in charge and showed him the tanks where live fish were – big pink sea bream, young dogfish with yolksacs still attached to their bellies, and a few octopuses which changed colour as they swam across the tank. He also showed Alasdair the plankton net and the tiny life which comes out of it, under the microscope. It was Jock also who produced cream tarts from nowhere to eat with the coffee – and finally the visitors' book was placed before us for our signatures.

The kindness extended to us by the Captain and company of *Explorer* knew no bounds. Before we came ashore we were given a basket of fish – twenty big haddock, all split, cleaned and ready for salting, and a dozen fine soles. And just before we came off the ship one of the crew called Alasdair to the fo'c'sle and gave him a bag of sweets. I was very deeply touched by this. Big Jock also gave him some chocolate, explaining to me that he brought this stuff every voyage and never ate it. How typical it was of this big man that he should excuse his kindness! We had not yet stepped off the ladder before Jock said:

'What about giving 'em a real treat, Cap'n? Can I run and fetch 'em half a dozen salt herring?'

He was gone before the Captain could reply. Up came Jock again, all smiles, with a dozen wet and sticky herrings.

'Let 'em dry well in the sun, then grill 'em! Man, they're just beauties!'

We had our lemon soles fried and served with chips before *Explorer* finally left the anchorage, blowing her siren in farewell. What a feed! What a morning!

We spent the rest of the day salting the fish in brine and hanging them out to dry. Our hut and the sheep fank looked like a Shetland croft by the time we had finished, what with the upturned boat and the haddies strung around. Perhaps this thought was in my mind that evening as I lay on the cliff edge in contemplative mood watching the puffins, my belly full of a second good meal of lemon sole.

The puffins are the most numerous of all the birds on Rona. They nest in burrows of their own making on the tops of cliffs and make for a certain amount of disintegration of the cliff edge, for sometimes the burrow-ridden soil sloughs off and falls to the sea after gales and heavy rain. They also manure this strip very heavily, and chickweed and scurvygrass become a luxuriant growth. The cliffs of Rona are littered with the skins of puffins neatly pulled inside out from the carcass. Such is the technique of the black-back in eating any animal. The peregrine falcons also prey on the puffins, but there is only one pair of them on Rona and their influence on the population is small. The falcon takes the puffin to a little pool of water, wets the bird thoroughly and proceeds to pluck the feathers. A pair of untouched wings joined by the cleaned pectoral girdle marks the remains of a falcon's meal.

The old people of the islands salted puffins in thousands. I was glad I did not have to, even though I do curse at an advancing urban civilisation which cuts across the self-sufficiency of island economy. It is difficult to know where to start and where to stop in this matter of taking life. If I lived here entirely I should eat puffins, but I would not take one puffin in the meantime, because I should not be taking toll of the race of puffindom so much as cutting short the free, and doubtless happy, life of one individual puffin when he was enjoying it most. Why should that individual suffer, of all his fellows, for a gastronomic experiment? I feel somewhat the same about the greater black-back gulls. There are too many of them here, I think, and I could at this date easily draw the necks of a dozen or more not yet in the air. But such a course would have no real effect on lessening the population, and the act of taking life would not be justified. I should have much less compunction about shooting three or four hundred of the adults.

Three days after this the weather was still brilliant, and after breakfast I went to a good place on the west side of Fianuis where I could watch seals, lie out of the light east wind and write in the slack intervals. But less than an hour afterwards I heard Bobbie's whistle blowing hard, and I ran back in an awful fright, thinking Bobbie must be in some dire trouble. There she was, running along the stony top of Fianuis, bursting her cheeks with the whistle whatever. 'A yacht going up the east side,' she called. And when I got up there it was to see a nice ten-ton, ketch-rigged yacht going north-about with her sails full of the fresh south-easterly breeze, a pretty sight indeed. Bobbie said she came round Sron na Chaorach into the east bay and sounded her klaxon. Then, as there was too much breeze for landing there, she continued northwards.

She lowered her sails at the north point, set her auxiliary going and came into the west bay like a cat walking on eggs. I did not smile at her extreme wariness, because the chart shows no soundings there. We watched her drop anchor, saw the dinghy, a Norwegian pram, come overboard, and then we climbed down the cliffs on the south side of Sgeildige to give him an idea where to make for. They did not venture very close to the cliff face, and when I called out that he could land if he came stern first to the cliff, the man in the stern said: 'Oh no, I'd rather not land unless you are in any trouble. Can we do anything for you?'

'No, thanks,' I answered, 'as far as I know we're all right; but you've come an awful long way not to be landing.'

'Not at all; we're sailing; we were in the Minch, and the last we read about you was that no wireless message had been received, so we thought we might come this length and be able to report you all right.'

'Fine, thanks, but really, won't you come ashore and have some lunch or a drink of tea?'

'No, no, I wouldn't climb up a dangerous cliff like that for all the wealth in China. You oughtn't to have come down there yourselves.'

Bobbie and Alasdair were standing beside me, and none of us had thought the cliff more than a walk; but there you are, that was his outlook, and mine at that moment was to admire his courage in coming fifty miles out of the shelter of the Minch and then not to land. These sailing men are like that. I would not wish to go a mile in a boat unless I were going to land somewhere at the other end. We chatted a little longer and learned that the yacht was SY *Judith*, Mr W.A. Scott Brown, of Paisley and Glasgow. He was a member of the Royal Clyde Yacht Club and told us he had been talking to friends of ours in Lochbroom a couple of nights before. So Mr Scott Brown drew back to *Judith* and I saw the little yacht disappear round the west point. This is just one of the short meetings we have had with strangers on islands, which have subsequently led to more solid acquaintanceship.

And Bobbie and I said to each other, 'What about the odd cup of tea?'

I did a little writing before lunch, but very little, because I was on the edge of the cliff above Sgeildige Geo, wearing polaroid glasses and watching the seals swimming in beautiful movement below water. I could see the shags going a good way down also, darting hither and thither among the swarms of tiny fish which I could just see. Arctic terns were dipping constantly and taking toll of these same swarms of seemingly indifferent little fish. The individual is nothing to them. As the guillemots left their ledges on the cliffs, I went round the island and found the exodus had been a general one. Here and there was a solitary bird brooding over a very young chick, and these individuals merely heightened the forlornness. I imagine that the 'ledge' is the group unit in the social life of the guillemot, and that where I had seen the solitary birds the youngness of the chicks had made them more 'valent' for the parent than the larger loyalty of the 'ledge' which had now left the cliff and gone to sea. It is to me a wonderful thing, and not easily explained, that thousands of guillemots spread about an island should suddenly leave it in one night. What prompts this large group activity? All I can say about the birds prior to the event is that they were extremely noisy in the darkness for two nights before. Not until I saw those solitary birds that afternoon did I realise that half the charm and beauty of seabirds is in their busy life together.

The puffins were gone the next day, just as suddenly, and now the cliffs had very much the appearance of 'the morning after the night before'. Here, in a heightened form, was that anticlimax of August. There is no doubt that the immense concourse of birds transmits some of its own excitement to the human observer, and when the birds go the human being feels lonely. I am not sentimentally fanciful in this, for I have heard a hard-headed lighthouseman at an island station make the same admission.

That night I removed the beard of a month's growth. Bobbie said it was repulsive, and I had to admit it was a failure, as a beard. My razor had gone rusty in this oceanic climate, and despite thorough stropping the removal of this beard was in the nature of a major operation. The weather had been so hot and calm on this day that I had been able to enjoy a complete and leisurely bath in a pool on the south side.

I sat up late that night carving for Alasdair a model boat with mast and sails and working rudder, and when I had finished at half-past eleven I went outside to enjoy the beauty of the night. The moon was at the full and the air still, quieter than I ever thought it could be here. The petrels were trilling among the stones and some were flying close round my head. I picked up one which came to earth and brought it into the hut for Bobbie to see. The little black mite coughed up on to my hand the food she was doubtless bringing for her chick, and I was sorry.

The next day I went to the Tor and looked round with my glass. It was one of those calm days of soft colourings which are among the most beautiful for those who live on islands. The clouds did not wholly obscure the blue, and the clouds themselves were high and delicate. The sea answered the clouds with its diversity of colouring. The island was softened and its cliffs seemed not so sheer and terrible. I could see the mainland clearly, a distant skyline of isolated hills of fine lines; ships like toys seemed barely to move, thirty miles away. I lay for a while in the rich grass on the Tor enjoying the scents of earth and of the abundant white clover. It was a day for scents.

On most days you can see no other land from there but Sula Sgeir, the stark rock 12½ miles away west-south-west of Rona, which just breaks through the ring of sea and sky. But today the air was so clear I could see the gannets or solans flying round Sula Sgeir and details of the rock were plain. An immense panorama filled the southern horizon. Several of the Orkney Islands were to be seen and the Hoy stood out as a flat cone; then Duncansby Head at the north-east of the mainland of Scotland. Next the fine line of the hills of the North Coast, growing ever higher and more noble in shape as the West was reached. Cape Wrath lighthouse was a white speck 47 miles away, and then the mountains began their southerly course until I could see shapes I knew well in Suilven and An Teallach. Now the circle of relationships seemed complete: I had seen Rona and the Brae House from An Teallach years before, and now, from that speck of Rona in the northern ocean, I was seeing the mountains of home which I see every day from Tanera. Rona is linked with our lives for ever.

When the three of us topped the ridge atop the Tor, on 1st September, Alasdair pointed towards Sula Sgeir. There was a large brown sail on the sea just south of Gralisgeir, the skerry half a mile south of Sula Sgeir. We watched the boat tack in the northerly breeze until she came into the east side of the great rock, and there we could see no more of her, because the sun was going round out of our favour and Sula Sgeir was over twelve miles away from us. It was the men of Ness in their forty-foot open boat, come to take their annual harvest of the young gannets or *gugas*. This boat is the last of its kind in existence, and it is this journey each year which keeps it in commission. The boat is a direct descendant of the ancient Viking type, skiff-ended and extremely buoyant. There are boats of similar type and lineage left in Shetland – the yollie, and in Caithness – the skaffa.

Since time immemorial the men of Ness, Lewis, have made the yearly journey to Sula Sgeir in late August or early September to take a toll of the young gannets, which are immensely fat at this time. The young birds are preserved for winter food. The present toll is about two thousand birds each year, more than the gannetry can stand, with the result that the stock is diminishing. There has been a considerable outcry from the preservationists to put a stop to this practice; but the final result has been to harden opinion against any interference, and the boat went again in 1939.

The conservationist's point of view would be to consider man as a predatory animal and to include him in the ecological web. In an age when skilled physical effort tends to be dropped and ability lost, there can be little doubt that this open-boat journey has a social value in the small community of Ness. If these people did not eat the gannets, what else would they have? The answer is corned beef and margarine, a poor substitute which would bring in the money factor – always undesirable in a semi-primitive community – and allow the boat to rot. What I say in defence of this practice in no way excuses the appearance of roast gannet on the menu provided by the local steamship service!

Perhaps the toll of gannets should neither be prohibited nor passively encouraged, but regulated. If a thousand instead of two thousand were taken for five years and the fluctuations of numbers noted on this remote islet, the safety of the gannetry would be ensured and the Ness men would continue their thousand-year-old custom.

As far as we know, and this is not a documented fact, St Ronan was the first human inhabitant of Rona in the eighth century AD. He moved to Rona from Eoropaidh at the north end of Lewis and adopted the name of the island as his own. Thus we gather that Rona has been the island of the seals for a very long period. Tradition has it that St Ronan built the existing cell on Rona, and as this building is in many ways typical of the cells built by ascetic hermits of the early Celtic Church in other parts of Scotland, there is no reason yet for disbelieving the traditional origin of a building which is unlike any other on Rona.

Muir, a Scottish ecclesiological antiquary, who visited Rona in 1857 and 1860, carefully measured the cell and described the place as he found it. His sketches indicate a very low entrance, and a paving to the cell is implied. He also wrote of entering the cell on elbows and knees; it was the unlikelihood of this being the original mode of ingress that decided me to dig.

The east and west walls of the cell are almost perpendicular, but the longer north and south walls slope inwards rapidly, and at a height of over eleven feet are bridged by rectangular slabs of gneiss to finish the roof. The length and breadth of the cell at floor level are 11 feet 6 inches and 8 feet. This building is in drystone, very beautifully done, and the technique is the same as that of the black houses still inhabited in Lewis. The inside edges of the flattish stones are set a little higher than those reaching to the outside, so that all water draining on to the top of such a wall must drain outwards and the inside surface remains dry and free from condensation. The beehive shielings are built on the same principle and the courses reach inwards from near the foot of the wall. These buildings are in direct descent from the culture of the Megalithic age. St Ronan's cell is the best example of this type of construction I know, and into the south wall, near the east end, he built a neat aumbry a foot square. There is a small window 19 inches by 8 inches running through the thickness of the west wall above the door. Whether there was a similar window in the east end is not known, because the upper part of the wall there has fallen in. Earth and stones were banked high round the north, east and south walls so that the building was practically underground. The outside of the west wall became the east inside wall of a chapel which was built some time after Ronan's cell; Muir estimated about two centuries later. This building, also in drystone but of poorer workmanship, is 14 feet 8 inches long by 8 feet 3 inches, and forms in effect a nave to the cell as chancel. But it is doubtful whether the two buildings were used conjointly in this way.

The roof and much of the walls of the chapel have disappeared, and when I first went to Rona the south wall was just a heap of stone fallen outwards. I had with me a copy of Harvie-Brown's book, in which there is what is probably the first photograph of the chapel ever taken. That was in 1885. The south wall was erect then, and from the photograph I could see very well the height of the doorway in the south wall and a curious bulge in the eastern half of that wall. I began nervously to make a clearance of the fallen stones and to find the foundations; I did not wish to take down much in an effort to rebuild, or there was no knowing where I should be able to stop. However, once the foundation was clear, even showing that increased thickness east of the doorway, I went ahead with confidence. The south wall is now back in the state it was in 1885, and I do not think it will be easy to tell where I began work.

The inside of the chapel had been occupied by fulmar petrels in the summer and was half full of fallen stone and earth. This very low doorway into the cell was intriguing, and it was there I struck first with spade and pick. It was not long, as I cleared my way north and south of the opening, before I struck two blocks of masonry; they were piers 3 feet high and 2 feet 3 inches square, one each side of the entrance, and they had at some time been faced with lime mortar. When I reached the foot of these piers, which I take to be the altar supports of the chapel, I found a rough paving running into the doorway of the cell. Here was no necessity for elbows and knees; the doorway with its original paving and a tiny step was 4 feet

4 inches high and 20 inches broad. The vertical section of soil and floor made by my digging revealed a thick bed of shell sand laid on the paving and over the floor of the chapel. I found charred bones of seabirds and seals in this layer. A hard floor of rammed clay lay above the shell sand, and I was able to clear all the inside of the chapel to the level of the clay. As the east end and the entrance to the cell showed workings below the level of this floor, I built a course of drystone across the chapel, so that both the clay floor and the original cell front are now visible and should not easily become encumbered again.

There was now the cell itself to excavate, and I have not done this entirely, because at some time the sloping walls have been roughly buttressed on the north and south sides by large stones placed on end. But I have cleared to the paving inside the door, and at the east end I have gone right across the cell. I found an altar of well-built masonry 2 feet 6 inches high, 3 feet broad and 2 feet 3 inches deep. Muir said there was an altar stone 3 feet long at the east end of the cell, and he gave a sketch of it in position. Doubtless this was all he could see of the altar at that time, and I found this stone on a level with the top of the altar but at right angles to it. The altar being completely revealed, I have replaced the big slab. A visitor to Rona will now get the impression of a simple early church in a very fair state of preservation because it has been almost buried for so long. I am glad to say His Majesty's Office of Works is going to take the place in hand.

The only hint of a late age in the burial ground round the chapel is the hideous flat sandstone slab, complete with twirls and so on, brought here and raised to the memory of the two penitent shepherds who, having had words with the minister in Ness, came to Rona in May, 1884, and died there in February, 1885. The weather of these parts is reducing the imported stone to decrepitude and the whole thing has taken a good lean eastwards. The legend on the stone is:

SACRED
TO THE MEMORY OF MALCOLM McDONALD
WHO DIED AT RONA, FEB 18 1885 AGED 67
ALSO M McKAY, WHO DIED AT RONA SAME TIME

Blessed are the dead
who die in the Lord

The composition of this legend is typical of West Highland English, primitive because it was a strange language to those whom the stone commemorates and those who piously erected it. But 1885 was a time when it was thought more genteel to have your gravestone inscribed in English, and this foreign stone would be thought to convey more respect than one of the rough crosses of Rona's own gneiss. These, indeed, were beautiful, and those which remain in the burial ground make the place a wholly pleasant one, far different from those places of stark, smooth monuments where civilised men bury their dead and attempt to immortalise them.

The first written mention of Rona and its people was made in 1549 by Sir Donald Monro, High Dean of the Isles. He mentions the ancient chapel and some of its magical qualities, and he speaks of the whiteness of the barley flour and of the method of its storage in sheepskins. Next comes Martin Martin, who made his famous tour of the Western Isles in 1695 and who took down an account of Rona and its inhabitants from Daniel Morison, the Minister of Barvas, Lewis, in which parish Rona was and still is. The minister had been there about 1680 or before, and had received five sacks of the white barley meal, the sacks being the skins of sheep just as Sir Donald had described well over a century before. The minister's tale is of cattle and sheep and cultivation of barley and oats, but there is no word of potatoes (first planteed in Lewis in 1753). He speaks of the altar in the chapel as being a 'big plank of wood about ten feet in length; every foot has a hole in it, and in every hole a stone, to which the natives ascribe several virtues'. The plank is gone, and how would we recognise the stones today? But I imagine that plank lay across the stone piers I have laid bare, and if so, it seems improbable that the cell would be used then for religious services. Presumably it was the clay floor now uncovered which the natives, according to the seventeenth-century minister, swept every day and kept 'neat and clean'.

From what we read of Martin Martin the life of these five families of remote people had a beautiful simplicity. He says 'they covet no wealth, being fully content and satisfied with food and raiment; though at the same time they are very precise in the matter of property among themselves . . . they take their surnames from the colour of the sky, rainbow and clouds'. It was very soon after this that a plague of rats came to Rona from a wrecked ship. These rodents ate up the whole sustenance of the people, who had no means of combating a new pest. A further calamity was the theft of the island bull by a passing ship wishing fresh meat. The people starved to death, and when the steward of St Kilda was some time later driven as far as Rona in a great storm, he 'found, a woman with her child on her breast, both lying dead at the side of a rock'. The rats also starved, because Rona has no foreshore which would maintain them when they had eaten the people's harvests.

The ruins of the houses of this ancient people remain. They are half underground and each covers a considerable area, for devious low passages surrounded them and it seems probable that barn and byre were part of the house, just as they were in the black houses of Lewis, but the general plan of these Rona dwellings is round rather than rectangular, and the wind-baffling passages are distinctive. Nobody else has had my opportunities of digging and seeking among these ruins in winter when the silverweed has died. I have found one perfect quern stone 22 inches across which was buried in the floor of the largest dwelling. Two more well-preserved ones were lying visible on the wall of one of the houses, and I dug several fragments from the ground about the village. Bobbie made an important find of two fragments of stone vessels, one of which was evidently shallow and round and the other oval and deeper. I have gathered all these artefacts together in the west end of the chapel, and we have also made a plan of the cultivated area, showing the disposition and number of the lazy beds, which appear to be in five main groups, possibly indicative of the five families which we are told made up the community.

RONA IN WINTER

SEVERAL YEARS OF ISLAND LIFE have caused me to try to analyse the emotions which so deeply affect us in the march of the island seasons. What is the cause of this elevation we feel over and above the joy of the mainland? First, I think the quality of light raises our perceptions, heightening as it does the brilliant colours of the season. The sky is cloudless on these ecstatic days. The sea is deep blue, unbroken and also limitless until the island shores are reached and a band of brilliantly white surf makes endless patterns of beauty as it falls from the rocks and rides back to meet the next oncoming swell. A seal's head rising in this their favourite playground gleams bright, and as the animal turns and rolls, its belly flashes smooth and as one with the wave it breaks. The saffron lichen of the cliffs above the tide and fed by the spray is a vivid reflection of the sunlight, never clashing with the range of colours displayed by the cushions of sea pink which grow as soon as a few grains of soil can lodge. Never have I seen such a carpet of sea pink as on the west side of Rona above Geodha Blàtha Mòr – there is little else but sea pink there and the flowers white, cream, and every shade between pale pink, rose and a deep red colour which is almost purple. Every day we would see something new and wonderful. I remember a flock of about two thousand kittiwakes closely massed on the skerry of Lisgeir Mòr at the north end of Fianuis. They were a pretty enough sight like that, but when all of them suddenly took to the air and of necessity fanned out to give themselves flying room, it was a vision prodigal in its loveliness. It was a gigantic unfolding of resting life into brilliant animation. Perhaps two seconds after they took to the air they began calling; even a single kittiwake can make a lot of noise with the cry which gives the bird its name, but when two thousand throats cried out as one I stood in wonder listening to a paean of praise. Our bare northern islands often produce these moments of spontaneous exuberance and, in the right sense of the word, magnificence.

There is no quiet on Rona in summer, day or night; the harsh rattle of the guillemots and shags, the cackle of fulmars, the high-pitched cries of kittiwakes, the coarse complaint of black-backs and the high, chittering scream of Arctic terns, all are blended into a splendid paean in our ears.

There are also the little storm petrels churring in the walls of the fank at night, and from midnight on the sound of the Leach's fork-tailed petrel may be heard on Fianuis and about the chapel and village. Alasdair, Bobbie and I would set out for the old houses about midnight on those calm July nights, rather a subdued party, for we had tried to get a little sleep in first. We would be wrapped up well and carrying camera, lenses, flash bulbs and so on. Usually it was good to get into the shelter of the main house and wait until the first-comers arrived from the sea. Several were flitting about by half-past twelve, then more came in rapid succession, and those already in their burrows in the drystone walls began to sing in an ascending trill most pleasant to hear. It seemed to me that more petrels gathered near the place immediately after these trillings. Soon the birds in the air began to scream, but this was no unpleasant sound like that of the Manx shearwaters. It was a succession of eight or ten notes in a definite cadence and of varying pitch, rather like a staccato, musical laugh. The swift-flying shapes increased in number and the volume of sound grew. We could feel the excitement waxing in this community of little black birds. Their flight is erratic and swift, and when two or three hundred are flying in this way within a restricted space, collisions are common. Our faces were brushed by the soft wings smelling strongly of the characteristic petrel musk. A pitch of excitement is reached after one o'clock in the morning, and the laughter and erratic movement wane before dawn.

How exciting it was for us the first night we went to hear and see this aerial dance! We stood silent a long time, and I was thinking how few people in Britain could have experienced this on a northern summer night. St Kilda, the Flannans, Sula Sgeir and North Rona; after these you must go to Iceland or Greenland, the Labrador coast or the Aleutian Islands in the

Northern Pacific Ocean. I shone a torch into one hole in a drystone dyke when I heard that little trill, and there was the full black eye of the petrel, its lovely grey face and the shining black bill.

The advent of September meant a new season in the life of the great seals. They began to come high on the face of Rona, the bulls first, to take up their territories for the breeding season, and then the cows a few days later. They came up not only on Leac Mòr but up the steep rocks from Geodha Stoth so that the huts were soon surrounded by the crying seals. Those in our immediate neighbourhood soon came to accept us as part of the island and did not go hurtling back to the sea when we passed to and fro.

The first calf was born on 14th September, and after that they came in quick succession. The continuous falsetto crying of the seals was augmented by these baby cries, a sound that pulls at your heart when you hear it in the night when the weather is wild and rainy. It was a magnificent experience to be living among these hundreds of seals, though there were times when Bobbie objected to the smell of them. It is an acrid, animal smell, smacking of the sea. Alasdair played with some of the calves but they would have none of him; even the mothers accepted him better than they did.

The breeding season of the seals was waxing, but autumn had come to Rona. A bleakness and hardness were there, and in the evenings we enjoyed more and more the institution of half an hour sitting on Alasdair's bed when we settled him for the night. This was the time when I played the mouth organ and Bobbie and Alasdair sang. The conduct of Alasdair's *salon* as we called it was a matter for care because we found ourselves sensitive to the atmospheres evoked by music. If we wanted fun it had to be at the beginning with 'The De'il's Awa', 'McRory's Breeks' and other Scots and English songs. Then we would drift into the melodies of the like of 'Afton Water' and 'Drink to me only', and then into the still quieter and more primitive Gaelic songs such as 'Caol Muile', 'Grigal Chridhe', 'Caisteal na Gleann' and one of Alasdair's own composition. Sometimes we had a round of hymns, and always we finished with two or three verses each of 'Lead, kindly light', 'Now the day is over' and 'The day thou gavest, Lord, is ended'. This nightly half-hour was an integral part of our

lives on Rona, and had a great influence in making us feel bound together
and strong in each other's love. It is one of the treasured memories we have
brought away from Rona, and I know that Rona *salons* are in Alasdair's
heart for evermore. If ever we made a right decision it was in taking him to
the island; his spirit and his life were enriched as well as ours.

The latter half of September 1938 was clouded by the development of
an international crisis. There was talk of war with Germany. From our
remote corner of the earth's surface we seemed to see it impersonally as a
tragic drama unfolding on another planet. And yet our perceptions were
never clearer. On the Sunday, 25th September, I felt extremely unhappy
and thought about the world which thoughtless men in Britain and the rest
of Europe had created in recent years. I was still unhappy on the Monday
morning when I went over to do a little more work at the chapel and cell. I
sat a long while in that place where simple folk had worshipped in old time;
I thought through recent events as far as I knew them, and then I stopped
thinking and was conscious only of the island and the sound of the sea.
Even these loved things became dim in a brighter light which filled my mind.
Such moments are not ones to be dwelt on in print, but when they come I
know them for truth. I came back to the huts that day with the unshakable
conviction that war would not occur at that time, though knowledge was no
cause for complacence.

The autumn migratory season is a thrilling time on Rona. Flocks of young
white wagtails came to Fianuis and were a joy to us for a month or more
by their tameness about the huts. Then there was a surge of Greenland
wheatears. Ringed plovers paid us but a passing visit in August, but
golden plovers stayed about for some weeks in very small numbers. And I
remember the fine surprise of meeting a green sandpiper by a soft place on
the ridge on 24th September. I stopped in my tracks, and the lovely bird I
had never seen in my life before walked about a few yards away in apparent
unconcern. I saw a pair of little stints twice, in August and September, and
one day in August my friend of deer forest days, the greenshank, came
through. I saw a sanderling twice in a flock of knots on Leac Mòr. Iceland

redshanks were common in August, and dunlin were fairly common from August onwards. Two swallows came and flew round us in July, in the same confiding way they did on Chlèirich. A female hen harrier stayed about the island for most of September, and many were the fine views she gave me. I think I was never happier in my life than at this time. I could do fine to become a modern Ronan and live there the seasons through for a few years more, watching the birds come and go and pass through, and the great seals populate the place in the wild autumns. Oh, Rona, Rona!

Late summer and early winter on Rona are made lively by the breeding seals and migrating birds, but the depth of winter is a time of deadness and sleep. Seals are gone, birds are gone, the ground is black and the rock has lost its brightness. The mainland spring and summer rise and unfold gently from the dark cape of winter; summer itself has a length and an evenness the little islands never know, and autumn does not come into the island's seasons. The illusion of summer may persist into October, when one gale from the south-east will shrivel the grass and each leaf and flower, and from then till the advent of a laggard spring it is winter. Quietness and the colourings of sea and sky make the beauty of an island winter, though storms can make those moments rare. Storms may be beautiful, but a continuance of them is not felt to be so by the island dweller whose nights are made wretched and whose thoughts are constantly running over the possibility of damage to boats, stacks of hay or corn and roofs of buildings. The cruel inexorable quality of a south-easterly gale lasting from ten days to three weeks deadens perception of beauty and leaves the nerves raw.

Those acres of Fianuis which had been lush fields of chickweed in the summer were now a sea of mud. The place was black in the dull daylight of winter. The northern face of the hill was a vast black slide down which we could see several seals making their way at a great pace. We climbed up there with difficulty to fetch water from the well on the south side and had the surprise of seeing seals on the top of the ridge, three hundred feet above the sea. It was altogether amazing. There was another young seal at the extreme edge of the sheer west cliff, one which a few days later I saw fall the three hundred feet to its death. There were seals young and old round the edge of Geodha Leis, a terribly dangerous place, because if they take the hundred-foot jump into the sea they are liable to fall on rocks which are just covered down there. One day I saw a big bull seal go down when he was chased by another, and he just burst when he hit those rocks. I was thoroughly upset; it need not have happened.

I can see now that these Atlantic grey seals could be transplanted to new groups of islands when they are at the stage of naturally starving at three weeks old, i.e. before they have any tradition of the sea. I can see that the population of these seals could be much increased and drawn upon carefully as a natural resource of oil. If that ever came about under the direction of a Bureau of Biological Survey, on which I am so keen, it would also be possible on a place like Rona to prevent a great deal of loss of stock, by fencing these geos and sheer cliffs where the seals fall to certain death.

Bobbie and I counted 850 live seal calves and 150 dead ones. All the first lot which were calves when we left at the end of September were away to sea now. Animals which breed in large congregations require our very special protection if they are to remain in existence. The grey seals were nearly exterminated in the last century, but fortunately for them a growing industrialism began to counteract the harm it was doing them, by supplying the Hebridean population with rubber boots which were more efficient than sealskin, and with paraffin oil which gave a better light than seal oil.

It was good to get in out of the muck at night and eat a terrific dinner. Life was not too bad, I thought, seeing our little world through the magic haze of a Havana cigar. One of our Cheddar cheeses which had been in a flour bin under the coble with the seals had ripened beautifully into a blue-veined cheese which could only be described as noble for its richness and fullness of flavour. I was in similar mood when I wrote in my diary three nights later: 'The waves were going green over Lisgeir Mòr this morning, and north of Rona where the water is shallow the rollers are piling higher than any waves I have ever seen. Now, after an immense tea and a Larañaga (box getting distressingly low), I can hear the steady roar of the sea outside and in the caves beneath us. Now for a few tunes on the mouth organ and then to bed. This is a rest cure.'

Another night, 27th November it was, a southerly gale was raging, and as I came in, just on dusk, I saw a seal cow and her calf on the edge of the Sgeildige Geo, outlined against the stormy sunset. It was too dark for me to see her face plainly, but I could see her movements and the patient carriage of her head. In that light, in that wind and in these desolate surroundings there seemed to me to be the living spirit of Rona in that silhouette.

The gale reached a hurricane force in the night. The hut shook and the roof went up and down as the great gusts came down the hill. The pounding of the sea on the west side of Rona was of itself rattling the crockery on the shelves. The wind and rain being what they were, we stayed in bed till ten o'clock that morning and got breakfast by the simple means of reaching forth for various eatables, and the stove was there with water ready for tea. The rain stopped and the sun appeared, though the wind showed no signs of abating. We went out to enjoy the spectacle of the island under these conditions. The waves were breaking two or three times the height of Fianuis and it was not possible to get along there west of the storm beach. The waves breaking in Geodha Leis and Geodha Blàtha Mòr were sending up clouds of spray to over three hundred feet, which spray was then driven over the whole face of the island, even over the Tor, which was farthest removed from the west and 355 feet high. From up there we could see that Lòban Sgeir and Sceapull were white with water going over them, and waves were breaking over the north end of Fianuis as well. The form of Sgeildige Geo saved the huts from the worst of the spray, though we saw green water come to within ten feet of the edge of the cliff there, just the rise and fall of the swell.

Heavy rain set in again during the afternoon, herald of another wild night. We could not sleep for the buffeting of the wind and roar of sea, but we were snug and warm, with plenty of books to read and tea to drink. Indeed, Rona was a good place to get some reading done. I read *Robinson Crusoe* again for the first time since schooldays, and felt he was well off. When such nights as this frightened us a little with the wind and sea I used to read Cherry-Garrard's *The Worst Journey in the World*, and realised that it was ourselves who were well off.

The wind suddenly slackened at ten o'clock the following morning, and brilliant sunshine bathed the island. We were out taking photographs for two or three hours before the afternoon came grey and sullen once more and the wind freshened from the south. There was a full gale blowing from the south-east when we went to bed, accompanied by incredibly sharp and intense showers. One of them was just as if some mighty hand had hurled a fistful of rice on the roof. Broken sleep or little sleep at all in these nights of storm seemed to have no effect on my mental brightness; in fact, I do not think I was ever more keen in my perceptions. I was happy, well fed, warm at nights, well supplied with work and new things to see in surroundings I knew and loved. The outside world did not exist for us now, the wireless being dismantled and ourselves not wishing for any contact until Christmas was near. The utter desolation of the land and the might of the sea seemed to uplift us in some strange way. Life was good. But as we look back on that time of complete withdrawal from the world of men, it is the weather which is the most vivid part of the experience. It was not only wind and sea, but the sky as well. I wrote on 2nd December: 'The wind has slackened a little, late this evening, though it is still strong, the clouds have gone higher and the moon is out for long periods. The northern lights are beautiful to the north-east – a great curtain of greenish-yellow light and glowing masses of this light rising and falling very rapidly. It is interesting to look one way at the aurora and the other way at the moonlight. How different they are! The one seems unreal, intangible, almost mystic; the other is homely and well known from childhood, and seems a light with more body to it.'

After a calm night the wind began to freshen again from the south-east about seven o'clock this morning. This was most disappointing, for we were sick of wind. It blew fresh all morning, but then the sun came out and we counted it pleasant weather. The strength of wind increased after lunch and was blowing a gale by tea-time. Bobbie and I enjoyed only a few minutes of absolute peace from wind in St Ronan's cell.

That night was an Inferno and we were very unhappy; we dozed now and again, but we read and made tea and listened for most of the night. How can I describe this dreadful south-easterly gale? The noise of wind and its physical effects on our hut were bad enough – roof lifting, all crockery rattling, creaks everywhere, and sometimes the upper half of the door bending in from the top. But as well as this there is the fact that we were not altogether ourselves. We heard that dreadful sea a hundred yards in front to the east of us, and there was the pound of an immense swell forty yards behind to the west. All this tends to rattle you in the middle of the night, although in the day you see quite well that the water is unlikely to reach you. The spray had driven across the neck of land and our windows were thickly encrusted with salt as with a heavy frost. When we rose in the morning the sea was more white than green, and in a measure flattened by the force of the wind.

Bobbie and I battled forth to the south side for water and had to crawl over the ridge. We were several times blown back, and yet the queer thing is that but for this exceptional wind the weather was perfect; hardly a cloud in the sky, and the sun shone the length of its short span. I was watching the swells come round the north end of Lisgeir Mòr to meet the full force of the gale from the east. One immense wave rolling forward to break was piled vertical by the wind, and its crest and half its body were just blown away as a great cloud of spray turned rainbow by the sun. The whole pillar must have been seventy or eighty feet.

Herring gulls and greater black-backed gulls sat close to the ground round the hut and inside the fank where there is a bit of shelter. They did not care if we picked them up and put them down again, and never tried to escape from our hands. Poor devils! Meanwhile, we have to yell to make ourselves heard even inside the hut! But Bobbie still produced one of her treats – fried sausages, peas and new potatoes; strawberries-and-cream trifle and excellent coffee.

The night was extraordinarily calm, and Bobbie and I found ourselves unable to sleep. We lay in our beds drinking tea until we could lie no longer. Breakfast was over and we were out long before it was light. We took a walk up the Tor – to find an empty, flat-calm sea. It is difficult to appreciate the sense of well-being in the blessed calm following one of these snorters. Rona was paradise, where for the last week it had been prison. The scene of grey seas and skies and snow showers in the half-light of this whiter morning was strangely beautiful; we put up ten woodcock from here and there – a sign of snow – and sure enough, before we were home again the snow began to fall. Then came a strong south wind and mist. I went over the hill for water later in the day, and on coming back saw a dim, white Fianuis washed by a green-edged sea, appearing from the mist. This glimpse of another Rona I would not have missed, a quiet, remote place indeed in this snow, despite the strong wind.

The snow settled the weather, and three days before Christmas we rose to a calm sea and a white, frozen Rona. It came light just after nine o'clock in the morning when we had climbed to the summit cairn on the Tor.

Never had we seen the view so magnificent as on this which was to be our last morning. The sun was rising behind the far, clean line of the Sutherland hills and tinted the whole of our snowy world a rosy pink. The atmosphere was clear and still, and even as we watched I spied a dot thirty miles away between Cape Wrath and the Butt of Lewis. A ship undoubtedly, the first we had seen for a month. The dot was certainly coming nearer, and it must be the cruiser coming for *us*.

We slid down the snow slopes on the seats of our Grenfell suits; we rolled in the snow and turned somersaults. And rather more quietly we went over to Ronan's cell, the still vivid heart of the island. I know also that both of us silently paid our last tribute to Malcolm Macdonald and Murdoch Mackay who did not live for such a joyful moment as this one in our lives. We may never see Rona again as we saw it that morning early, no one else alive has been there at such a time, but we felt in those quiet moments by the chapel that our farewell was not forever. As I write these lines we are plunged into a war the outcome of which for our society we do not know, and this slowly mending leg and the depth of winter make me feel that active and carefree days on Rona are far away. But I would not like to think I had been there for the last time. 'Ane little ile callit Ronay', wrote Dean Monro in 1549; 'afar off in the lap of wild ocean', wrote Thomas Muir in 1860, 'not to see thee with the carnal eye, will be to have seen nothing! 'Even beloved Eilean a' Chlèirich has not affected us so deeply as this little green island in the northern ocean.

The cruiser dropped anchor in the east bay within three hours, by which time we had carried some of our gear down to the landing at Geodha Stoth. All this we got off eventually, but a lot of stores and heavier stuff had to wait – we were glad to leave something so we could return.

Cap'n M's welcome to us seemed particularly warm that day, and no one was more thankful than he was to get us aboard. We heard later of Cap'n M's remarks when the ship came in sight of the camp. Someone had said: 'Well, the huts are there all right.'

'I'm not thinking about huts,' Cap'n M had said. 'I want to count the population first.'

The census of two souls was entirely satisfactory.

Our journey home was the most comfortable I had had. Early next morning we came into Tanera Anchorage, and that island, even in winter dress, looked subtropical to our eyes. A hard frost was down but no snow. The high hills themselves were clear of it here, though Harris and Lewis were white to the sea. We left some of our gear at Tanera and made for the boathouse at the head of Little Loch Broom. We could feel the air getting colder and colder the farther up the Loch we went; the Ardessie falls were frozen solid, and the head of the Loch itself was frozen over.

The Macleans at Dundonnell Hotel breakfasted us, and how delightful it was to meet the Morrisons again when we got the length of Brae. And once more the trees had their quality of wonder for me; I looked at the different branchings of oak and beech, and birch and ash, and enjoyed the quiet shelter of the pine trees. But soon we had to be busy. There was the car to get and to travel across Scotland to Aberdeenshire for Christmas. We reached Williamston on Christmas Eve to find a white world again and frozen curling ponds. Our hosts and Alasdair came down the steps of the house to meet us and we were in a Christmas world of storybooks.

Three nights before, I had peeled off those hardworn Grenfell clothes, let down my kneebands, put on dry woolly socks and slippers, and had a wash in preparation for one of Bobbie's Rona dinners. Now I had a real bath, climbed into my camphor-scented dinner suit and boiled shirt, and could hardly believe it was myself. I looked across the polished table, through the light of candles and the glint from silver and glass, to where Bobbie sat in her black evening-dress and Spanish shawl. Our eyes met and there was nothing to be said.

Summer Isles

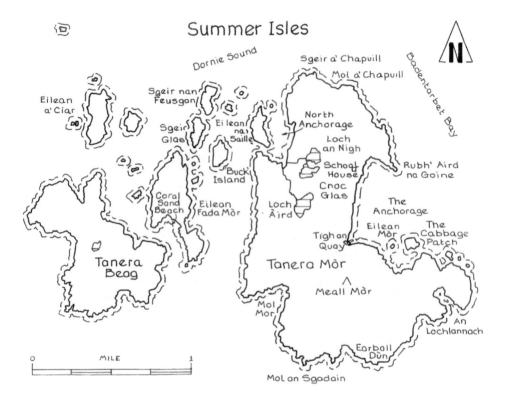

Dornie Sound

Sgeir a' Chapuill

Mol a' Chapuill

Badentarbet Bay

N

Eilean a' Ciar

Sgeir nan Feusgan

Sgeir Glas

Eilean na Saille

Buck Island

North Anchorage

Loch an Nigh

School House

Cnoc Glas

Rubh' Aird na Goine

Coral Sand Beach

Eilean Fada Mòr

Loch Àird

The Anchorage

Eilean Mòr

The Cabbage Patch

Tigh an Quay

Tanera Beag

Tanera Mòr

Meall Mòr

Mol Mòr

An Lochlannach

Earball Dùn

0   MILE   1

Mol an Sgadain

TANERA MÒR

ACQUISITION

I WELL REMEMBER THE WINTER DUSK of an Edinburgh day when I walked through that part of the New Town where the Writers and Solicitors have their Chambers, to meet the Factor of the Dundonnell Estate. The characteristic little winds came round each corner of George Street, whichever way I was going; Melville on his column was silhouetted against a clear sky, far above the elegant places he thought he adorned in his lifetime, and away to the north beyond half a town was the blue-black ribbon of the Forth spangled with the lights of ships and the little towns of the farther shore. In that air the modern Edinburgh faded, romance was abroad, and I slipped back a hundred years and more to the time when my own people had strutted these fine new streets of the Athens of the North.

The interview in a room lined with books and a fine collection of Scott portraits and relics did nothing to destroy the illusion, nor did the courtly manners of their owner help to dispel it. The question of a house came up among many others. 'I wish you were interested in a little outlying property of the Estate on the island of Tanera Mòr,' he was speaking dreamily now, reminiscently; 'it abuts the Anchorage and has a pier of its own. I have always had a special liking for that place.'

My pulse quickened, but this was not the time for departing from my purpose. 'Some other time,' I said. 'I shall not find the fact easy to forget.'

Neither did I, for it recurred often enough in the years following. It was a fact few people knew, and I remember the surprise on the face of James Macleod, the proprietor of the rest of the island, when I mentioned Dundonnell and Tigh an Quay in the same breath. This bit of land was a forgotten corner of Scotland, forgotten and, as I found in good time, forlorn.

There came a day in June, 1937, when the sea was so calm that I paddled forth in my canoe from Eilean a' Chlèirich, bound for Tanera Mòr, six miles away. It was a perfect day and grand going, and in an hour and a half I had rounded the bare, red rocks of Earbull Dhuin, the south end of Tanera, and come into the Anchorage. Here was a different world from the one to which I had been accustomed for many months and which that south coast of the island had led me to expect. There were clumps of rowans and willow trees growing as high as twelve feet, and I was much struck by the unrippled surface of the Anchorage, the shores of which were covered with a heavy growth of knotted wrack, a seaweed which docs not thrive on the open, storm-washed cliffs and inlets of Eilean a' Chlèirich. I was never more impressed with the sense of haven.

James Macleod's cottage had a small garden in front of it, bounded by young trees which he had planted for cover. My eyes feasted on that garden of flowers for several minutes, on the brightness and gaiety of colour in lupin, primula and many more blooms which arc grouped in the mind as old English garden flowers. The bees hummed with a great sound for there were so many of them in such small space. We rowed out to the net slung in the Anchorage and took from it a basket of silvery herring. James Macleod came back to the house immediately to cook some for a meal, but as he left the boat he bent down to give one of the fish to the cat which had come down to the water's edge to meet him.

The meal done, James went to the mainland about his own affairs and I climbed to the highest point of the island to look over the land and sea which here among the Summer Isles made an intricate pattern. It was such a still day that I could hear voices on a yacht coming down Fox Sound well over a mile away. I moved northwards a little from the summit and looked down on Tigh an Quay in the glen, set at the heart of the Anchorage. From four hundred feet above I could see neither the utter desolation nor the true value of the place, but its unique position in such a fine Anchorage attracted me. I decided then I would like to live on Tanera and continue my work from there on birds and seals. The hinterland of islands backing Tanera would be a naturalist's paradise.

Bobbie was eagerly awaiting me when I got back to Eilean a' Chlèirich that night. What had I seen, what like was Tanera? I talked long and with enthusiasm for the island. Perhaps James Macleod would let us an empty cottage if we could dig out the earth floor and reline it. There was one among the trees, set with its face to the north, to Suilven and Quinag and the Foinaven group near Cape Wrath. Bobbie went to Tanera another day and liked the feel of the island. She and I let our intuitions have full play, for we have found that if the 'feel' of an island or house is wrong in the first place it does not come right afterwards. But I had still been no nearer Tigh an Quay than the top of the hill and we did not think about buying it then. Yes, we would come to Tanera, but the time was not yet, and the island had best be put out of our minds entirely until our Treshnish expedition was accomplished. Effort should never be divided.

We went to the Treshnish Isles, lived a new and interesting life with the great Atlantic seals, and came home again to the Brae House. Then began one of those annual journeys to London which are at once a nightmare and a most enjoyable experience. The long journey down in our old car with the snow on hundreds of miles of roads, the series of colds which Bobbie and I always caught on these winter trips and the soft fat we accumulated on our bodies – all these had to be offset against the delight of meeting friends we knew, of good conversation and argument, of good food and wine and many another pleasures. For me also there was the time spent in my mother's house, where I laid aside all the responsibilities of being grown up and became her obedient child again, anticipating Christmas with all the childlike joy that our own son Alasdair was showing.

We returned to the Brae House in March with the southern Christmas fat thick about us. I remember I had called in the Cowcaddens Street in Glasgow on the way down in December to be measured for a new kilt: then I was lean and fit after the Treshnish trip. But when I called to be fitted on the way home the kiltmaker was pained – and I a little shamed.

'Just carry on with the kilt as being for the fellow who came south in December,' I said. 'I will attend to this chap when I get him home.'

The tailor took hold of his lower lip and fidgeted with his tape.

'Do you really think you'll get it down? I think I should slacken her off a bit all round.'

'No, no; I'll grind it off with work all right.'

Nevertheless, I found a great lot of writing waiting for me at Dundonnell. There was a book to finish and type, some proofs to be read and much correspondence about our forthcoming expedition to North Rona. Wood cutting with cross-cut saw and seven-pound axe took me a good hour a day, but being a good doer that was only enough to keep me from getting heavier than I was already. The real tribulation of thinning down had to wait until we reached Tanera in the first days of May, 1938.

I happened to be writing to the Factor of Dundonnell in April and the subject of the Tanera property came up again. Bobbie and I thought it over, and on the first good day set forth from Little Loch Broom in the launch we had recently bought for our island work. We went to Tigh an Quay, climbed about the ruin of a house and walked over the sadly neglected ground.

Bobbie agreed with me that if we were not fit and able the place would not be worth thinking of, but we happened to have those gifts. The sense of dereliction and ruin was not enough to take away the feeling that the place and ourselves needed each other. We knew also the queer history of Tigh an Quay, of which I shall write later, but it did not deter us. We came back to James Macleod's cottage then and asked him if he wished to buy Tigh an Quay, because if not, we did. He said no; that he had the rest of the island and the use of the ground meanwhile.

We now had a clear path before us and I wrote to the Factor in Edinburgh in scarcely veiled excitement. A journey down to Glasgow had become necessary for other matters, so I was able to accept an invitation to lunch with the Factor in Edinburgh. He and his junior partner and I went to his club and talked of birds and seals during the meal; the Factor had been on an expedition to Spitsbergen with Scottish geographers and scientists of an earlier generation, whose names were well known to me.

The business of stating and accepting a price for Tigh an Quay was a matter of but a few moments.

'The place is stated to be ten acres Scots, that is, a little over twelve and a half standard English acres, but I would not be surprised if you found it measure up to more than that. Surveying in the Highlands a hundred and fifty years ago was not very accurate. The place came to Dundonnell by a process of exchange for the salmon fishing of the Little Gruinard River. I should imagine if you offered the Estate something between sixty and seventy pounds sterling it would be accepted; for it is such an outlying corner.'

I said that if he would accept sixty pounds sterling, sharing expenses and giving me absolute rights of ownership, I would give him my word. The Factor turned to his junior partner: 'I think we may say that would be all right, don't you?' And then the Factor told me a little of the way in which Tigh an Quay had come down in the world from the great days of the herring fishery in the late eighteenth and early nineteenth century until the present when it lay a gaping ruin.

Thus Frank and Marian Fraser Darling became the superiors *pro indiviso* of 'All and Whole that piece of Island Tanera or Taneray lined and marked out opposite the Bay of Taneray . . . being part of the annexed estate of Cromartie lying in the Barony of Coigach, Parish of Lochbroom and County of Cromarty, together with the storehouses and other houses and conveniences built thereon and the quay or pier erected on the shores thereof. . . .'

I could have danced on eggs as I went back to Glasgow that night to tell

Bobbie, and James Gilchrist with whom we were staying. Jamie is a sailor born and a man with half a mind to be a farmer. He groaned with envy and looked hard at William Daniell's colour print of 'Pier at Tanera, Loch Broom' which I had with me. This print is one of a famous series made by Daniell in 1820, and in composition and colouring one of the best. It shows the whole of the pier and part of the terrace, with herring-smacks both in the harbour and in the Anchorage, and little men in the costumes of the

period sit negligently on the parapet, walk along the pier or boil tar over a fire at the foot of the harbour. Jamie was conjuring visions of his own little ship lying alongside the quay and of the pleasant life that goes on round a small harbour where boats arc constantly in use. Bobbie and I promised him then that when he and his wife cared to have the place and our boat for a holiday it was theirs for the time being; and all in good time they came for a spell and had it to themselves while we were on North Rona.

I cannot well describe my own feelings that night and shortly afterwards when the deeds were finally transferred. Now, a little while before I was thirty-five, an island property had become a fact, a bare fact in truth, but the place was there and our own. We owned part of one of the British Isles and at least a quarter of a mile of British coastline. Ownership of land in Scotland consists of two parts, the superiority and the *dominium utile*. A superior may sell the *dominium utile* for the full worth of the land and still retain the valuable superiority which gives him the title 'of' So-and-so, which means much in Scotland, and the right to charge the owner of the *dominium utile* a feu duty. The superiority of Tigh an Quay is worth £2 10s. a year. This means nothing at all monetarily as long as we continue to live in the place, but had we not had the superiority granted to us we should have had to pay Dundonnell the £2 10s. each year.

There was this exultation of ownership of land of our very own, won after years of intense longing; and there was a more defensible emotion of gratitude. I have taken the path in life of not accumulating worldly goods, of actually choosing poverty in return for the right to live as I wish. I believe that to take joy in gathering riches is bad and exultation in ownership is bad. Yet here was I exulting, and I asked myself how it squared with my philosophy of life. Land, land; what it has meant to me and my family! A fierce love of land above all other riches, and a pride in the ownership of good animals. I should be just as high-chested about a herd of cattle (if I had bred them myself) as about the land on which they fed. Land and stock are in a category by themselves. All this I feel deeply, but if I consider the subject objectively I cannot defend my feeling. It is primitive and not abreast of man's spiritual development, and yet there is undoubtedly a voice inside me which says, 'Never you mind, me lad, it may be primitive, but it's good common sense.' The very fact that I love land so dearly is sufficient reason for my renouncing it. I overcame that first exultation very quickly, or perhaps it passed of itself, being mere froth, and Bobbie and I have both been left with the enduring feeling that ownership is really custodianship. I have always said that this should be the attitude to ownership of land, but now I do more than state it academically, I feel it through and through. That custodianship is not merely for Alasdair, whose name is in the deeds as heir to Tigh an Quay, not merely for the British nation, but for posterity. We have become more and more humble in our tiny ownership and are grateful for the chance of work it offers.

As land is held in this country at present I should continue to exercise fully and precisely the rights of ownership because I feel my policy to be constructive and responsible. Nevertheless I would support nationalisation of the land of Britain as an advance on private ownership if I had more conviction of the State being a good landlord. There is no better farmed land than some of that which men own outright, and most of the best rural communities are on privately owned estates, but the fact remains that some of the worst-farmed lands and most abject rural communities are also to be found on privately owned estates. Land ownership, particularly if there are tenants, calls for the highest expression of *noblesse oblige* and a full sense of responsibility to those living and those yet to be born. The Government itself, when nationalisation comes about, will have to acquire that good type of pride of ownership and not be merely official. It will need imagination and sympathy, with a power to express the nation's love for the land of Britain. We, the common folk, must build for aye and see to it that the country's land policy shall not be mean in conception nor niggardly in execution. The State is already the most extensive landholder in Scotland, largely because of the Scottish Department of Agriculture's buying of West Highland and Island estates for crofting purposes, but, as I see it at present, that ownership works with all the bleakness of officialdom and there is a laxity of responsibility among the tenants. The Forestry Commission, which is also a considerable State landowner, seems to me more human in administration, and that semiofficial body, the National Trust, appears to administer its lands with all the charm of the best type of private ownership. Meanwhile, then, we will fiercely love our few acres and hold them fast for another generation and another age.

A great peroration, indeed, about a wee bit ruin, but it is cared for as much as if it were many times larger, and it is the scene of our work and high enthusiasm. Our task and responsibility are greater for the place having been the ruin it was when we came. The first part of that task is to replace the scene of degradation with greenness and beauty.

THE ISLAND

COME WITH ME TO TANERA and let us see the island before we look more closely at Tigh an Quay. If you sail north of Skye, beyond Rudh' Re and Greenstone Point you will come upon the last considerable group of islands before reaching Cape Wrath – the Summer Isles.

'Summer Isles,' exclaimed Pennant in 1772, 'Find ourselves near a considerable number of small isles, with a most dreary appearance, miscalled the Summer Isles.'

There are days when the casual visitor would agree with the hyperbolical Pennant: only by living there and seeing the seasons through would you say they were well called the Summer Isles. The name possibly came from their being used by the earlier inhabitants of Coigach for shieling purposes – the cattle and the people would go to the islands for the summer grazing. But the cattle husbandry of the Highlands is more or less dead, and sheep have taken their place, so that now the Summer Isles might be more correctly named the Winter Isles. The weaned lambs of the mainland crofters' flocks are put to the islands in October and brought back in February and early March. Those islands which carry flocks of gulls are the best ones for grazing the weaned lambs or hoggs, because they are greener and their soil has a higher content of lime and phosphates.

No other group of Scottish islands is quite like the Summer Isles; they are very rough and broken, covered with peat rather than soil, except where the red rock itself bursts through the black of winter and the green of summer in numerous cliffs, scarps and slabs. They are on an open seaboard, yet among them may be found quiet unruffled anchorages. How delightful it is after crossing the rough water in a westerly wind from Glas Leac Beag to the north end of Tanera Beag to turn south into the narrow sound between that island and Eilean Fada. The water is flat, yet two or three hundred

yards away across the island the roaring sea of the Minch can be heard
falling on the bay of big shingle and rattling the boulders up and down.
Here in the narrow sound are little red cliffs where rowan trees cling and
festoons of fragrant honeysuckle lie over the heather. Sometimes the water
is deep beneath us, then it shallows to but a few fathoms and looks pale
green, for the floor of the sea is coral sand.

All bird notes are clearly heard in there and are something of a paradox.
Against the background of the drums of ocean the loud song of island wrens
comes over the quiet water, the thin *pi-i-i* of tysties or black guillemots,
the cooing of eiders and the purity of a thrush's song. The shores and
the water between the islands and skerries are full of interest, though the
islands themselves have little to offer the explorer. Tanera Beag is unusually
rough, and despite its wonderful anchorage is quite unsuitable for human
habitation. The only water is a shallow brown lochan on the summit of the
island. The outer islands of Eilean Dubh, Carn Iar, Bottle Island and Glas
Leac Mor have wild cliff scenery but uninteresting surfaces.

Tanera Mòr is the largest of the Summer Isles and the one nearest the
mainland; from the Anchorage across to Badentarbet Pier is less than two
miles. The shape of Tanera was undoubtedly its fortune in early times and
may be again if the fishing were to come back. It has a large horseshoe bay
on the eastern side and the water is deep close to the shore and free from
sunken rocks. Ships of 2000-3000 tons could lie in the Anchorage of Tanera
without anxiety. The beak-like point of Ard-na-goine provides effective
shelter from the north and Rudha Dubh protects the south, together with
two little islands on the south side of the Anchorage. These little islands
make another small anchorage of remarkable cosiness for boats up to 25
tons; it is called Garadheancal – the cabbage patch.

The mainland shore opposite Tanera is singularly devoid of safe
anchorages and it is a bad shore on which to land at all if there is a south-
west wind blowing. It can be imagined how much used the Anchorage of
Tanera would be in the days of sailboats. Here was one of the safest places
on the coast and yet well out to sea. A sailing ship, for example, would
not welcome a journey up Loch Broom to Ullapool and out again for the

sake of shelter. Ullapool as such did not exist until 1780 or thereabouts, but the Anchorage of Tanera Mòr has been busy for a thousand years. The Vikings called the island Hawrarymoir – the island of the haven – and it was under this name it was mentioned in the famous manuscript of Sir Donald Monro, High Dean of the Isles, in 1549.

I have a fancy myself that the name Tanera is very old, coming from an old Celtic root and meaning island of fire. My reasons for this derivation are that the highest point of Tanera, Meall Mòr, 406 feet, is one of the most conspicuous landmarks from the mainland hills, from the Torridonian range to the Foinaven group cast of Cape Wrath. Long before I set foot on Tanera I had seen Meall Mòr from numberless points on the mainland and had been struck by its prominence.

The brown sails of Viking galleys rounding Rudh' Re, Point of Stoer or Rudha Mor Coigach could be seen from Meall Mòr, and were a fire lighted there the inhabitants of a great stretch of coastline would be warned and have ample time to retreat into the forests which then backed the coastal settlements. The peat has been cut away from the top of the hill, yet it is hardly credible that the inhabitants would have cut their normal supply of peat from up there when there were peat hags in plenty down below.

Tanera itself is an island of many small and very rough hills, dominated by the dark mass of Meall Mòr. The ground looks black because the heather is dark and poor, much of the top turf of peat has been skinned for fuel in earlier days, and the Torridonian rock here is darker and less pleasing than the bright red faces to be seen on our beloved Eilean a' Chlèirich which lies six miles to the south-west. Tanera has three freshwater lochans in the northern half of the island, but they are not very interesting from the faunal point of view. But there is a brackish loch, Lochanach (or Lochlannach), at the south end of Tanera which is full of interest to a naturalist. Its shingle shores alone are the haunt of redshanks, peewits and ringed plovers, and duck may be seen there most days.

Cliffs and rocky shores practically surround Tanera. There is a beach of large smooth boulders on the west side of the island and two small shingle beaches in the Anchorage. A tiny bay on the north side of Ard-na-goine

also has a shingle beach of light-coloured stones and is called Mol Bàine
– the white shingle bay. The fine cliffs of the western side of Tanera do
not hold large breeding flocks of seabirds, only a pair of ravens, a pair of
peregrines and a few black guillemots or tysties.

The Anchorage itself is certainly the heart of the island. One of the
islands in this large bay has a colony of common gulls and the other a
varying colony of Arctic terns. Eiders, mergansers and oystercatchers nest
on the islands and about the shore of the Anchorage, so in summer it is a
place constantly busy with birds.

Tanera has a tradition of the sea first and foremost, and I think this fact, as
much as the physical roughness of the island, accounts for the lack of road
or good footpath. There is no road anywhere on the island, and the only
footpath passing round the Anchorage is a poor and somewhat perilous
affair. It scarcely merits the name of footpath, because it is a succession of
steep and boggy places which keep you constantly on the hop. This last
phrase has come from me without thinking, but I will let it stand because
it fits well with the name of pullets, which was given to the women of
Tanera in the old days by the people of the mainland shore. These women
were so accustomed to clambering about the island that when they got on
to a road their feet were unconsciously lifted much higher than necessary.
This footpath traverses cliff edges of real danger, because of the tendency
of the peat to slough off, and it would not be possible to wheel a barrow
round the Anchorage. Handbarrows carried by two men were used when
necessary, but a boat is the common and obvious means of getting from
place to place on the Anchorage shores.

The Anchorage was busy from the end of the fifteenth century when
the Loch Broom herring fishery was well established. In those early days
the boats fishing the herring grounds off the West Coast were Dutch, and
it seems it was not until the eighteenth century that the local inhabitants
became deep sea fishermen with the improved tackle brought by the fleets
of Dutch busses. Tanera Mòr must have an extraordinarily interesting
history if only it could be unravelled, but, like much more of this North
West, there are few records in writing. The Highlands have no Domesday

Book. Tanera became doubly busy after the Forty-Five Rebellion, when the English-owned companies were taking an interest in West Coast herring and exporting them in large quantities to the West Indies for feeding slaves on the plantations.

There were twenty-one families living on the eight hundred acres of Tanera at that time. They each had a few acres of cultivated ground near the sea, and the hill ground was grazed communally. This state of affairs continued into the beginning of the present century, when a rot set in and family after family left the island. The great herring fishery of Loch Broom began to fail about the middle of the nineteenth century when the shoals moved away from the area, but the effect on the Tanera crofters was not immediate. It was Tigh an Quay only that was dealt a death blow. The crofters of Tanera were nearly all fishermen, but they used both great and small lines for haddock and other white fish, and some went away to the herring fishery working from the East Coast. They formed a contented and thriving community, but as the fishing declined, the other economic and sociological factors which have broken the old Highland economy came into play.

The last crofters left Tanera in 1931. They had really no option but to leave, because they were up against the physical limitations of living on small islands. But our lonely life on the islands was not concerned with boats and the tilling of ground. We took all we needed with us and paid for it in money. The slender thread of one family on a remote island was always apparent to us, but the tasks were few that we were really unable to tackle. Only since we came to Tigh an Quay has the necessity of man power in island life struck for us its insistent note. The boats of earlier days were heavier than now and men were needed to haul them. There were ways then, as now, of lessening labour in hauling, but winches, blocks and tackle and so on cost money and islanders have little actual money. When the male population of an island falls below a fishing boat's crew it is as good as dead, for they all leave together then, being unable to remain alone. Their power to work for export has gone. An island is like a tiny nation; if its imports exceed its exports it is bankrupt. Conditions are different for us; the work of our hands would not have kept us fed and clothed when we first came here, no matter how hard we might have worked; research fellowships acted in effect as subsidies until the war came, but since then we have had to depend wholly on what we could export, and our easiest manufactured commodity is my writing. Were it not for this we should be following the last of the old folk from Tanera – and for similar reasons. But my writing has given us sufficient to put some back into the farm, which, with the labour we have put into it in these years, is approaching the state when it will be exporting enough of its own produce to give a man and his wife a fair island living.

The slopes surrounding the Anchorage are dotted with ruins of crofts and little houses of a later date, gradually falling into ruin. One house is let by the proprietor as a summer cottage, but it is so rarely occupied that it does little to mitigate the sense of emptiness which the island conveys. Those older folk still alive who lived here in their youth are homesick for Tanera, and I was told of one old lady who, when taken to the mainland many years ago, pined away for love of the island. She used to go each day to Rudha Dunain, look over to Tanera and weep. I heard also of a cow from here which was never cured of attempts to swim back. Our own son Alasdair, whose connection with the place is brief as yet, loves it so passionately that we have some fears for the hurt that might come to him some day if he cannot make his living here as we are managing to do at present. We too love the island and the home we are now making, it is the salt of life to us, but we are not untouched by an atmosphere of gloom which seems to us part of Tigh an Quay. I do not wish to suggest the place is miserable, far from it, but at the back of everything I get a sense of great age, dark things done, and secrets held.

This sense of the feel of places is queer. It hardly bears description in a gathering of intelligent people, but it cannot be disregarded in the Highlands. Explanation should be sought along physical and physiological lines, but the psychological result is nevertheless there to be contended with, and cannot be escaped. The long-gone people of Tanera were apt to get religion as a disease and they were superstitious beyond the level of the Highlands as a whole. I wish I could get a bird's-eye view of the human history and present it as a psychological and sociological study: that is impossible, but from bits of hearsay pieced together imperfectly and perhaps clouded by the stamp of my own mind, I get a picture of a small community at first living a busy life in which they were not isolated from their fellows because of the constant traffic of boats and the work of the fishing. Then this contact with the outer world stops with the divergence of the herring from Loch Broom. The community grows smaller, less thriving, and minds react among themselves, like atoms buffeting each other inside a closed sphere. There are memories of the dark deeds wrought in the island's history, inevitable in a place far from the beaten track of civilisation and visited by wild characters from the Vikings onwards. The small community was now truly isolated and would tend to lose stability. An extreme brand of Presbyterianism coupled with deep superstition is a dangerous mixture. The repressive quality of the one on the dynamic potentialities of the other is apt to cause explosions and disintegration. And, as a social unit, the community of Tanera did disintegrate before it was wholly warranted by economic causes.

If there is a touch of gloom about the empty houses of Tanera, there is added the feeling of doom about Tigh an Quay, the incomplete story of which I shall try to tell. Here is a bare description: the place lies at the most westerly point of the Anchorage, where the land is lowest and becomes a shingle beach at the sea's edge. The beach ends abruptly at the south side in a steep bluff and grassy cliff which is really a shoulder of Meall Mòr. The southern boundary of Tigh an Quay comes to the very edge of this beach. The ground rises steeply to the north side also to form a hill about a hundred feet high, called Cnoc Glas – the green knoll – and it is part of our property. Its three hundred yards of low cliff glow red in the sun beneath the green of the hill, and pockets of soil are held in the cliff, growing a few aspens, dwarf willows and brambles.

Cnoc Glas had lost some of its greenness and gone back to heather over a large part of its area; but there was still a vividly green cap of grass on the top and we by our work have begun to make the whole knoll green again so that now the cap docs not stand out in such sharp contrast. The reason for its old-time greenness and the persistence of the cap of short turf is interesting. The knoll was used in long-past days as the place where the nets of the herring busses were spread to clean and dry. Herring nets in constant use tend to get slimy with the floating life of the sea, and such a drying ground is common to most fishing communities. The dried sea slime from each net acted as a small dressing of a manure rich in lime and phosphates, and through the years the knoll would come green without any intentional cultivation.

The southern bluff of the bay forms one side of a tiny harbour; the other is made by a stone quay shaped like an obtuse-angled letter L. This quay is a beautiful piece of work and was one reason for our buying Tigh an Quay. It is 80 yards long, 5 yards wide, and with a parapet running the whole length of the north side. Great blocks of undressed stone form the seaward side, and smaller but still considerable stones compose the rest. It is all built in drystone except the parapet, which had been done with lime mortar.

The terrace at the head of the pier was called the Planestones, and so we call this flat quadrangle today. William Daniell helps us no more to visualise the buildings bordering the western, southern and northern edge of the Planestones, so we have had to deduce a good deal and have made rather drastic clearance. The house of Tigh an Quay, nearest the Planestones, and the one-time living quarters of the staff, formed a continuous block of three-storeyed buildings 38 yards long and 6 yards wide running south-westwards. Parallel with this range and 6 yards to the south of it, was the factory, equally long and narrow but not so high. The two blocks were joined by high stone walls at the ends – south-west and north-east. This north-eastern wall has a fine archway leading on to the Planestones, looking down the quay and across the Anchorage. It is one of the architectural features, this archway, and it will be integral in our scheme for reconstruction.

When we first came the inside wall of the factory had gone, so as one entered through the archway there appeared a space as long as the buildings and 12 yards wide, enclosed by high walls. We immediately said 'Walled garden', and that terribly ruinous place has kept that name. Since then we have tackled the job of removing the rubble: the wall fell about seventy-five years ago, on the night a child was born in the house across the alleyway.

I often wondered why it should fall, as every other wall has stood magnificently, long after the roofs had gone. Now I know. Our clearance of two or three feet of rubble and earth above the flagging in the walled garden brings us to the foundations of the wall that fell, and we find it must have consisted of a series of five arches, 10 to 12 feet wide, divided by piers of masonry 8 feet by 2 feet 6 inches. The ground floor of the factory, then, must have been more or less open to the alleyway. All the buildings are done in very ill-shaped undressed stone, and it was no mean feat to take the walls so high, using such stuff. The walls were harled afterwards with shell sand and lime mortar. The mortar in all these walls is made of the coral sand from Tanera Beag and hot quicklime. It is good stuff but tends to crumble if it gets wet. Now this long wall of the arches must have placed an immense weight on the few piers, and as they were not made of shaped flat stones it is not surprising that with slight crumbling of the mortar the whole thing fell out suddenly. And there it remained for three-quarters of a century until we came along. All the buildings were slated with blue Ballachulish slate, which is rather thick and rough-edged.

William Daniell's print is charming, but I wish he had gone to the top of the high bluff to the south of the harbour and done another picture from there. He would have been able to give almost an aerial view of pier, Planestones and buildings, and we should have had still further working drawings for reconstruction. The buildings would have appeared white and neat, and beyond them is the Little Irish Park which he would have shown as a productive garden, for in his letterpress of the volume of prints he mentions the garden particularly. We ourselves have been told of the fruit which came out of Tanera, including apricots grown on a south wall.

There were buildings of nondescript character north and south of the Planestones, and north of the house itself were others. When we bought Tigh an Quay all the buildings except the house were roofless, and that was far from watertight. In high gales loose slates were regularly flung down and some were delicately perched on the eaves waiting for the right puff of wind to tip them over. That roof troubled both Bobbie and me.

A doorway leads from the south-western wall of these ruined buildings

into a field known as the big park, a field which is really the floor of the
glen formed by the steep face of Meall Mòr to the south and the lesser hills
of the island to the north. There is also rising ground between the head of
the big park and the sea at Moll Mor. A rocky knoll in this field is called the
lazy knoll or Cnoc an-t-Sidhe, which means the fairy knoll. The name lazy
probably comes from the fact that the big park was regularly dug, but this
knoll was too steep and brashy to be any good, and therefore contributed
nothing to the place. We prefer the alternative name of Cnoc an-t-Sidhe
because we like a fairy knoll, and in our plans for the future it will not be
lazy, for it will grow some furze bushes, a few birches and rowans and some
alpine flowers in the brashy slopes which form a perfect natural moraine.

There lies between the big park and Cnoc Glas a small triangular half-
acre of ground, bounded on its southern side by the Little Irish Park of
an acre or thereabouts which is to the north of the blocks of buildings.
This triangle is a very old burial ground which was used until late in the
nineteenth century. The graves are marked by rough unlettered pieces of
stone for the most part, as was the custom with Highland graves, but
the sophistication of the nineteenth century reached this remote place,
probably because of the touch with the outside world through the herring
traffic. A few flat dressed slabs of ugly grey stone, lettered by a stone-
cutter, reached the island at that time. The first roughly inscribed local
stone is dated 1790. The serif of the figure 7 has practically disappeared,
but the eighteenth-century style of curved strokes is plain to anyone. I have
been told in several places, nevertheless, that there is a stone in the burial
ground of Tanera dated 1190! Even without the help of this questionable
corroboration, I should judge the place to be a burial ground of great
antiquity because crumbly fragments of human bones crop up in the
surface layer of the soil a few yards away. Again, places are few and far
between in the West Highlands where you can dig deep enough for burial.
I have been told that in olden days people were brought from the mainland
to be buried on Tanera; there were several reasons for this, one being the
freedom from wild beasts or dogs which tended to dig up mainland graves.
And another reason applied to the period when the resurrection men were

busy stealing corpses from wherever they could for the anatomists. It so happened that Tanera was not too good from that point of view because of the busy sea traffic a century or two ago. The resurrection rascals came in the boats like sewer rats, and here began one of the tragedies of the island. I have been told that one of these corpse-thieving parties was caught red-handed and the members killed before they could reach the boats.

The burial ground lay forlorn and desolate, the stones slowly but surely disappearing below the soil. Perhaps it is as well they should go. Our immediate wish was to fence this half-acre, plant trees and shrubs in it and plenty of bulbs, so that it might become a more beautiful place and one more attractive to the birds.

And now for the Little Irish Park, which is one of the gems of the place. Why Irish, you may ask? Again we must look to the herring traffic. Part of the catch cured in Tanera was exported to Ireland and boats came back in ballast with Irish soil. This was dumped and spread in this little field, so that today we have some good deep ground for a garden, and when it was grass it was green the winter through. A good drystone dyke all round gives fair shelter, and it is here we hope to grow new things and make experiments as to what can and can not be grown. This little field slopes gently to the south and slightly to the east, so that its lowest part is but a foot or two above the high spring tides which reach the gate. We want to plan it as a satisfying garden or, as the old word puts it, a pleasaunce.

There are four old apple trees on the south-western side of the garden, as we will henceforth call it, which are reputed to be 150 years old, and this estimate fits the history of the place as we know it. These apple trees give us immense satisfaction: first, they are real trees, reaching a good ten or twelve feet high; second, their blossom in spring rests our very souls after the wildness of a Highland winter; and third, they bear well. Such apple trees as these would be an affront to any rigidly orthodox gardener. Their trunks are about two feet high and very thick, growing close against the drystone dyke. When the branches reach the top of the dyke they turn eastwards, all of them, and the uttermost twigs droop to the ground seven yards from the trunk. It is possible to set a table in summer in the bower

made by these old trees, and many are the pleasant meals we have taken
there with the willow warblers calling softly in the branches overhead.
That orthodox gardener I mentioned might forgive the singular shape of
these trees, compelled to adopt it as they have been by the force of two
human lifetimes of Atlantic gales. But he would be aghast at the state of
the branches, which are matted as close as those of an old wild apple tree.
Several visitors have already said to us that these trees would bear pruning.
So they would, but they will not get it. The shape of them is dear to us and
the shelter they give to the garden east of them would be worth while if we
had neither the glory of the blossom nor the abundant crop of apples. The
apples themselves are smallish, but the best of them run four to the pound.
They are fit for eating from December onwards when they have become a
delicate yellow in colour. But their main value is as a cooker: I am one of
those who are apt to think plain apple pie rather an anticlimax and that the
best part is the crust. Not so with these apples, which have a most delicate
flavour when cooked, comparable with that of a berry fruit. The apples
do not cook to a froth but remain as tender pieces. They keep until the
beginning of June if wrapped in newspaper when picked.

The low walls of a former building remain attached to the main range
and jut into the garden; growing within these old walls is a single willow
tree which has spread its recumbent trunk in such a way that one tree forms
a clump of willows. This is our highest tree, reaching to more than twelve
feet from a place the one-time inhabitants used as a midden. The tree was
planted long ago to provide withies for lobster creels, a purely practical
end. But our eyes see the waving fronds of the willows and how they attract
the birds. The desolation of mouldering boots and broken crockery at their
foot could be covered with stone; and this we have done.

The walls in which the willows grow have an interest of their own to
the naturalist. They lie on the north side of the high range of buildings
and therefore get no noonday sun. Tiny ferns and mosses grow there and
many of the stones are beautifully lichened. One May day soon after we
came to Tigh an Quay I found a beautiful pyramidal orchis growing on
the wall; and when I read about this species in my flower book I learned

that it was to be found on dry chalk downs. There are no such places here, but this orchis was growing on the nearest approach to a chalk down – on the top of a wall made with mortar composed of lime and shell sand. This discovery pleased me then and I still think of it with pleasure.

All these damp north walls must have a large population of insects, for our commonest birds about the house are wrens and hedge sparrows. The wrens especially are like hummingbirds, going up and down the faces of the walls in hovering flight, halting here and there to make closer inspection of a cushion of moss or plant of spleenwort. Centipedes inhabit the lime mortar in great numbers.

A few elders grow in the south-east corner of the garden; they do their best to give shelter and greenness, and they blossom prodigally. So far we have not seen the berries ripen. We have topped and pruned the trees to make them grow thicker, but they have a hard time when the east wind blows after they have broken into leaf. All the prunings have been planted elsewhere, for with us the elder is no weed but the beginning of all-important cover. We have a few chaffinches about the house and garden now and our cultivation has probably induced them to stay and breed, but they have not nested in the elders as one might have expected them to do. I think the reason is that as they are placed at the moment, the trees do not come into leaf from their first shoots of the season but from secondary buds after the east winds have ceased for the summer, and this means that the bushes do not provide the chaffinches with sufficient cover early enough in the year for them to nest in them. By June the elders are full of feeding and resting birds.

Cover, shelter; with these the West can be a kindly country: without them our hands are tied. Such are the bare lineaments of Tigh an Quay whose 'ten acres Scots or thereby' turn out to be over seventeen acres of the standard variety.

The first mention I have managed to find of Tigh an Quay is in the Old Statistical Account. It tells that Tanera, along with the rest of the Cromartie Estate, was then in the hands of the Commission of Annexed Estates, the

body which had administered a large number of Highland properties since
the fatal year of 1746. Everybody knows that the estates eventually came
back to the rightful heirs, but the Commission seems to have made itself
rather free of the Highlands while it was in possession. Tigh an Quay is an
example, for when the Cromartie lands were restored, this bit of ground of
Tanera was not, because the Commission had sold it to a London company
of business men who hoped to make profit from the famous Loch Broom
herring fishery.

I have mentioned earlier that this particular fishery had come into
prominence in the sixteenth century when the adventurous and industrious
Dutch had come to this part of the world in their fishing busses, with gear
far in advance of anything the primitive Scots had developed. The Dutch
taught the Highlander how to fish, but from all accounts they received
no gratitude, because the Highlanders thought the Dutch were emptying
the seas. (That opinion occurs whenever a new or more efficient means
of catching fish is used. The Dover fishermen of the fourteenth century
petitioned the King to stop the use of the beam trawl which came to be
used about that time.)

The herring used to come into the wide mouth of Loch Broom, passing
between Tanera and the mainland, going to the head of the Loch nearly
twenty miles away, and returning on the other side to pass out to the
open sea again by Cailleach Head. This migration occurred with absolute
regularity for hundreds of years, and as the fish were present in huge
numbers it is no wonder that with the quietening of the Highlands business
men should begin to take a hand. Ullapool was built by the British Fishery
Society about 1780, the herring being the town's sole reason for existence.
Another herring station was built in the sheltered east side of Isle Martin,
also, I believe, by the British Fishery Society, which got a piece of land
along with it from the Cromartie Estate.

Tigh an Quay was bought in 1784 and one Murdoch Morrison, merchant
in Stornoway, was installled as manager. There must have been some sort
of buildings here then, and probably a small quay, because when we were
repairing and rebuilding the quay we found the fabric of a much smaller

and lower pier inside the existing one. Presumably, Murdoch Morrison was concerned with the building of the extensive ranges of house and factory which make the present ruin. What a fine place it must have been when newly finished!

The change in the migration of the herring made Tigh an Quay a backwater instead of one of the hubs of the Loch Broom fishery. This fact must have reduced the value of the place enormously and one can understand that repairs would not be carried out with regularity. The London company went bankrupt, there were years of quick changes of ownership, and then a tacksman got the lease of Tanera and Tigh an Quay about 1849. He was a Skyeman called Nicolson, very canny, and out to make money one way or another; he even rented stretches of the foreshore to the crofters for cutting seaware. This was a time when kelp burning was profitable. I have been told that glass was made at Tigh an Quay about the middle of the nineteenth century, but have not been able to confirm this.

Then came a romantic period: the Skyeman had gone and one Captain MacDonald had Tigh an Quay. Stories of this time have come to me from two quite different sources, a Highland lady of my acquaintance and from Murdo Macleod, who was the last crofter-fisherman to leave Tanera. These two met in our house here one summer evening, and I listened to them corroborating each other's memories of what they had been told. Murdo Macleod is well over seventy years old now, still full of interest in old-world affairs. He has the mind and inclinations of an archaeologist, and to him I owe a debt of friendship for many kindnesses, not least for these memories of Tigh an Quay and its neighbourhood. It was he who showed me an ogham stone on Badentarbet beach and the site of the first church 'that was ever in Coigach'. And he told me of MacDonald, a gentleman of the Clanranald family, who loved the sea and to live outside the law, as well as to maintain his position as a Highland gentleman. He was known as the Rover and he had a schooner called *The Rover's Bride*, of which Murdo Macleod's uncle was skipper.

MacDonald carried on legitimate trade with the help of his schooner, but he smuggled as well. Now even I, staid and law-abiding as I am, have played with the idea of smuggling here. Everything is right: the atmosphere of a private island stronghold, a good anchorage into which little ships can come without comment, night time in which to transfer the stuff and no one to see, and no customs officer for miles and miles. Before the war Brittany smacks used to come up the Minch fishing; no doubt I could have made an arrangement with a skipper to bring me silks from France, some wine, and perhaps a few cigars for myself. Silk would demoralise no one, neither should good wine, and any profits could go to a charity – for, of course, it would be unpleasant to smuggle for private gain. It could be done all right, but I am so busy with other things I am afraid this profitable sideline will have to remain in abeyance! Captain MacDonald did more than dream, he smuggled whole-heartedly, apparently making trips to France himself and sailing through northern British waters for sheer love of it.

But you get caught some time in the smuggling game, because you cannot do everything yourself. You share your secret with someone and it is only a matter of time before information leaks out. So with Captain MacDonald; but he enjoyed the risk, was prepared for it and had a good skipper as well as himself aboard the schooner. *The Rover's Bride* was lying in the Anchorage of Tanera one day with a cargo of contraband when news came that a revenue cutter was in sight. The Rover weighed anchor immediately and sailed away northwards with the revenue men hard on his heels. He rounded Cape Wrath and struck eastwards for the Orkneys, still closely pursued; the Rover and his skipper knew the cutter was gaining on them, but neither was seriously troubled if only the islands could be reached before the cutter drew level. The skipper knew a passage between two of the islands, through which he doubted whether the revenue men would risk their ship. *The Rover's Bride* went through with every stitch of sail and reached freedom, to return peacefully to Tanera in ballast. It is from this period there has come a legend of a cargo of rum being buried somewhere about the buildings of Tigh an Quay, a legend known as far away as Orkney.

I do not know how the Rover parted with Tigh an Quay, or how the eccentric Meyrick Bankes of Letterewe came into possession of the place. This rich Englishman, a Liverpool merchant, did the most extraordinary things in this countryside and was considered one of the meanest of men. Some remarkable anecdotes of Bankes are recorded in Osgood Mackenzie's *A Hundred Years in the Highlands*. All I know of his association with Tanera is that he used to bring his yacht alongside the quay every year for it to be bottomed and painted. The property came to Dundonnell from Bankes's heirs by an exchange, the other subject being the salmon fishing of the Little Gruinard River. At this date it seems as if Letterewe got the best of the bargain.

But who knows what may come out of Tigh an Quay one day? There is another legend of buried treasure, and Murdo Macleod has shown me the area where it may be found. He says that when he was a lad and this bit of ground was regularly turned with a *cas-chrom* or crooked spade they would sometimes find silver coins about the size of a shilling. I asked him what sort of coins, was there any inscription, date or head in relief? 'Och, we wouldn't be knowing about that,' he said, 'there was very little real money about in those days and the coins were nothing to us but curiosities.'

Some day before many years have gone by I shall be breaking that ground myself, going deeper than ever the *cas-chrom* dug. There are big boulders in the ground there and I would like them out of the way, because that bit of the big park is sheltered from the east and had the reputation of being good for early potatoes. Perhaps I shall find a silver coin or the hoard from which the early ones came. The value may be negligible in terms of money, but how rich in history and interest! Remembering the long, unwritten story of Tanera as a haven from Viking days, through the period of the Dutch fishery and the later turbulent history of the Highlands, there is a good chance of treasure being hidden here. Suppose it were a Viking hoard, hastily buried, telling a tale of robberies farther down the coast where the Celtic civilisation had reached a high standard, or containing Byzantine coins, which seem to have come to Britain with the Vikings? Or it might be some islander's small savings, buried as they often were in the seventeenth and eighteenth centuries.

Such treasures have been found in the Highlands, some without the fact being made known. This very one on Tanera may have been lifted long ago and the only treasure I will ever get from that ground will be that of the fable – the good land resulting from deep digging and thorough breaking up of the soil. The Brahan Seer knew of the Tanera treasure, apparently, and foretold it would be found by a one-eyed Macleod. Coigach is full of Macleods, but all those I know have both eyes in their heads as yet.

There is a story in Coigach of some men gathering sheep on Horse Island, less than two miles from Tanera and closer to the mainland: one of the men fell with one leg deep into a hole in the peat – a very easy and common thing to do – but he got up and ran on after the sheep. That night, two golden guineas fell out of his sock as he kicked off his sea boots. He quartered the ground thoroughly after that, trying to follow his track exactly, but the story goes that he never found the hole of the golden guineas.

As I say, my friend Murdo Macleod the elder is a man full of old tales. He and his son of the same name bring us a mail once a week and they usually find time for a crack before going back to the mainland. I could see the old man was happy one day, soon after we had reached an advanced stage in rebuilding the quay. He was inspecting the new work, walking the stone flags where lately the sea had covered a litter of fallen stones; and the parapet – such a wall is built along a quay for two reasons, of which that of an additional windbreak is perhaps the lesser! The parapet has the social value of a leaning-place where men in moments of inactivity may place their elbows and gaze across the water. Such a place has an evocative quality, drawing forth reminiscence in a fine reflective style, and tales we had thought forgotten.

'The 'prentice will soon be above MacCrimmon,' said my companion.

I looked at him enquiringly for I did not get his meaning, but it was better not to speak.

'I was looking at the boy,' he said.

Alasdair was rowing the dinghy about the Anchorage, getting the feel of oars into his hands and making practice approaches to a mooring buoy. Murdo is an accomplished raconteur, a man with the art of a Seannachie, and his remarks thus far had made me the eager listener. He reached unhurriedly for his roll of twist and his knife and began paring thinly the tobacco into his palm before continuing.

'Och, it was just an old story and a saying they had in the island here.'

The knife closed with a snap and was exchanged in his pocket for a pipe, with the stem of which he pointed to the foundations of those rude and ancient dwellings at the sea's edge, under the dyke of the Little Irish Park.

'There were houses there once, though it's not myself that remembers them. In the far one, under the rock, lived a MacCrimmon.'

The old man turned to me quickly and his bright blue eyes shone from among the wrinkles and through the haze of new tobacco smoke.

'You'll be thinking that a queer name to be in Tanera, but it was like this: it was that Skyeman called Nicolson, a tacksman he was, who rented the whole of the island from the proprietor; and then he parcelled it out to the crofters and charged very high rents. In this way, d'you see, he was getting the herring factory and quay for practically nothing at all. It was himself that brought people from Skye for curing the herring, and one of these men was MacCrimmon, who lived yonder with his son, just a young lad of perhaps fourteen or sixteen years old.

'Well now, this MacCrimmon was out on the sea one summer evening and the boy was alone at the house there, practising on the chanter. *Hidraho, horodo* and so on he was playing. And then he was feeling he was not alone, whatever; there was a stranger standing beside him. I'm sure you'll know that when you live on an island you are accustomed to see who will be coming ashore, and to feel a strange man beside you is a queer thing altogether. But this lad wasn't feeling surprised at all, nor when the stranger stood behind him and brought his own fingers on to the boy's as they rested on the chanter, like this, look you.

'"Now then," says he, "be trying it again with me."

'The boy played, and he was finding himself playing as he had never played until then. He was forgetting everything else now and he took out the full pipes. The stranger had disappeared, but the boy, he was hardly noticing that as the bag swelled in his oxter. This was not the chanter any more but the pipes. The father of the boy came round Ard-na-goine yonder in the boat and was hearing the pipes over the water. He turned to the other fellow in the boat, very strange like, and he says: "The 'prentice is above MacCrimmon." And that was a saying in the island ever since when a lad was getting as good as his father at doing anything.'

The old man lifted the cap from his pipe, lit another match and slowly puffed the tobacco to redness. The cap was carefully replaced; blue smoke hung on the air as he turned to me.

'And that boy grew to be a famous piper of the MacCrimmons, but it brought him a lot of envy from others not so good. There came a day when he was to play in a great competition of pipers, and these people knew it was young MacCrimmon would surely be winning it. Those men came in the night to where MacCrimmon was lying asleep and they were sticking needles into the bag of his pipes, making such little holes in it you would never see them.

'And so in the morning, when MacCrimmon came to play before the judges, he was finding it hard to keep the bag full, and as you know, a pibroch takes a long time to play through. But this MacCrimmon, he was a proud lad altogether, and he blew the harder, rather than say there was something wrong with his pipes. He finished his piece, though all was black in front of his eyes, and then – then he spewed up the blood of his heart.'

Many other queer things have happened in Tanera. In another of those old black houses near MacCrimmon's there lived a bachelor who was credited with the second sight: it afflicted him in this way – a knock would be heard on his door and he, taking down the bar, would see a cortege passing in the darkness on its way to the burial ground above the Irish Park. He would see the face of the corpse in this ghostly procession and then knew which of the islanders would be the next to make the journey in reality.

Fiona Macleod must have known Tanera and its strange tales, for in that series of macabre stories grouped in *Under the Dark Star* he tells of the family of Achanna who lived in Eileanmore of the Summer Isles. In the first of these stories, *The Dan nan Ron*, murder is done aboard a fishing smack in the Anchorage, and the atmosphere of gloom about the place is well described. The Achanna family apparently occupied our property in Fiona Macleod's fancy; the folk seemed cursed and tragedy after tragedy befell them – and prophetically, the ultimate abandonment of the island is mentioned.

But the family that came to Tigh an Quay in 1868 and finally left it in 1923 did suffer dire misfortune. There were two brothers and their wives, industrious folk who dug the whole of the big park – from deck to deck as Murdo Macleod said to me. The wall of the arches fell after they came, when the child was born. What a shock that great fall of masonry just outside the windows must have been to the poor woman, the cracking of joists and roof timbers as the inside came down, and the thin sound of innumerable slates clattering over all! How typical of the West that it lay where it fell for seventy years and more!

Soon after that the death-watch beetle got into the red pine timbering of the house and remaining range of buildings and utterly riddled the place. Floors and roof of the buildings collapsed, so that little more than the house and immediate penthouses remained. When we came to pull the house to bits, very gingerly for fear of it coming down about our ears, we found many of the poor little bodging jobs the occupants had done to maintain the interior structure a little longer. I have heard that towards the end one poor woman went halfway through a floor when carrying a bowl of milk across the room. Incidents like that are upsetting to the nerves.

The last quarter of the nineteenth century must have been rather a nightmare for the people of Tigh an Quay; ruin was growing all about them, ruin of the industry, ruin of the buildings, and the beginnings of ruin of the quay when fishing smacks from Stornoway brazenly came in one day when all the menfolk were at the fishing, and took away many of the dressed stones which formed the coping of the quay. Once rot has begun in a place, human beings seem to take on the habits of carrion crows and are not satisfied until they have pulled it to pieces.

A *poltergeist* began to play tricks on the poor folk in Tigh an Quay. Candles blew out when there was no wind, doors slammed and opened, there were sharp raps on the panelling, an occasional windowpane was smashed, steps were heard where no one trod, and in one of the upper rooms it became increasingly difficult to sleep well. I have never heard that a ghost was actually seen, but the people were oppressed in this room by some presence which was not good.

All these sort of things get on the nerves of simple folk, and how much more so in a dark, high building going to ruin, far from any other house, and where the place had a history of violent deeds. It seems reasonable to believe that in their hypersensitive state they imagined and attributed to the *poltergeist* more than should rightly be borne by it. Let that be as it may, queer events continued to occur and the family at Tigh an Quay was feeling the strain of it all.

When your house becomes afflicted with a *poltergeist*, several courses are open to you: one is to leave it and let someone else endure it; another is to study it as an interesting phenomenon, to which scientific treatment the *poltergeist* often objects and disappears, or you can call in an exorcist, though this appears to be one of the skilled professions which have almost disappeared in this machine age.

Our folk in Tigh an Quay were Presbyterians, but when it came to *poltergeists* they knew something more ancient was required than plain matter-of-fact Calvinism. They called in a man of great natural goodness from South Uist, a Catholic ship's carpenter, who had much experience of laying ghosts. He inspected the job thoroughly from cellar to slates, just as a plumber might investigate a rattle in your water pipes, and his report was most interesting.

'I can lay this ghost all right,' he said, 'but you would be better to let it be and endure it, and let it go in its own time. If I send it out of here, it's a feeling I have that you will be having worse trouble of another kind.'

But the people had had enough of it, years and years of this pin-pricking worry in a scene of gathering doom. We shall have to chance that, they said in effect, but please set us free of this meantime. So the man of great natural goodness from South Uist exorcised the *poltergeist*, and as far as I have heard – and know from our own life here – the supernatural joker played no more tricks in the house.

The family at Tigh an Quay then began to pay the price of the exorcism. They paid in sickness when they had previously been so healthy; two members drowned; cattle died; rotten woodwork of the house was crumbling.

When we first came here there was a small roofless drystone building to the north of the Planestones, which, from the structure of the floor, we rightly judged to have been a byre. Why, we thought, should they make this when there are so many old buildings? The answer is a pathetic one – the poor folk thought that if they built a new byre they might break the spell which was killing their stock. But doom was gathering momentum for Tigh an Quay and its occupants; there was no respite. The last member of the family, who left the place in 1923, was suffering from a nervous breakdown, an extremely uncommon ill in the Highlands.

Doom had fallen. Tigh an Quay lay empty, windows disappearing, slates flying in the gales, the timber mouldering. As we trod about the rotten floors in our early explorations we felt the pathos of this unfortunate family's life here. We could feel so much of it in that usage of the place by them which was still apparent. We read the newspapers which lined the walls below about six layers of lurid wallpaper. There was a *New York Herald* with pen-and-ink illustrations and an account of a notorious gunman of the 1880s having been shot in a saloon out West somewhere. There was an English newspaper reporting the Duke of Cambridge's statement in the House of Lords concerning the death of the Prince Imperial in the Zulu War. A bit of a Scottish paper, undated but probably fifty years old, announced that the valuable Burra Islands in Shetland were for sale. And in the haunted room were two coverless and much-thumbed Gaelic Bibles.

We might well wonder what is going to happen to us now that Tigh an Quay is our home. The place had reached a nadir of poverty and lovelessness when we came, a state which did not cause us to shun it, but to offer it love. That we can and do give it in plenty, and such money as we have to spare. But love to Tigh an Quay means the ardent labour of our hands, first given for little in return. Tigh an Quay is hearing happy laughter again, our hands are cleaning its besmirched face, and unless I am greatly wrong our love is driving away its long sleep of doom.

HOUSEWARMING

WE WERE STILL AT THE BRAE HOUSE, Dundonnell, on a Thursday in May, 1938, finishing odds and ends of correspondence and proofreading, but feeling certain we would get away to Tanera by the Saturday if the weather held good. And then we saw a car pull up at the foot of the brae and a figure walk up the hill towards the house. I knew the broad smile before I could see the features clearly. It was George Waterston, the Midlothian birdwatcher. For sheer energy in the craft and organising ability among his fellow-ornithologists there are few to equal George. The valuable migration records which came from the Isle of May before the Second World War and the concerted keenness of birdwatchers on the southern shore of the Firth of Forth were due in no small measure to his energy. He is the sort of man who is always birdwatching whatever he is doing. During his trip to Finnish Lapland, he found himself peering over the Russian frontier through his magnificent binoculars, and the Soviet frontier guards came across the boundary and took him into their post. Birdwatching indeed! Anyway, George was their prisoner for a few days, but in that time he had his captors creeping about in the birch scrub getting their first exciting lessons in the art.

'The only thing I was scared of,' he said to me, 'was if they should take my binoculars.'

And now, as I write, George is languishing in a German prison, a victim of the Cretan disaster. He was getting on well with his study of the birds of Crete until the German invasion interrupted it, and the latest news is that the Germans have changed his camp again, just as he was getting upsides with the ornithology of Oflag —. How deeply we grieve for a prisoner, but we need not fear for George and any more there may be like him, because his unflagging interest in a hobby which may be followed in almost any country of the globe will sustain his spirit and save him from brooding.

Well, here was George at the Brae. He could stay a night and come back for the weekend. But we suggested he go on to Achiltibuie and we would pick him up from there and take him to Tanera instead. So George went off the following morning and we continued our packing and sorting and got our stuff down to the boathouse on the south shore of Little Loch Broom where the launch was moored.

We were going to Tanera, but as Tigh an Quay was roofless and forlorn, the Brae House still remained the home and headquarters. In fact, we kept it for another two years, spending a few nights there from time to time on our journeys to the east. This departure on a new and quite different island trip was a calm and easy affair compared with those journeys in previous years. We were not going for a six month stay with limited contact with the outside world, but to an island less than two miles from the mainland, with a good anchorage and having our own boat. It was so easy that we felt we must be forgetting something. Alasdair was at school, doubtless wishing he was with us.

The sea was flat and calm and the bright sunshine made it a grand world. Cailleach Head was merely a lump of rock today by which we could steer closer than ever before instead of having to stand well out to sea to avoid the choppy water often found there. The little isles of Carn nan Sgeir were coming a wonderful spring green on our starboard side and I thought to myself they would be like a miniature North Rona, for, unlike the rest of the Summer Isles, Carn nan Sgeir are not of Torridonian Sandstone but Hebridean Gneiss, the same rock of which Rona is made. Our joy was complete when we came into the Anchorage of Tanera and into the harbour of Tigh an Quay at high tide. The decrepitude of that quay was hidden from our eyes by the tide and this sunshine. We drew alongside, near the head of the quay, and with an ease we had never known on Eilean a' Chlèirich or the Treshnish Isles, put our gear ashore, moored the launch and came on land to choose a site for the tent.

The grazing of our property was still let to the proprietor of the rest of Tanera and it would be some time before we could take it over ourselves.

So in deference to him we felt we could scarcely set up our bell tent in the
Little Irish Park by the apple trees, where he would be taking a crop of hay
eventually. Instead, we placed it in the ruin, sheltered to some extent from
the west and in nobody's way.

We began to learn something of Tanera that very night when the rain came;
steady, calm, unending rain, all night long. I woke the following morning to
remark there was a pool in the tent, and as I looked about it was obvious
I had made an understatement. The tent was in a pool or slowly running
stream of water which was not the accumulated rain fallen near the tent but
part of a very large catchment area which all came down into the deep stone
drain which actually ran beneath our tent. I learned then what I have since
had plenty of time and opportunity to ponder, that if our glen were ever to
be good arable ground I should have to dig a deep open ditch all the way
from the sea to the top of the park, with one or two open subsidiary drains
leading into it. The whole place is well drained by the old-fashioned stone
culverts known as eye drains, so called from the shape of the inside. These
work well, but they are not sufficiently large to carry off a spate of water
from about two hundred acres of hill.

There was nothing for it but to move round to the good dry ground of
the Little Irish Park, in the lee of the apple trees which were then full of
blossom. It was a good place altogether: we could hear the willow warblers
in the apple trees before we rose in the morning, and morning and evening
the pied wagtails would hover like little hawks a foot or two above the
grass around us and perch on our tent pegs.

With George Waterston we explored Tanera, which was almost as new
to me as to him. I remember going to the north-west corner of the island
overlooking that lovely little bay called Acairsaid Driseach – the anchorage
of the thorn trees. The sun lighted the sea and the northern half of the
Summer Isles, and there below us in the calm water of the bay all manner
of things happened to delight the eyes of a birdwatcher. A pair of red-
throated divers were fishing there, down from the freshwater loch at the
back of us where they had begun nesting. Eider ducks and drakes were
there in numbers, idling on the blue water and voicing that croon of theirs

which is as the very breath of the northern spring. Another island sound was the perpetual cluttering of Arctic terns which were newly come to the skerry immediately north of Eilean na Saille. Common seals were basking on the bare rock in the middle of the bay, and the sleek heads of others shone in the sun as they rose from the water of that calm place. And we saw there that day what I have never seen since around Tanera, a shelduck with a brood of newly hatched young. I was there in the following year with another birdwatching friend and saw a pair of velvet scoters, a species which I think must breed occasionally in the Summer Isles, for not only have I seen the adult velvet scoters since then, but once when we were on Eilean a' Chlèirich I met a half-fledged duckling on the sea when I was out fishing in the canoe.

A brisk west wind was blowing on the last day of George's short visit, and partly to see the cormorants nesting on Carn Iar, partly to see what the launch would do, we went north about out of the Anchorage of Tanera, with my neighbour at the tiller. We reached the open sea off the northern overhung cliff of Tanera Beag, where for some reason the waves have a tendency to pile up steep and big. Even on a flat calm day there is always a heave on the sea just there.

'Shall I ease her off a bit?' I asked my neighbour.

'No, she's all right; keep her to it.'

So I just let myself enjoy it. It was my boat, but it was in charge of a man of experience far beyond mine. We found she was a very wet boat, but her action and response were wonderful. Sometimes she seemed to stand upright climbing the top of a wave, and this she did perfectly, with no tendency to split them and go through. The launch was also remarkably free from roll, a characteristic in her for which I have always been thankful in view of my capacity for being seasick.

They were busy weeks which followed – checking observations among the islands, frequently going to Dundonnell on errands, enjoying the mobility given us by the launch. Sometimes in the evenings we would put a few stones in position on the quay and think wistfully of the finished job. Then my friend Leicester Payne came to us for his holiday, and out of the back of his car he produced with a flourish – a crowbar! He lives a life of business and wishes he did not, and now, clear of all the world for a fortnight and primed by my earlier enthusiastic letters, he was going to enjoy himself in his own way. How happy we were together, delving into the ruin and the quay and talking of its possibilities! Leicester is a little man, I am a big one, and a job that I will do by brute strength and with little forethought he will do by science, with careful preparation and with most irritating neatness. Thus we worked together perfectly on that quay, with many a quip at each other for that quality the one of us lacked. Leicester surprised me one day in the middle of our work when he lapsed into the Yorkshire tongue he knows so well. 'Dost realise, me lad, that this year thee and me 'ave known one another for a quarter of a century?'

And we fell to talking of those early days when we would walk the high edges of millstone grit searching for the caterpillars and cocoons of emperor and oak eggar moths. To this day I thrill anew each time I see an emperor caterpillar, heather green, black-banded and bearing tiny spots of purple or yellow. Our own bit of hill here on Tanera carries enough northern eggar and fox moth caterpillars to have made our mouths water in those days.

He and I together found Charles Darwin when we were fourteen years old. *The Origin of Species* caused an upheaval in our young minds. Orientation in this new intellectual freedom took time, but with Darwin we felt on firm ground. I remember also that we got a little green-backed book, priced sixpence, which was a biography of T.H. Huxley by Gerald Leighton. That gave us another hero and a lot more reading. I would not have those striving days back, but they were great days nevertheless.

Now we were together in those happy days of an island June. The sun warmed the stones of the quay where we worked, and I think it was then the quay began to reassume the social quality such a place acquires in addition to that of mere use. It is a place where friends can walk and talk or sit and idle if the mood is right. Leicester and I decided to rebuild the terrace and two sections of old wall against the gable, and once started we found it difficult to stop. Leicester's muscles had limbered up in the past week to make him fit for anything. But he was here for a holiday and I thought I ought to

get him about in the boat more, and round the islands. We did make such journeys, most of which were necessary ones for me, and we had a night out fishing as well, but always he came back to those walls and that terrace. The long daylight enabled us to do a day's work after tea, so I gave him his head, let him boss the job of dropping the walls, and I willingly acted as heavy labourer. By the time his last evening came the terrace was built and filled in with rubble. It is the world's misfortune as well as ours that Leicester Payne and I do not work together all our days. He was mentioned afterwards in this district as 'thon little fellow who could work'.

One glorious summer day while Leicester was with us I had the nearest approach to a row it is polite to reach in the West Highlands. I saw a launch early in the morning crossing to the north end of Tanera, then I heard shots, and looking through my binoculars I saw men shooting herring gulls as they flew by the boat. They will be probably going round to the seals in Acairsaid Driseach, I thought to myself, and ran across the island to frighten the animals off the skerry, where they would be basking, into the water. They were then pretty safe from these people who like their sport cheap. We had decided to go to Eilean a' Chlèirich ourselves that day, and went off northwards, weaving about the islands and skerries as far as

Glas Leac Mor. Then we struck across to Glas Leac Beag and noticed the launch of the morning going south from there to the east bay of Eilean a' Chlèirich. This island had been proclaimed a sanctuary by Lord Tarbat and it was my unofficial job to see it was kept as one, so we gave chase and reached the island four hundred yards behind the party.

The boatman was still in the launch, a fellow we like well enough, and his comment was one of admiration for our speed. We were soon ashore in our dinghy, and from the noise being made by the peregrine falcons I knew what the objective was – young falcons for visitors at a pound apiece. My speed on the hill is as good as that of most, so I reached the foot of the little cliff as soon as the other fellows. One showed his displeasure quite obviously, but I take my hat off to the other, who came forward with a smile and an open hand: 'Ah! How are you, Doctor? Lovely day, isn't it?'

I was just as charming myself, and we went on to recount to each other a few anecdotes of natural history. There was no touch of rancour.

'The peregrines are making an awful row, aren't they?' I said.

'Yes; terrible noise that. I wouldn't be surprised if they had an eyrie somewhere up in those rocks, if anyone had the time to look for it.'

As I had all day to spend on the island and showed no signs of leaving that braeface, I won the round and the falcons got away all right that year. But from what I heard later, the remarks passed on me were not complimentary. I felt no animosity to the fellow sent to get the falcons, because it meant a couple of pounds to him and how should he be expected to let such a sum pass through his fingers? It is the man behind who is the trouble, and those of this countryside who encourage visitors with promises of cheap sport at the expense of the natural fauna. The peregrine is fairly safe anyway, but the resident race of greylag geese is in peril.

It was our intention to rent and repair a small cottage from our neighbour. There was the earth floor to be dug out and made ready for a wooden floor, the walls to be lined with matchboarding and the place partitioned into rooms. The floor was in – almost – but no partitions and no lining, so we had in effect one long room with an open fireplace at each end. The door had rotted away at the foot sufficient to allow a dog room to get in and out, but we were able to prop sacks against the hole and realised the luxury of having rigid walls and a good roof about us.

Potatoes should have been in the ground before this time, and here were we with not a spit of earth dug. I began work at the east side of the Little Irish Park, where a large bed of dockens and nettles were now pushing ahead for the summer's growth. Nettles do not grow on bad ground, neither do dockens of the strength these were, but to get an old nettle bed to look like a garden means a spell of tribulation, to which I, soft and flabby from the winter months of luxurious living, came with full knowledge and some shyness. I dug a trench 18 inches wide and 15 inches deep, then pared off the nettles and dockens of the next one and deposited them upside down in the bottom. Bobbie cut and carried seaweed which was put on the upturned nettles, and finally the bared soil of the second trench to be was loosened with a pickaxe and then dug over the seaweed in the first trench.

This technique was followed throughout till we had enough ground for potatoes, cabbage and kale. How I suffered! The winter's fat fell away from me, and after a week of hardly knowing how to get on my feet once I was down on my back, I began to limber up and enjoy the work. Blisters burst and hardened into 'hooves' which have not left my hands since. Furthermore, the soil there was very deep and of beautiful quality and it stimulated me to see the patch of fresh brown earth growing larger each day. The growth of everything we planted there was enormous, and even now in 1942 there is no better bit of the garden than Nettlebed Piece.

Those three or four weeks Bobbie and I lived on the floor of that cottage, becoming so gloriously tired with the gardening, have made a very happy memory. Our meals were simple, but among them there stood out a daily dish we had never been able to have before in our island years – nettle purée – for nettles grow only where man has lived and tilled for a long time. Let me tell you exactly how we make this really delicious but generally despised dish: pick a large quantity of *young* nettles, and put the top four leaves only of each stalk into a saucepan. Press them down

well, add a very little water and cook for seven minutes, keeping the
nettles moving and pounding them gently with a wooden spirtle; do not
strain, add a lump of butter and pepper and salt, and eat immediately.
Nettle apologists often say they are quite as good as spinach, but I should
never apologise for nettles, because they are a delicacy far in advance of
spinach, with a fine flavour all their own. I knew of one old Highland
gentleman who said he felt no man at all for the rest of the year if he did
not get at least three boilings of nettles in the spring. We also had plenty
of winkles from our own beach and found they were an excellent meal
in conjunction with the nettles. The winkles were put in cold water and
boiled for one minute.

I also painted the launch before putting her on the water, and in this
practical sense I wondered anew at the remarkable drying power of the
Highland May and June when the sun often shines its full span of about
sixteen hours a day and the prevalent northerly breeze desiccates everything
which does not have its roots well in the ground. This is the time when boat
seams open and the paint almost dries under the brush as it is applied. The
north wind of May and June can be cold if you are standing about on a job,
yet as soon as you step out of the wind and still remain in the sun the air
is baking hot. The afternoons are best spent lazing about if the time can be
spared, though on Tanera we have had to cut down the time of our usual
island siestas. We do try to have a rest each summer day after lunch, because
the daylight is so long and the evening such a delightful time in which to
work that we often have to compel ourselves to come indoors at midnight.

Cuddy fishing is another hindrance to regular hours in May, when these
young coalfish are in the vicinity of isolated skerries and will take a coarse
white fly trailed below the surface on a bamboo rod. We go about ten
o'clock on a dead calm evening and wait for the cuddies to rise. They leap
in thousands from the water to make the surface for many yards around
dance and sound as if heavy tropical rain were falling. A basketful of fish
takes little getting on such a night and we come home in the half-light with
plenty of song, gutting and cleaning the fish as we go. Some to eat, some
to salt and some to give away to friends on the overside. The guts we keep

in a bucket to put on the compost heap; such excellent, readily decaying organic matter is not to be wasted.

It was in May that we managed to rent the schoolhouse of Tanera, an ugly, meagrely built place set high on a cliff looking south-east over the Anchorage. We were glad to get it, for we could now bring our furniture from Dundonnell and set up house more conveniently than in the cottage. The large, draughty schoolroom would do as a dining room in summer when we should have lots of friends coming. We painted and papered and scrubbed, though we never managed to make the place look really nice. The woodwork was too poor for that, and there was an atmosphere about the house which we did not like very much. There is no garden or fence round the place, just a very poor black moor, scarred by turf cutting: the great thing to be said for that house is its view, which is a superb panorama of sea, wild coast and the mountains of Sutherland and Ross. The house has lain unused as a school since before the 1914 war, the registers of that period still lying in an outbuilding at the back. What we cannot understand is why the school should be set up there, far from most of the other houses and entailing a journey for the children from one half of the island along a cliff edge where the path is continually crumbling and dangerous for man or beast. The house was built about 1870, I believe, and the story goes that the women of the island carried up the stone and lime for the job, their husbands being away for the fishing. Having now carried several tons of stuff up and down there on my own back, I can salute those women and wonder the more at the odd choice of site.

I had been to a funeral on the mainland one day in May, and was sitting with Donnie Fraser in his mother's house when a young man walked in whom I did not know. He was fair, bright blue of eye, lean as a falcon, with a well-poised head, and dressed in blue jersey, breeches and heavy boots. I liked the make of him and was able to take such full stock because I was sitting in a dark corner. I was a little surprised when he asked for me, though I had guessed from those boots that he was a climber and therefore no native of these parts. It was Alastair Cram, one of the best climbers in

Britain, with every one of the five hundred and forty-three Munroes or 3000-foot hills in Scotland to his credit, and more than anything else, we knew him to be a friend of Kenneth Dougal MacDougall, our own Dougal of the island years. When he walked into Donnie Fraser's he had been living in the hill for a month or more.

What an extraordinarily open and innocent face for a lawyer, I had thought to myself immediately, but soon I saw how his face could be that of the mystic and idealist he is in one moment, and of the sharp, practical man of affairs the next. The dualism was in his character as well as in his face, and the warring of these two sides had brought him here now, the mystic in the ascendant. He came across with us to stay for two or three days, and it seemed as if he were glad to sever by a mile or two of sea his few remaining bonds with the lawyer's life. Tanera became a stage in his journey, for he remained with us three months and would have gone to Rona with us for the winter had not the war fallen upon all our plans. He left for Switzerland in August and got back only just in time. And now, as I write this, word has reached us that Alastair Cram, the seeker of experience, has fallen a prisoner in the second Libyan campaign and is now in Italy, with the high Alps in his view from the prison camp.

Alastair Cram was a godsend to us: he could live on our level and not count it uncomfortable; he could handle a boat, use his hands in many ways, and showed a willingness to learn such skills as he did not command. Bobbie was painting and papering one day at the schoolhouse when he looked in and offered advice. Bobbie is a careful and good worker but with no pretension to professional skill, so without the least touch of irony – for it is not in her – she suggested he should take over. This he did while Bobbie and I went off to another job, returning at teatime when we found Alastair Cram sitting on his heels in the middle of the room, his paint-soiled hands hanging over his knees and the mop of fair curly hair showing unmistakable signs of terracotta paint. There was also more paint about the room than there should be. Bobbie was respectfully quiet, but I immediately thought of that bouncy one in A.A. Milne's *Winnie-the-Pooh* books. 'Tiggers don't paint houses,' I said.

'Frank!' said Bobbie, at once shocked and remonstrating with me, but I was not bothered, for Alastair Cram was now on his back laughing uproariously, acclaiming my aptness.

We had also to cut peats during that good weather, and I started a bank near the house where there appeared to be about four feet of peat. It was black, stinking stuff I found when I got into it, that black, fibreless peat which is highly charged with sulphuretted hydrogen and which crumbles easily under the turf spade. Pieces of bogwood were also interspersed through it, making it difficult for me to keep a clean, straight face of peat. Alastair Cram had carefully observed the beautiful peat faces in the bog which is cut by the Coigach crofters and he was not greatly pleased with mine. I could see he was itching to do it himself, so I turned over the job to him and when Bobbie came along to help I left them to it, not returning till much later in the afternoon. I looked at the pockmarked peat hag which had been at least straight earlier in the day and regular in its spade marks. Alastair Cram* looked at me and at the job, and he knew what was coming. From that moment his name was Tigger or, in our own diminutive, Tigsie.

Next day Tigsie and I were walking down to Tigh an Quay and as we passed the peat face he said: 'Look here, Frank, why didn't you take the spade out of my hands yesterday and tell me to get to hell out of it? I deserved it.'

'For this reason,' I said: 'you came here of your own free will; you took up the tool to do a job for us, with intent to help. You found you couldn't do it as well in practice. But the more expert a craftsman is, the easier does his work appear to the onlooker, and you had been watching crofters born to it cutting peat of quite different quality from this. Had you been a paid labourer I should have given you a good blowing up, but you were not; you were a free man trying to help and trying to learn.'

Tigsie accepted this outlook and tried many a skill in the following months his hands had never known before. But of some things he was complete

* Following Alastair Cram's capture during the Second World War (at Sidi Rezegh in 1941) he is said to have plotted and escaped from 29 consecutive PoW camps.

master, and I found it interesting to watch the difference the sureness of mastery made to him. The engine of the launch was an example: I am a very poor hand with engines and am inclined to neglect them, partly because I do not know enough about them and partly because they do not interest me as long as they do their work. Tigsie was not satisfied with our engine, and it says much for my confidence in him when I let him take it down and reassemble it. One of my most enduring memories of him is that of the sunlight of June, the launch in the harbour leaning on fenders against the quay, and amidships a fair head of hair just visible above the gunwale. Hour after hour he stayed there, silent except for the occasional sound of a tool, and with immense concentration. Then one day he climbed out of the boat, quite casually, and said, 'I think you'll find her run a bit better now.'

Moving furniture from the Brae House to Tanera was no light job, though the help Tigsie and Donnie Fraser gave us made it possible to do it ourselves. Bobbie and I went round to Dundonnell in the Ford for a night or two at a time and carried stuff in the car to the boathouse. Donnie and Tigsie brought the launch from Tanera if the weather was fit; we stowed the cargo together and drank a quart of tea, and then we would return to Tanera our respective ways and join forces for the back-breaking work of getting everything from the shore up to the schoolhouse.

Leicester Payne came for his second Tanera holiday at this time and joined the launch party. His interest in rebuilding the quay was just as keen this year as last, and in face of the many distractions such as the furniture removal we did get a few days' work at it. We pulled down the drystone walls of that pathetic little byre on the Planestones which the old folk had built in the hope of eluding the evil spell on the place. It was good to see it gone, and the stone was used in rebuilding the sea wall or parapet along the front of the Planestones at right angles to the quay, on which the man is sitting in Daniell's print.

Those were the best days of his holiday, because a short summer visit to Rona was impending, but uncertain as to actual date. Rightly we should have gone in May, but the cruiser had had to go in dock for engine trouble. She came in now on Sunday morning, 18th June, as Leicester and I were planting kale, so it was bundle and go for Bobbie and me. The last I saw of Leicester was in the dinghy below me as I leaned over the rail of the ship; it was an effort not to reach down and lift the little man inboard by the scruff of his neck and whisk him away to the remoteness of Rona. Had I done so I know he would not have cared a damn, for he would have lived for once in the moment and faced the uproar in his business and family circles when the time came.

And yet, of course, he would have cared, and so should I; it would have been escapism, running away from what he did not like. I get a fairly large mail from people who want to live an island life and who ask me how they should set about it. First of all, their approach is wrong – you have to discover entirely for yourself how you are going to live such a life; and secondly, their outlook is usually wrong, because the island life in prospect is escapism pure and simple. You will never be happy on an island if it is something to which you have run away. Come to an island when you have conquered in the life you are already living, and come not as a lotus-eater but with heart and hands ready to meet a challenge. Perhaps I did not see all this as clearly as I do now when I used to yearn for an island, but this ripening of the experience should be passed on – come to an island with a definite job of work in your head and the determination to carry it through.

It seemed possible – even likely – that funds would materialise for seven years' of research on grey seals, for which work I should need a 40-foot boat of Zulu type. I went to St Monance to see the builders of our own launch and talk over the problem. The firm built little ships of wood and the partner I met was the fifth of the line: here was no man refined by family success out of all likeness to the practical shipbuilders his forebears had been. Well educated and polished he might be, but he was in dungarees, with rules and tools in the thigh pockets of them, first and foremost a shipbuilder and man of his hands.

I enjoyed this morning in the little town of the Fife coast, watching skilled hands working on good wood, seeing a beautiful yacht taking shape. It seemed there was no depression in the building of little wooden ships, whether they were yachts or fishing boats, and plenty of young lads were happy to come into the job. My host said he had no complaints about labour at all, the youngsters were as keen and proud to do a good job as the older men. The evidence of my own eyes bore out his statement. The sheds were full of whistling and singing, and some of the men doing delicate and difficult jobs were intently silent, completely absorbed in their work. I could not help pondering the whole scene: here were no wage slaves, machine minders, automata who screwed on a couple of nuts in a moving assembly line, but whole men. Everything they did was individual, they produced beautiful things and their boss was alongside them as leader and not as driver. The longer I live the more convinced I am that a man cannot achieve wholeness unless he uses his hands as well as his head. Hands are part of the quality of humanness.

Then I went outside and contemplated my old Ford car to which I owed so much for its gift of mobility. Back in there I had been the sincere but doctrinaire enthusiast for the handmade; now I was climbing into the classic example of the machinemade and I humbly remembered that if motor cars were all handmade Rolls-Royces I should still be walking. The serious human problem remains to be solved.

Back at home, Ivan Hulburd was asking if he could not be of some use to me in my seal work – he was the owner of a 33-foot green schooner, *Southseaman*, and he was suggesting shipping Tigsie as crew. The idea suited me well, for I was anxious to map out the summer distribution of grey seals between the Summer Isles and Cape Wrath and along the North Coast. Ivan and Tigsie could take the sea way to Cape Wrath and I would go north in the Ford, working the coast and making numerous enquiries. We arranged to meet in the bay of Fiondalach Mor in Loch Laxford to compare notes, and for me to take a trip out in the schooner to outlying skerries up the coast.

I worked hard and gleaned a lot of useful information, and Ivan and Tigsie scoured the coasts and open Minch very well too. I reached the few cottages of Foindle just before noon on this lovely hot Friday in July. The sea was flat calm and unbroken by the presence of *Southseaman*. An old gentleman from one of the crofts told me she had not appeared yet, so I went back to Scourie to meet a man I had missed the day before, and to see the salmon watcher at the foot of the Laxford River.

There were two tinkers in the river fishing for freshwater mussels, which yield the beautiful Scottish pearls still greatly prized as jewels. These fellows

had no rubber boots and did not bother to remove their shoes and socks and roll their trousers up. They went in and got wet and came out and dried without thinking any more about it. One was gathering the mussels with his right hand and holding in his other a little square box bottomed with glass which was held just below the water to cut out reflection and distortion from the fast-moving flow. The other also had his little glass box but was working in deeper water, and instead of his arm used a cleft stick for picking the mussels, which lie individually among the shingle of the river bed. It is unfortunate that a pearl-carrying mussel cannot be identified from the outside, because as so few do carry pearls there is very great wastage in opening – and killing – the mussels.

The Laxford men had a few small pink pearls in their pockets which they tried to sell me at a high price. I haggled with them for the mere fun of haggling, and as they seemed to enjoy it too I think they were well enough satisfied with three shillings for about half a dozen pearls which were either misshapen or too small for the jewellers. Anyway, they helpfully posed for a picture which I thought worth taking to show a Scottish rural industry which will soon be gone.

When I got back to Foindle, *Southseaman* was lying in the bay. The old gentleman had studied her lines carefully and gave me a shrewd summary of what the little schooner could and could not do. I liked this old man straight away, tall, slow, carrying his head high, and yet perfectly easy in manner. I asked if I might leave my car within his gates, and not only did he say yes, but invited me to take tea with him and his sister later in the day.

A high whistle from me at the shore below the crofts brought Ivan's head out of the hatch of *Southseaman* like that of a Jack-in-a-box. He waved his recognition and in a few moments Tigsie rowed ashore for me. Yes, they'd had a grand trip but hadn't seen one seal all the time. What a fine time they had had looking at the birds on the sea cliffs of Handa! I climbed aboard chattering unconcernedly, and then down through the hatch from the brilliant sunlight to the dimness of Ivan's little cabin. I have probably never been more surprised in my life, for sitting there on the lower bunks were Alec and Beryl Valentine, friends to whom I had said goodbye at Garve a week ago and whom I now thought were in London. The joke was undoubtedly on me. Alec and Beryl had decided to stay longer in the North and see Handa and Scourie again, and that is how they had struck *Southseaman*.

Well, this was the point where degeneration overtook the seal enquiries. First we had to have a meal and some tea and then go to Scourie for food for the boat party. The old gentleman at Foindle was going to walk two miles to the junction of the Lairg road to wheel home a new barrow, but I managed to save him this journey with no more fuss than his sister making him change into a pair of shining black boots before he stepped into my car – the old Ford of many a rough trip, which was cleaned once a year whether it wanted it or not! Little as I would have wished him to change into those boots, I accepted the gesture as one which is typical of the unspoilt Gael who wishes to do you honour.

It began to rain and blow from the south-west that evening after a long spell of dry weather. The prospect of sailing up the North Minch to Cape Wrath and back on the morrow was no treat to me as I lay curled up in the back of my car, the sound of the rain accentuated as it drove against the hood and found its way inside. I knew the rain had come to stay this time, and in fact it did not stop for the next thirty-six hours. Burns were running well as I went to the shore to go aboard *Southseaman*. My innermost feelings were disconsolate compared with the hilarious state in which I found the boat party; after all, it was fun to them whatever happened, but I was locating seals as a job of work. The rain dripped down inside the collar of my oilskin.

Chug, chug, chug went the diesel engine as we almost headed into the wind; and we got wetter and wetter. Rain with plenty of action can be pleasant, but to have to stand around in it and get cold is deadening to the spirits. Alec was quiet and Tigsie laconic but secretly very happy: Ivan and Beryl got more and more cheerful as we reached the open sea where the engine could be stopped and sails raised, for these two were sailors for the love of it.

The scene which would have been glorious to me from the top of a cliff became a wretched moving greyness as we rolled and weaved through a bigger sea than the wind merited. There was no hope of seeing or counting seals in this, or of poking a boat close in to the skerries I wished to examine. However, I had come a good way to do the work and Ivan had put his little ship at my disposal, so onward I preferred to go, feeling like death. We saw no seals at all on or near the skerries where I thought they might be. The weather was getting worse rather than better, and, trying my best to dissociate the feeling and desires occasioned by the state of my stomach from what scientific detachment demanded, I came to the conclusion it was better to call it a day and return to Loch Laxford.

I felt as bright as could be as soon as we dropped anchor and began to prepare a meal, and after that I played the mouth organ for a singsong which went well with Ivan's voice leading the choruses and his hand conducting.

Such exercise of five pairs of lungs in a small cabin over which the hatch has been drawn to keep out the rain caused a unanimous demand for air. We went ashore in *Southseaman's* little tender the *Atoll*, Alec to poach a couple of lochs (though he knew quite well it was a no fishing day), Ivan and Tigsie to walk through that queer country of rocky knolls, and Beryl and I to go through to the south side of the peninsula and to Scourie for some more shopping. Seals being off, we were enjoying the picnic.

My hosts at Foindle asked me in for the evening and would not hear of my sleeping in my car that night. How much I enjoyed our quiet conversation of homely things, sitting comfortably on the settle, getting a whiff of peat smoke from time to time and hearing the kettle sing for another drink of tea. For me this evening had the spice of contrast with our ribald idiocy during the day. And not least did I enjoy the Gaelic prayers which my host read last thing in his deep and beautifully modulated voice.

My friends were starting their run back to London that evening, so we thought a quiet tea at Kylesku Hotel would be a good farewell. But this was not to be: the brown sails and green hull of *Southseaman* sailed into the anchorage from Loch Cairnbaun and we knew the chances of a quiet meal were few. Ivan's bellow of a laugh set us all going and Tigsie seemed to drop his reserve and become frisky. We ate an enormous tea, everybody's wit seemed sharpened and we laughed so much that Tigsie finished on the floor. Here were five normally well-behaved people, ranging in age from twenty-six to forty, acting like a lot of kids at a bun fight – and on the Highland Sabbath at that.

Next day Ivan, Tigsie and I sailed up to the head of Loch Glen Coul, a beautiful and remote place: the hills rocky and varied in line, the slopes lightly flecked with birches and the red July coats of the deer standing out from the new green of the high ground. I envied the stalker who lived at the head of the loch with his well-built house and nice bit of arable ground. He told me of the pine martens in the cairns of rocks close by and I was tempted to stay up there for a night or two to see them for myself, because I have never seen more than the tail end disappearing into some small trees.

This was the end of our trip. I hurried home to get on with some work and to enjoy the company of more friends who had come to see us. There was Margaret Stewart, lover of little children, who, born in Labrador and reared in China, had travelled across Siberia as a child in the last war; there was Archie Leggate, surgeon, physician and saint, son of a family devoted to the service of their fellow men; and Ted Fynn, *quondam* Rhodes Scholar, a man with a gift for human contacts and having a deep social conscience. I hardly know when we slept, for there were the days to enjoy among the islands and the nights for good talk. One night I was playing the mouth organ while Bobbie, Margaret, Ted and Archie were dancing in the schoolroom of the house on Tanera and it seemed to me we were snatching golden moments of a precarious peace from which the sands were fast running out. 'Play on, play on, and keep them dancing,' said the gnome inside me; 'this party will never meet again.'

I used to come back to the fruitless subject of wartime again and again in our conversation. What was our intellectual attitude and what would our actual behaviour be? It really was fruitless because we could be only academic and ignorant of our destiny. Since then, our dear Archie has gone; he was last seen moving among the wounded men on the deck of a sinking destroyer, giving his all to those lost men as he gave his all in the slums of Liverpool. Ted Fynn has gone from our ken; the last we heard of him he was in an anti-aircraft battery as a private, enjoying equality with working lads; and here am I still on Tanera, a fact which three years ago I should have thought impossible in the circumstances of war.

Our company began to melt away in August. Ivan set sail for Shetland in *Southseaman*, Tigsie went to Switzerland to climb, and we to Edinburgh and Berwick, at which latter place I was to study the grey seal problem in relation to the salmon fishery of the Tweed Estuary. I was looking forward to seeing the isolated group of these seals on the Fame Islands.

Then Bobbie and I were going on to Dundee for the Meeting of the British Association. Whatever clouds were gathering outside, our own little world was a very happy one at that time.

THE CHANGED LIFE

Bobbie and i stayed in College at St Andrews for the Dundee Meeting of the British Association. We met Dick Purchon, a Bristol zoologist, in the train and shared the delight of going from the station to the College in an open growler. It was grand; we had not been in a carriage since childhood, and Purchon was too young to have known them in general use. We came to know this young man as having the rare gift of making intensely interesting an account of the mouth parts of an obscure marine invertebrate, and as I listened to him I hoped sincerely he would soon get a lecturer's post. But war has overtaken him too and he is in a German prison camp.

War was in the air and everyone silently apprehensive; it seemed wrong to me then to calmly assume war was inevitable, because every thought and action of us, the common folk, should be to prevent war occurring. I thought then that Germany would come to the very brink of war but would not be foolish enough to precipitate it. I passionately believed peace could be kept at that moment and that we should use the peace immediately to get together a new round table of nations. I was wrong, of course.

The reception given by the Lord Provost of Dundee in the Caird Hall was a brilliant affair. Scarlet academic gowns and brightly coloured women's dresses, tables well loaded with good food, the strains of the orchestra and the movement of the dance – I found myself wondering if it was real. Was this another ball of the eve of Waterloo? Well, the lamps of Europe went out in a gay and happy moment of our two lives. A meeting of the British Association is an interesting phenomenon: men of science like a lot of children at school, going into their various classes and trying to be serious, but as soon as they are let out they romp joyfully into the tearooms, into the general office where an indulgent secretariat is kind to them all, and off they go in charabancs for afternoon treats which are called 'geological excursion' and 'visit to the soap works'.

I shall never forget the following day. There were no morning news broadcasts then, so we went to our sectional meetings unknowing. But in the middle of the morning I went up to the BBC room to make final arrangements about an evening broadcast I was to give. Ian Cox told me the news, and while I sat there sipping sherry with him fresh news was coming all the time of the German advance into Poland. It had always been the language of politicians and newspapers that Britain's declaring war on Germany was 'unthinkable'.

I said goodbye to Cox, whose careful preparatory work for this week of broadcasts from the Meeting had been rendered fruitless. Down in the General Office the news was filtering in; the secretaries were obviously troubled men, members' faces were grave and I saw one girl, wearing the red gown of a St Andrews undergraduate, standing with her eyes looking far into the future. There was no fear there, but the same tragic clarity of vision I knew so well. We spoke together for a while, two sorrowing folk without hate in our hearts, both with a sense of outraged honour through the behaviour of this country's leaders, wondering how it was that such a small group of men in Europe could so grossly misrepresent the kindly heart and the honour of simple and lowly folk.

We went in the afternoon to a film of the grey seal, a commentary being given by R.H. Hewer, the Recorder of the Zoology Section. He mentioned that Dr Fraser Darling would be giving a lecture on this animal on the following Tuesday afternoon; it was a brave gesture, for I am sure all of us in that darkened room knew we should not be gathered there four days hence. When we came out from the film show a blackboard notice in the General Office proclaimed that the remainder of the Meeting was cancelled, and in such an atmosphere of anticlimax everyone was trying decently to say goodbye and disappear.

Bobbie and I drove to Edinburgh as fast as we could via Queensferry, and were warned we should have to dim our lights if we were to drive in the dark. A long string of cars was waiting at the ferry, but we did not have to wait long before going aboard, and there was plenty to interest us anyway.

It was a dull evening of poor visibility, making the destroyers and cruisers then passing down the Forth into impersonal, mysterious silhouettes. They were moving out to the North Sea, where who knew what adventures would be awaiting them. A number of blue-globed hurricane lamps were standing on the deck of the ferry, and seeing my interest in them a deckhand picked one up to show me: 'And what do you think?' he said in a voice expressing both amusement and exasperation. 'The bloody things were made in Germany!'

We were soon in Edinburgh and back on the road again to the ferry with Alasdair between Bobbie and me in the front of the car. It was lighting-up time soon after our second crossing, and as blackout restrictions were in force we had to drive on the sidelights, which a policeman told us were still a bit too bright. Bobbie had the brilliant idea of smearing the lenses with face cream, a device which was entirely successful.

The advent of war taught us much. We found our normal life and means cut from beneath our feet and it did not seem to matter at all. I hardly felt regret for the loss of the research I had hoped to do. Grief enveloped me; grief, not gloom or anger. Perhaps I was slightly bitter a little later on when I found that a man of thirty-six was a young man no more and not immediately required for service if he had no previous military training. Worse still, the kind of knowledge I had seemed to be of no value, even my agricultural knowledge, which was probably deeper and sounder than in the wider field of biology in which I had delved of recent years.

It so happened that we went back from the world of science to the simple tasks of primitive harvesting. Our friend Donnie Fraser, Raon Mor, had gone to Rhodesia, the young men of Achiltibuie were mostly away to join their units of the Seaforths, and Donnie's mother's harvest needed cutting. The house was full of grandchildren, buzzing with happiness which no war could dull. Some of these grandchildren had been born in Peru, and their mother, the wife of a Scottish medical missionary, had travelled far from the mode of life of the croft.

Bobbie and I went over in the dinghy nearly every day with Alasdair, who joined the pack of youngsters. They all looked alike in their tattered kilts; the varied backgrounds of their lives were hidden. They were a bunch of Highland children barefoot and free where their forebears had been reared. It was little different among us who were grown up. The erstwhile man of science took up his scythe and stone and mowed into the field of oats. His own wife and the wife of the medical missionary bent their backs to gather the corn into sheaves, and their fingers tied the sheaves with a bond of straw. The movements of the hands in tying that bond had come back to them over long years of disuse, sure and unforgotten.

We were peasant folk again, doing first things. The children's happy laughter was a joyous sound of the harvest field.

Yonder sat Mrs Fraser herself on her low chair, joyful in that which she knew: one baby on her wide lap, another clinging to her knee as it made experimental steps, and the golden corn was all about in a golden air. As I straightened my back to sharpen the scythe I would look to where she sat, a Ceres who is ageless and of all time. Not one of us there who did not bow to her greatness, knowing or unknowing.

The corn fell under my scythe and rose again in stooks of ten sheaves each. The sun shone, the straw dried and the harvest was carried. The mood was gone.

Bobbie and I turned to the ruin of Tanera, where from decay and degradation we might build when destruction in the outer world seemed imminent. There was no half-heartedness or regret in this decision for such time as we might be able to pursue it. The stone quay which might be so beautiful and which would be invaluable in working the place as a home and farm was still an eyesore, a tumble of great boulders left by past gales and those human crows who came forty years before to steal the dressed Caithness stones.

No work could have been better than this for helping to rearrange the mind at such a time. Stone is of the stuff of beauty. How often have I gazed at the varying structure of the millstone grit which together with the mountain limestone of northern dales was the stone of my boyhood! The shine of tiny crystals, the cleanness of newly broken stone, the strata of colour and texture in each stone, and finally this beauty of colour and crystal blended by men's hands in a well-built dyke of drystone, or a house built of it and roofed with slabs of sandstone. That gritstone of my youth cut clean and some of it split well along the strata: the limestone of the dales hard by was different, breaking into hard jagged lumps which needed a wholly different handling to build it into a drystone dyke. But it remained interesting because it was difficult, and in the pale grey stone itself were fossils of an early world of which I had then newly become conscious.

The Torridonian Sandstone of Tanera is red, dotted with tiny cornelians and uncertain in its break and split. It looks well newly built, but never harmonises with the landscape like the browns of the gritstone. Our ruin is built wholly of Torridonian stone, some of it pale red and irregular, some the colour of port wine, closely and evenly stratified and easy to dress. These darker stones appear mostly at the corners, door jambs and windows, and there are several in the pier, though a black lichen has there overspread them like paint, masking their beauty.

The rough blocks littering the quay were shifted back into place with crowbar and by sheer strength. You work slowly with big stone; slow steady movements and the weight of your body move the stones a few inches or an inch until they find their niche and are chocked. Sometimes stone strikes stone, a spark flies, there is a flick of blue, blue smoke and the air fills with the clean smell of that moment of heat.

We made a stonebarrow of battens of wood which had encased the huts we had on Rona; it was a job of a few minutes only to make that simple, useful tool, and now, over three years later, it is still in use, having carried hundreds of tons of stone between the toughened bodies of Bobbie and myself. I lay the barrow flat near the stone, I roll its one or two hundredweights on to the slatted face of the barrow; we stand one at each end, each one's feet close beneath the body, we bend low and take each our pair of handles and wait for the word 'Right' from each of us before we lift the barrow. Bobbie moves forward with her left foot first, I with my right, and so does another stone travel its hundred, its eighty or fifty yards along the quay to reach a place we hope it will keep for many a long year.

We also rigged the derrick, a twenty-foot pole of Scots pine carrying four stout rope guys at its head, each one ten fathoms long. The derrick moved a few feet at a time with the course of the work, its foot buried in the gravel of the harbour or in the coarser stone outside the quay, the free ends of the guys tied north, south, east and west, each to a great boulder, over which we piled more boulders until it was possible for a man to swarm up the guys without the head of that derrick swaying, or wrenching the opposite guy from its hold. When the derrick was as sound as that we would hang the endless chain block and tackle to its head and we were ready again to lift the large blocks of stone from the harbour.

Slow, slow work it was down there, for the tide would cover that part of the harbour for several hours of the day. Our rhythm of work followed the daily lag of the tide, so that we would be working sometimes when darkness was upon us or the tide itself washing around our legs and bidding us be

gone for the day. Bobbie would be on the quay running down the block
till it reached the floor of the harbour; I would be slipping a chain under
a boulder or dressed block of stone and making the tie fast; I would take
the hook of the block, fasten it with a simple turn to the chain in my other
hand, and I would call on Bobbie to haul gently. The stone would leave its
old bed in the gravel and come to the foot of the pole, and where it had
lain a strange fauna of darkness would writhe in an agony of disturbance
– red lobworms, tiny red-and-white-striped crabs, apparently inert blobs
of jelly, and sometimes, if the stone were not too deeply set, a little dancing
fish called a *cuilleach* in the Gaelic: dancing himself out of sight, in contrast
with the eels which glided away so smoothly.

Then Bobbie would lower the block a few inches for me to take up
the slack in the chain so that the next vertical haul would see the stone
level with the surface at which we were working. It was now my turn to
haul, for the vertical lift needed a greater strength than Bobbie's, though
sometimes a big stone would need everything the two of us could do on
that endless chain. Inch by inch the stone would rise till it cleared the level
of the quay; Bobbie would pull inwards on it while I quickly lowered the
block, and there the stone lay on the quay once more, waiting to be levered
to its place. The chain and salt water were hard on our hands, as were the
stones themselves. All papillation was worn from the pads of our fingers
till the blood showed a bright pink through the thinness of skin, and when
we came in at night we would have to be careful of picking up hot things,
so immediate was the transmission through our fingers. But peace came in
through the fingertips as well, from that touch of the stone as we fitted it
to its appointed place and found it good and firm.

Nightly we walked home slowly to the schoolhouse on the cliff half a
mile away. Then I would take a crock and go down to Ard-na-goine to
milk a couple of pints from a little black cow. She was almost dry, but her
half-gallon of milk a day made her worth the small rent which we paid
our neighbour for her. She grazed with the other rough cattle, and as
there was no byre or place to tie her (and she, though quiet enough, not
disposed to stand for long) I would milk her with my right hand and hold

the crock in my left, Highland fashion.

I love drawing milk through my fingers and hearing the sound of it piercing the mounting foam in crock or pail. And here on Ard-na-goine, with the sea plashing on either side and the mountains darkening into the night, milking the little black cow was a moment of joy in my day and war was forgotten. There was the distant calling of the barnacle geese newly come to this green point, there were the near sounds of rough tongues licking backs on which the hair was growing long for the winter, of diligent muzzles plucking the grass, and if they were not grazing I would hear the soft, rhythmic cudding of the cattle, together with the comfortable rumblings of their vast bellies.

How long, I wondered, would this go on?

Autumn is usually heralded on the West Highland coast by a south-easterly gale which comes with extraordinary suddenness and blows with great intensity for a long time. When it came in this year of 1939 on 8th October it was our first experience of it on Tanera, where its results were far more striking than on other and wilder islands where we have spent the autumn. All summer growth withers in a night and the leaves are gone from the few little trees before they have reached the glory of autumnal colouring. That gale came before we were satisfied about the safety of the launch, and showed us an Anchorage of Tanera which could be inhospitable.

The real suffering was in the house we lived in. We had never before suffered the hardship we did in this stone house on the cliff top. Its shoddy doors let in the wind, the sashes rattled and the noise of wind everywhere was hell. We endured a week of this big gale in growing discomfort; then it calmed suddenly for half a day, long enough for us to get mail and breathe in our lungs full of sweet air again. I also discovered my throat was sore.

The gale was blowing as hard as ever by nightfall and continued for another week. My sore throat developed into a quinsy. Bobbie and I realised that we could not live in that house even if it were offered to us rent free. We designed a little house of wood on the lines of our earlier island huts, but with three rooms instead of one. At least, we thought, it would do for the period of the war until we could think about rebuilding Tigh an Quay. We imagined standing on the Planestones facing the quay and it seemed an ideal very far away. The first mail out placed our design before our old friends Messrs Cowiesons in Glasgow, after which we had to wait patiently for about thirty sections and various bales of oddments to come to Badentarbet by steamer.

My whole being rebelled and was humbled by the weakness in which the quinsy left me for a week or two. I carried on with work on the quay as hard as I could because I was too proud. Margaret Leigh, author of *Highland Homespun*, came to us for a visit at this time and worked just as hard as we did on that quay, carting and carrying the seemingly endless loads of stone needed for the ever-yawning maw of the quay. There was the parapet also, which I was building close on the heels of the main construction as I reached the final level.

That parapet is built in drystone. It would have to be very strong to withstand easterly gales and it would in a measure be carrying my reputation. Already we had been told the first winter's gales would destroy our work and that it was not to be expected the limited work a man and a woman alone could do would stand. The parapet was five feet wide at the level of the quay and tapered to two feet at the top. Every outer stone needed wedging from within, most carefully, and the middle of the parapet was closely packed with small stones, barrow after barrow of them. When I was a lad the old drystone dyker who taught me how to build constantly reiterated the axiom 'You must keep your middle well filled.' It was I then who was doing the boring job of gathering small stones.

We carried on. Margaret and I would be down on the job early and Bobbie would follow, bringing a picnic lunch and a primus stove for plenty of hot tea. We saw that quay growing clean before our eyes and were happy altogether. Each night going up the cliff again our eyes would glance back along the extending line of the parapet, straight and good and clean.

We had by this time become the proud possessors of a small flock of Shetland sheep. I have always loved Shetland sheep. They have wisdom which other sheep have lost; they have primitive grace and their soft chestnut-coloured 'moorit' wool gives them a most satisfying appearance. It is one thing buying sheep, but a very different one getting them where you want them. Ours were to go on Eilean a' Chlèirich, which we had been able to rent as an addition to our small Tanera property, and were to be fetched from Poolewe. This meant taking our launch the ten miles to Gruinard, spending the night there with a friend, taking the car which he kindly offered us and going two journeys of fourteen miles to fetch the sheep on the following day. It was a very great act of friendship to lend a man a car for such a purpose, for the carriage of twenty-one sheep made it into an indescribable mess and there was no time to clean the car once we had got the sheep down into the launch.

A northerly wind blew up as we went the eight miles to Eilean a' Chlèirich, and I was rather anxious for the sheep, which were being thrown about the launch. We had to go slow, though we knew it would be all we could do to put the sheep ashore on the Chlèirich and get back to Tanera before dark. Patience in a boat is a very great virtue. I was thankful when we drew alongside the pier rock on the west side of the Chlèirich. The sheep went ashore a good deal easier than much of the stuff we had hauled up that rock in previous years. When the last had scrambled up the barnacled surface Bobbie jumped ashore herself and drove the sheep through the neck in the rocks to where they could reach the green of the island. The twenty ewes went through there, no worse for their journey, and carrying that eager, questing expression of the beast on new ground. Also they were hungry and the island was lush with a summer's growth. We left them feeding and moving over their new territory. Only the tup lamb was left in the launch, a disconsolate, unsure little figure, not long weaned from his mother and now bereft of all companionship.

I remember how hard we worked on the quay the following day. We came home very tired and the heavy rain in the night caused us to sleep-in on the Sunday morning. Thus it was after ten o'clock when I ran down the brae with the crock to milk the little black cow on Ard-na-goine. It is a habit of mine to run on such little errands, not always for the time it saves but because I feel like it. Movement on my feet nearly always gives me physical pleasure. Perhaps this joy in mobility is linked with the fact that I usually find it difficult to fall down; I may stumble, but seem to finish on my feet several yards ahead and a second or two later.

But it was different this Sunday morning. I was wearing a pair of lace-up rubber boots and the rain had made the dying grass of the steep brae very slippy. I was down – thump – almost before I knew I had slipped, and a sharp crack told me a bone had gone. Then came a few moments of intense pain in which my mind saw all the trouble which a broken leg would mean in our circumstances. These disordered seconds passed and I took in a few deep breaths of air which seemed greatly needed.

Here was I with that fracture of the leg associated with the eighteenth-century surgeon, Sir Percival Pott. The fibula snaps on the outside of the leg near the ankle and is in danger of sticking through the skin, as that bone comes near the surface; a process of the tibia, or main leg bone, which projects into the ankle joint, also breaks off, and it is this second and less obvious break which may cause permanent lameness. Pott's dictum, given in the dramatic circumstances of his own accident in a London street, was that the patient must not move or be moved until practised aid is available. He himself had to fight off would-be helpers until a door could be taken off its hinges upon which he could be carried to his hospital.

I had to decide whether to stay there until someone came to look for me – which might be a long time, and what could two women do anyway in carrying the dead weight of a heavy man? – or to get moving somehow. It did not take me long to decide to make for home, because I felt the sooner the leg was freed of boot and sock and into splints before it swelled up, the better it would be for me. So I rolled over on to hands and my right knee with the broken leg stretched out behind me and began the two-hundred-yard journey. It was nothing like so bad as might be imagined. Quite the worst part of the affair was the sight of first Margaret Leigh's face, for she met me a few yards from the house, and then Bobbie's. They were so rudely surprised seeing me come home like a lame sheep.

Once indoors and in the study, Bobbie removed the boot and cut away the sock while I lay on the hearthrug with the leg flexed at the knee. I read her the instructions from a little St John's Ambulance book while she straightened the limb and got it splinted and bandaged. Then she brought down a little bed to the study and got a fire going for me, and within ten minutes I was in bed with a hot-water bottle on my belly, but chattering my teeth with cold.

Bobbie can always be depended on to be efficient on such occasions. She did not sit looking at me with a long face and asking what we were going to do: she got me a cup of tea in no time and carried on making the steamed pudding at which she was busy when I came creeping in. Margaret Leigh has since said that her most vivid memory of that day was Bobbie's production of a hot dinner (complete with steamed pudding) dead on time, and the fact that we all ate well and heartily. That is as it should be.

The next few hours were unpleasant, for in addition to the pain I suffered from a type of sciatica to which I am prone, in which one or other leg jumps violently every fifteen seconds or so. And this day, of course, it was the broken leg which jumped.

I learned a good deal about myself in the week after this accident. First, I imagined I should have to feed lightly lest I should grow fat lying in bed. Not at all, my appetite was enormous and I rapidly grew thin. I slept about eighteen hours of the twenty-four and read Volume IV of Toynbee's *Study of History* during the wakeful time I was not eating. Within three weeks my hair was greying, though when I recovered every grey hair disappeared. Margaret Leigh having gone home, Bobbie was having a heavy time, not only attending to me but rowing to the mainland in the chancy south-easterly weather we were getting. By her efforts and the promptitude of dear friends in Manchester, we had plaster bandages within ten days. Bobbie soaked them and lagged my leg with them, and I shall not easily forget the immediate comfort which came from the support they provided.

I woke up after the first week, reached for pencil and manuscript book and began writing *Island Years*.

This was a new experience for me, lying around day after day, and I was much interested to note the effect on my output of writing. Normally, when up and about with lots of odd jobs to do, or with my work of watching animals to keep me busy, I find it quite difficult to write a thousand words a day of a book or essay. Now, my meals were carried in to me, and however much I might regret Bobbie having to do everything, the responsibility was lifted from my shoulders, so that I was able to concentrate fully on the job of getting the book written. I found myself able to touch the previously unimagined total of about five thousand words a day. Once I did over six thousand. Such work tired me and I slept like a top all night. It was curious how little my leg bothered me while I remained laid down; as soon as I got upright an awful drawing pain set in the ankle and I was soon too weak to stay upright.

I shall never forget my first move out of doors on a pair of crutches exactly a fortnight after the accident. The air was delicious, every breath of it sweetness after a fortnight of peat smoke. It was a calm, kindly winter's day and I moved determinedly, though somewhat surreptitiously, across the heather westwards, for there, two hundred yards away, was the crest of the brow, from which unfolded that magnificent view of the Summer Isles in the foreground, then the Minch, and in the far distance the dim Hebrides.

This little journey was a queer mixture of joy and sorrow. There was a child-like gladness in being up for a little while and in achieving the physical task of getting over the rough heather to see that resting panorama, but there was the dreadful feeling that I should never be the active, light-footed person I had been until now. That feeling remained with me for nearly a year, but then the lameness suddenly vanished and all ill effects seemed to go also, and now every bit of suppleness has come back and only a slightly enlarged ankle remains to tell the tale.

All the same, this relatively slight accident has had an immense influence on the course of my life. Bobbie and I were in a waiting stage when it happened, working on the quay because it was a job which needed doing, but hesitating whether to turn our energies and few pounds into developing the farm itself. It seemed improbable that we should stay on Tanera for long.

And within a fortnight of my accident the Russo-Finnish War broke and resolved all my doubts about the rights and wrongs of wars and their causation. I burned to go to Finland and cursed my helplessness. But I had grown accustomed to lameness and, knowing my physical limitations, had finally made up my mind to stay where I was, to put everything that was in me into making this farm from scratch, to demonstrate that in which I had faith – that this wild and neglected country could grow things as well or better than elsewhere if one could but lay aside tradition and think out an husbandry afresh, and that this was worth doing now. War is not the time to drop all that is creative, because man needs a field for creation to toughen the essential quality of hope, and to give reality to the faith which is beyond hope and which says, 'This shall be because it is good'. I could produce more food for my labour elsewhere, but in starting from scratch on Tanera I was going to work on faith in a principle, and its influence could go beyond the few acres of this island.

But for a broken leg, then, there would have been no Island Farm.

FIRST WINTER

L ESS THAN FIVE WEEKS after the broken leg I made my first journey in the launch to fetch Alasdair from the mainland on his way home from school for the Christmas holidays. It was the half-mile journey down the cliff path to Tigh an Quay and back again which was troublesome, for there is not room or evenness enough on that track to put the foot of two crutches down at once.

We also picked up a quantity of blackcurrant and gooseberry bushes and some small apple trees which had been ordered in the early autumn. Slowly, slowly, I made the holes for all these and Bobbie and I planted them. The appearance of these tiny bushes in their orderly rows in that bare garden gave us a thrill of pleasure, but what innocent babes we were! Rona, Chlèirich and the Treshnish Isles – all wilder than Tanera – had given us quite a false impression of the island which was now our home. Perhaps it was the safety and shelter of the Anchorage which made us think the land itself was more sheltered than it was.

Our lessons have been hard ones since then. All the soft fruit bushes have had to be moved to another piece of ground. The apple trees were put on a sunny slope near the sea, a slope which dipped to the south-east. We have seen those trees grow smaller each year till little is left but the central stock. It is east wind which is the killer. Summer and autumn gales from the south-west prune things, but they do not kill. Our very lives on this island for the first three years seemed to be a battle of a personal nature against east wind. A hedge of Lawson's cypress was planted up the middle of the garden in the autumn of 1940 and was dead by spring, after which we planted up with beech and hawthorn in the spring of 1941. Three days later there came such a storm as we shall never forget and which I shall have cause to mention again. The little thorn buds which had been peeping green were killed and the new hedge made no growth at all that year. Nearly all the beeches succumbed to that storm. That we live and learn is one of my favourite platitudes: we have learnt, and feel the more confident for that learning. The beech and thorn hedge is growing at last, having been mulched and limed each year and watched with eyes of love.

We bought shrubs of various kinds and fifty poplars in the early spring of 1940. All those shrubs are dead now because we did not understand what we were up against. You don't plant something and expect it to grow in this place; you imagine the site in every wind and go and stand there in every wind till you know something of what the plant will feel like. Then you create shelter with stones and treat the little bush more like a calf than as a plant. The poplars were put on the west side of the garden, continuing the line of the old apple trees. The drystone dyke gave them shelter from the west and they did not get the worst of the east wind. They thrived, and now, three years later, some of them are seven feet high and providing perches for singing thrushes. Poplars and soft fruit bushes, now close together, provide a leafiness this place has not known for many a year.

All our friends seemed to imagine we were starving on Tanera. At Christmas the house was loaded with food which had come as presents. War had hardly touched the shops and people's private larders at that time. My mouth organ came out once more to give us the beautiful, simple tunes of carols, while Bobbie and Alasdair sang together with a young friend far from home who was spending Christmas with us.

I still found it more than I could do to stay up and dressed all day, but I was determined to start the new year well by going to Eilean a' Chlèirich, gathering our tup lamb from the ewes and doing one or two other oddments. New Year's Day was magnificent, flat calm, sunny, and giving every confidence that it would remain a good day. We were away as soon as it was bright, after picking up a couple of fellows from the mainland who were themselves anxious to catch two sheep which had been left on the Chlèirich since the previous year.

This was the first of several journeys to the island on which I had to accept the fact that I was useless on my feet and could only manage the boat. Indeed, I crawled out of the launch on to the pier rock like an old, old man and did nothing all day but potter about the hut and look twice where I put down my feet and my sticks. How scared I was of falling down! That was one of the things the accident afflicted me with for well over a year, a fear of falling down and a tendency to jump almost out of my skin at any sudden noise or the appearance of someone past a window or through a door.

The other fellows gathered all the sheep which were on the Chlèirich, one going across the island and then working the southern ridge towards the west, another going northwards and bringing sheep south-westwards. The man outlined on the ridge could see most of the movements of sheep and man and dog in the northern half and could coordinate his work so that the two knots of sheep converged in the little flat of green grass in front of our hut. The Cheviot hoggs which belonged to the crofters were in a white-faced bunch, very nervous, unsure and ready to run wildly anywhere. Our own brown Shetlanders stood close together, also nervous, but not unsure. One or two of the ewes were sizing up the situation with studied care and it was for us to watch those particular animals with especial vigilance. If they broke we should probably lose the lot.

They stood there with their heads high, nostrils on the work, ears going far forward, one foot raised and stamping occasionally. Shetland sheep have not had the brains bred out of them: look at the width of their forehead and between the ears; look at them sideways and see how the face is dished, the nose being relatively small and the brainpan bulging outwards. How different is a Cheviot's face, which is Roman-nosed, small in the forehead and so narrow between the ears that their tips seem almost to touch, like those of a fancy dog.

Shetland sheep may tend to keep together and apart from other sheep, but they are determined. If one animal breaks away from a flock of other breeds when they are being gathered, the shepherd does not bother overmuch because he knows it has not the notion of staying by itself. When it finds itself alone it turns and runs back again to the flock. Shetlanders are not like that. Each sheep is ready to break, and those two or three watchful individuals in particular. If one goes, it keeps on going and does not come back. If two go at one moment they will not run together but in different directions, looking after themselves.

Today we wanted very few sheep, just our tup lamb and a couple of ewes to run with him, and the two Cheviot gimmers which had summered on the Chlèirich. We worked our sheep down on to the pier rock and caught Ronan and two companions easily. I rowed them over to the launch, for it was about all I could do that was useful. The two Cheviots were wild and strong and could not be got down with the hoggs at all, so the men went off on an individual hunt, catching the two sheep on the tips of rocky promontories and carrying them to where I could pick them up in the dinghy.

The afternoon was waning now and the cold increasing. We drew anchor and were away, to sit through half an hour of feeling colder and colder as the sweat dried on us. Half an hour means almost halfway from the Chlèirich to the Anchorage of Tanera, but this was not halfway home for us today. We stopped the boat just south of Sgeir nam Mult, bundled Ronan and the two Shetland ewes into the dinghy and rowed them to the rock. There was one quiet spot at which we could heave them out, and as soon as their feet touched hard rock they needed no second bidding to scramble up its face and on to the good green grass of this skerry.

And even then it was not home for us, because we had to take the men across to the Achiltibuie shore. It was dusk when we shouted goodnight, and I wondered if my face was as grey, and my eyes as red-rimmed with cold, as theirs were. I held the tiller coming across while Bobbie, Alasdair and the young friend got busy with a pail and brush cleaning up the boat. If you carry sheep in your boat you will be wise to clean it up immediately, however tired you may be, for sheep dung is like cement; once it sticks to the boards and planking of a boat it needs Augean labour to get it off. But when it is new, plenty of water and a brush work wonders.

It was practically dark on New Year's Day when the boat was put away snug for the night and I began that half-mile journey to the schoolhouse. The night was crisp with frost and bright with stars, but I was beyond feeling the beauty of it. Bobbie and the rest went on ahead of me to get a fire going and a kettle on. And thank goodness they did, for I swear I have never cut such a figure rolling home as I did that night. It took me a long time. The fire was bright and a cup of tea steaming – and more than that, my bed in the study was turned down ready for me. Within five minutes I lay in an ecstasy of rest.

The weather outside at this time was hard frost and snow. One would wonder why they should be about that bare schoolhouse on the black moor at the edge of the cliff, but there they were in dead of winter – a pair of hedge sparrows, two thrushes, a blackbird, three peewits and eight skylarks. We fed them because they came to us, and glad we were to do it. Larks are not common feeders at the bird table, but these eight were the tamest of all these birds, coming fearlessly on to the step and showing a fondness for rolled oats beyond everything else. The peewits ate some boiled potato and little shreds of meaty scraps.

A big new task now faced us. The wooden house lay in sections on Badentarbet Pier, where from this vantage point of the schoolhouse we could see them piled high. Murdo Macleod had been over with the mail and set our minds at rest by saying he had lashed down all the sections, and such loose oddments as might spoil were stowed dry in the shed on the pier. Snow and ice on land means a calm sea across to Achiltibuie and Badentarbet, so the awkwardness of handling the encrusted sections and getting them down into the launch had to take second place to this outstanding mercy of calmness.

There were six or eight loads of stuff to lay across the coaming of the launch, but halfway through we were delayed several days by bad weather. Each journey you would have seen the launch piled high forrard and amidships, and abaft the engine were Murdo Macleod, Donnie Shaw, Alasdair and myself crouching low to the boards in an effort to trim the top-heavy load. Only Bobbie stood, at the tiller, watching where we were going.

Enough of our own quay was finished to make unloading a much easier job than getting the stuff aboard at Badentarbet. How I cursed having only one good leg, though I found it possible to exert a good deal of strength and leverage if I could get the knee of my bad leg on to something firm at knee height and use the thigh muscles as usual. This was probably a very good thing for me, because that leg had shrivelled so that it looked like the limb of a done old man.

Murdo Macleod and Donnie Shaw were going to help us put up the new house, though in the few days of bad weather between the ferrying and their coming Bobbie and I made the foundations for the floor by rolling large stones into position to support four rows of joists. The Planestones are not plumb, for they slope upwards a little to the north-west, so the spirit level was in constant use, testing the setting of those wooden plates in each dimension. At its highest the floor would be nearly two feet above the Planestones, and about nine inches above at the north-west corner. Then we jockeyed the four heavy floor sections into position to make the full floor plan 25 feet by 10 feet. Now I could dive underneath and (in a thoroughly unworkmanlike but nevertheless effective manner) introduce fresh little piers of stones under those floor plates.

We knew that once we started putting up the house we must finish it in one day in its bare essentials, because if a wind blew up it would take away like a bit of cardboard any half-finished structure. There were Murdo and Donnie, Alasdair and I, and Bobbie, all going hard at it: sorting sections into place, holding them into position, bolting and screwing up the nuts. The roof sections were hardest of all, not only because they were heaviest and had to be slid up planks behind the house, but no matter how carefully you may work at this kind of thing, you find yourself possibly half an inch out when it comes to slipping the roof sections down into their appointed place. One last roof section was sliding up the planks when it was almost dusk. It was defying us by half an inch when it was dusk; then it slammed down into position and we worked feverishly at the long bolts which tied roof and walls together. Murdo and Donnie had still to be taken back to the mainland, we would have to see the launch snug on the mooring and then clamber that wretched half-mile in the dark up to the schoolhouse.

Next day I heard the roads were open after the snow and frost, and was able to take Alasdair back to school, nearly a fortnight late. He would certainly have preferred being back to time, because you feel rather out of things and at a disadvantage going back after term has begun, but of the two evils he was glad to have had the lesser imposed on him. To have left home without helping to put up the new house would have been a bitter pill. The roads were soft and slippery and dreadful, and this, my first car journey since breaking my leg, was something of a nightmare. But we got to Inverness all right. When I put Alasdair on the train there I felt a great responsibility lifted from me and I was able to give my attention to finding a porcelain sink which would fit into our minute kitchen.

This was our first house in the Highlands which would have a sink at all. Bobbie says she does not mind carrying water in, but she does object to having to take every drop out. I made a strong cradle, reinforced with shelves, to take the heavy sink; I cut a neat little hole in the floor for the waste pipe; then I went outside and dug a hole in the Planestones which was anything but neat. The terrace had originally been built up with rubble, so by getting down four feet into that, good drainage was assured and the broken surface of the rubble would prevent an impervious skin of soap waste forming in the hole. When war catches you without a good roof, it is no good arguing about plumbing refinements.

But we did make this resolve, not to come down into this little house until it was absolutely ready. It nearly always happens that one is moving gear into a house before the painting and odd work is complete. We went ahead steadily, finishing headings and facings, painting the whole of the inside of the house except the floor. There were numerous shelves to make and paint, and in the tiny kitchen I built in a narrow table level with the sink, fitted a chest of drawers on the other side and built a tier of shelves above them. A space was left for the stove, an iron Hestia oven heated by a Primus which we had used with such success on Rona. Two sheets of corrugated iron were nailed to the wooden partition behind the oven as a precautionary measure. And I made an airing rack just above the height of our heads over the oven. Bobbie and I congratulated each other on what we had managed to pack into a kitchen 10 feet by 6 feet.

The living room was bigger, 10 feet by 10 feet, and would have to hold best part of a thousand books. This was my one regret, that many of my books would never see the light. The two doors of the living room were nine inches from the back wall, just wide enough for built-in bookshelves. A wireless set and its impedimenta are a nuisance in a small room, and much as we grudge the space, we had to give ours a little table to itself.

Moving down to the Planestones was a slow business because the gear had to come down the cliff path. But at last it was done, the smell of paint had gone, windows were cleaned, the carpet was laid, there were books in position on the shelves and it looked like home. William Daniell's print of the quay and Anchorage was hung above the bookshelves on the back wall of the living room, facing the scene it portrayed.

We were due to go to Eilean a' Chlèirich with the crofters to gather the hoggs and ferry them back to the mainland, so what a blessing, at the end of that long day, to come ashore and for the first time step into the little house at the head of the quay. We were too excited to sleep. Next day as we sat at the table we looked forth at a view which has never palled: the parapet to the Planestones appears just above the bottom of the window, the quay stretches away obliquely, then the two-mile band of sea, the patchwork quilt of the Achiltibuie crofts, the moor; and beyond this the three isolated groups of mountains, Quinag, Suilven and Canisp, Stac Polly and Cùl Mòr. It is a mountain view for the epicure, no tumble of mountain after mountain; just these three groups whose shapes are so beautiful that none can excel them in the length and breadth of Scotland.

We see that view every day: we see it as a whole and in all its parts, in every change of weather and season. Now in February the moor is dark and the crofts are drab, and the mountains rise above them a remote and distant country, dark blue with all their features etched sharp with clinging snow. Only rarely do these precipitous hills and terraces take on a totally white face, when a driving blizzard has blown the snow at them horizontally for several hours.

Then in spring and early summer with a north-westerly breeze we see the richest colours: the moor is green and the sea very blue. The crofts have awakened into life with patches of newly growing corn, of brown turnip ground and of dark green potatoes. The mountains become Highland blue, a deep ineffable shade. Blue sky and white clouds arc behind them and the sun plays and dapples. Curiously, often we see An Stac dark in shade and Cùl Mòr behind in sun so that the fantastic shape of this mountain is even more sharply outlined; or the mass Cùl Mòr may be dark, with the battlements, screes and corries of An Stac shown in the detail of sunlight.

The summer months of July, August and September are unpredictable in the Highlands. They may give good weather or bad, but if the day is to be good we see the mists of the morning wrapping the feet of Quinag, Suilven and Canisp, and as the sun mounts the sky the mists rise to the tops and disappear. And on rainy days at this time you may see the clouds beginning to flocculate round Suilven, and that is a sign that it will soon become fine and turn out a bright evening.

North wind and snow squalls in winter will take away all the view except that of the moor and the mainland shore. Beyond is a dull dark curtain of grey in which the snow is lashing the mountain country. Then the squall is gone and the sun shines through an atmosphere vividly clear to show the mountains in sun and shadow all the way to Ben Stac and the Fionaven

group, beyond which there are no more mountains in Scotland.

Few ships or small boats come into the Anchorage of Tanera now, but for us sitting at our window there is equal interest in the constant traffic of birds, the character of which changes with the season. In the few February days left after moving down to the little house on the Planestones we would see the great northern diver, two or three of them, sailing majestically about the Anchorage; sometimes diving quietly and rising again with a fish, sometimes becoming half playful and diving with a little white splash which partook of the nature of display. We hear their weird call sometimes and think of the bird then as the loon, the name by which it is known in Canada. Later in the spring the laughing cry becomes more strongly developed, and before the birds finally leave us in June I have seen a full display between a pair of birds. What a wonderful sight it is to see the great birds standing in the water, wings stretched wide and the head working sinuously!

Those close relatives of the divers, the grebes, are common winter visitors to the Anchorage. Even as I write I can see a band of five Slavonian grebes three hundred yards beyond the quay. They are active, strong birds, much given to beginnings of display which strike the watcher as being in the nature of conversation within the group. And every day one or two pairs of little grebes come fishing in the shallows. Sometimes you can lean over the parapet of the quay and watch the little grebes immediately below, swimming on the water with their heads under or diving with a little chuck of their bodies almost clear of the water and working the shingle for very tiny crabs and marine worms. Black-necked and red-necked grebes are seen occasionally in winter, and the crested grebe each spring on migration.

A pair of greater black-backed gulls and a pair of herring gulls haunt the Anchorage all winter, either floating quietly on its surface or flying above, but rarely standing on the shore. When summer comes, these gulls are still there, now spending much time walking about the seaweed at low tide or standing on the parapet of the quay. Is it a greater profusion of water edge life in summer which accounts for this differing behaviour?

Common gulls nest on the larger island in the Anchorage and become more numerous during February, until the whole flock is roosting near the water edge by the middle of March. They bring a new sound to the Anchorage, heralding the tardy spring, and throughout the summer they tamely work the seaweed in the harbour or join the hens at feeding time if they are given a chance.

The heron is there day and night through the winter, stalking the shallows and finding eels in our harbour, for a freshwater drain runs into it and attracts these fish. The movements and long spells of immobility of our herons seem a constant delight to our guests, and indeed their slow flight, their landings and takings-off, their postures and lightning beak thrusts, are spectacular. These birds have bred on the shores of the Anchorage in the past and began nesting on our cliff in February 1941, but the wretched east wind blew all their sticks away and caused them to lose heart.

The summer scene in the Anchorage is much changed. There is more liveliness to watch as we sit taking our food. A colony of Arctic terns which nest on the little island is now in a fever of activity, using our parapet as a social centre and hovering and dapping for little fish in the harbour. If the launch is anchored off the quay a number of them perch on that and chatter continuously. Courting eider ducks and drakes are there in May and June, and resplendent mergansers, and by the end of that month both of these ducks are appearing in and about our harbour and in the Anchorage with broods; the eiders never have more than five and usually only three or four, but the mergansers appear with a dozen to fourteen ducklings. What mites of energy the little mergansers are! They can swim at a great speed for such little things, and if they wish to hurry they raise themselves on the water and hydroplane along its surface at as fast a pace as a man could run.

All this we watch from our window and it is a pageant of which we never tire. Night in the little house on the Planestones was also something of a new experience for us, for it is nearer the shore than any of the tents or huts in which we have lived on the other islands. When the weather is calm we hear the plash of the sea just a few yards from our heads, a constant accompaniment to the calls of the birds of the night. There are curlews on the beach and on Fank Point, sometimes the note of a purple sandpiper comes through the window on a winter's night, and often a ringed plover. I have never seen a ringed plover on our beach in the day, though they come at night. This is strange behaviour for such a tame bird of the shingle.

To come down to that little wooden place on our own ground was in the nature of a fulfilment. We were happy and hopeful of the future. We not only owned a bit of derelict ground but were occupying it, and felt a tremendous surge of energy rising within us to make that ground fruitful.

As yet the gaps in the dykes were not built up and our neighbour's cattle and sheep wandered round our very doors and over all the land except the acre of garden. It was difficult getting this work done, and when it was finished there was nothing in the nature of production to be seen for the immense labour. What a sense of privacy we got from having a gate at either end of the Planestones! And when we saw our ground completely free of Cheviot sheep for a whole day we felt we could see about getting cattle of our own on the place.

MAKING A FARM

No one can divorce his own doings from the international events of 1940, however remote in body he may have been from them. I put it down as one of the queerest years of my life, one of mental confusion clouding the perfect physical conditions in which I seemed to be living. In March I was active enough to go down to Berwick-on-Tweed in my old Ford, to finish off the investigation I had begun before the war on the influence of the grey seals on the salmon fishery of the Tweed Estuary. There was little hint of war then on that part of the East Coast; this peering, keeking biologist nosing about the coast and crossing the wet sands in his car to Holy Island was never once accosted or looked on as a spy. There was good food in the hotel and I received delightful hospitality from friends in the town. Only the blackout was strange and unbeautiful, and on one journey up the coast in the Tweed Commissioners' motor coble I saw a red gash in the cliff which was the spot where a mine had washed ashore and exploded. Six months later, all this would have been impossible to do.

This journey to Berwick was the first I had seen of wartime Britain; it was like making a visit from Mars; little things like anti-blast preparations on shop windows and various blackout gadgets impressed me though they had become everyday affairs to other people. Then back to remoteness again, where we *heard* all about the war in the wireless news and commentaries. Later in the year and during the following winter of heavy air raids, the attitude of outsiders who came to see us was definitely optimistic and cheerful, but in the remote Highland townships there was a deep gloom not wholly to be accounted for by the fate of the 51st Division, forced to surrender on June 12th in France.

To all intents and purposes, the war began for us with the invasion of Norway. The news altered its tone and spoke no more of the qualities of

Saarbrucken. Yet it remained unduly elated. Even Mr Churchill thought Hitler had made a vast mistake in going to Norway, and the epic battles, in which such severe naval losses were inflicted on the enemy, did make things look brighter. But we on Tanera got our weekly newspaper a week or a fortnight after it was published, and as the news at that time was progressively getting worse, to read week- or fortnight-old news was doubly depressing.

The Norwegian news was bad enough in this early and delightful spring, in which we had worked as hard as our bodies would take us and were as happy in our immediate surroundings as we could hope to be. Three tons of basic slag and two tons of ground limestone had come to Badentarbet Pier, and this we had to ferry over, some by launch but most of it in the dinghy because it saved petrol. Slag is very heavy stuff, packed in 1¼ cwt bags, and I found it hard on my mending leg to get the bags out of the boat on to the quay and each bag from the ground to the best position for carrying, on the top of my shoulders. Fifteen hundredweight of this slag and half a ton of the limestone went into the acre of garden, and that was easy – a short journey from the quay and no hills to climb. But the remaining three and three-quarter tons were destined for Cnoc Glas, which ugly lump of blackness we were hoping to turn green.

What perfect weather it was in late April for this job, sunny and calm day after day! Bobbie joined me, wearing her oldest trousers and shirt and a bandana handkerchief, she helping to spread the slag from a bucket while I carried it up and spread a little. I found each day that after fifteen hundredweight precisely had been carried to the hill my leg simply refused to do any more. This was an interesting experience, for it said no in defiance of the will. So then I did stop each day, and Bobbie and I would repair to a pond in the park with a bar of soap, there to strip off our clothes, have a bath while we were still warm from work and become white again instead of a dirty blue-grey. Slag is hard on the hands and unless you sow it carefully it goes for the eyes, so we were careful, as far as we could be. But to bathe the eyes with rainwater each evening was refreshing and almost a necessity.

The desire for flowers after winter on Tanera is so great as to be almost a pain, and was heightened by the derelict nature of the scene in which we lived and the outer wildness of the island. We made a flower bed on either side of the house: one where the two big walls had been and which were felled to make Leicester's terrace, and the other on the site of the little byre which the last occupants of Tigh an Quay had built in drystone to combat the spell on their other byre. The very neatness which was the result of this work made it worth while. A journey to Dundonnell at this time gave us a chance to bring back a little birch tree I had brought from the hill into our few square feet of garden there. And there were a few alders, a tiny larch, two little geans and a beech – this last a child of those majestic beeches which grew behind the Brae House. All these came round to Achiltibuie in the back of the car and were planted within a few hours of their having been lifted. The little birch tree was now nearly six feet high and very shapely, a fitting thing to have in the bed on the Planestones which could be seen from the kitchen window. A gean (wild cherry) was put in the bed on the north side and duly came into blossom.

How little we knew! The gean could not stand the east wind at all and had to be moved. As it was, a great deal of it died back. The birch throve and grew in beauty, and I foolishly loved it so much that I began to personify it and associate it with our progress here. It was the apple of my eye, that tree.* By June, 1941, it was eight feet high and in bright young leaf; and this was the time when a decrepit and slowly dying cow belonging to my neighbour chose to stand for hours at a time in our harbour. I was so sorry for the poor creature that I let her in to the tiny bit of land south of the Planestones and against our boundary. The cow ate the young grass readily, though slowly because she was weak. I went about my work and came back half an hour later. There was the cow round on the Planestones and my birch tree was snapped off three feet from the ground. I cried out as if I had been struck a blow, and for a fraction of a second my anger blazed. But it never reached the poor beast which had so disastrously rubbed her itching head. I led her out slowly, oh so slowly, for she was wretchedly lame. Poor devil.

* This birch tree is still growing at Planstones today – it is almost 20 feet tall.

The desire for flowers even made me so rash as to try sweet peas – only a sixpenny packet, it is true, but a little trench at the top of Nettlebed Piece in the garden was properly dug, manured and limed for them. A wall was to the east and another at the back of them to the north – the gable end of the tiny house by the shore where the old bachelor with second sight had lived. Those sweet peas began to flower on 13th June and thereafter gave us hundreds of blooms. There they were, a tiny world of fragrance and peace while France was falling and our ideas getting the biggest jolt they had ever had.

My mother came to visit us in the first week of May in that year and, as might be imagined, there had been a good redding-up in preparation. I was the happiest of men next day when Bobbie and I took her round with us in the launch to the coral sand beach of Tanera Beag. My mother sat there on the white sand enjoying what is one of the quietest scenes among the islands while Bobbie and I filled sacks and waded out with them to the boat. But the next morning Holland and Belgium were invaded. Instead of having quietness, my mother was to grow increasingly unsettled.

The weather was the most perfect we have ever had here – and the news grew worse each day. We had every meal outside for three weeks. We had breakfast on the Planestones, near the parapet and overlooking the sea. Lunch would be in the shade of the south wall of the walled garden-to-be, and at teatime we would carry the table through into the garden and set it in the domed bower made by the old apple trees. They were in blossom then and humming with bees throughout the day. It seemed all wrong to have this perfection in that time of horror. The blow which fell on the whole West Highland area at that time was a crushing one. Many thousands of the Highland Division, the 51st, were taken prisoner and many good men of the district were killed. Of thirteen men in the 4th Seaforths from Achiltibuie alone, eleven were taken prisoner. One man, Donnie (Beag) Macleod had the good fortune to be wounded at Abbeville and escape the prison camp by exercising his stalking abilities. He returned to Britain on that famous 'last boat from Bordeaux'. The wound was not serious, Donnie was awarded the DCM, and now a singer of Gaelic songs he has fought with the Desert Army in its proud campaign from El Alamein to Tunis.

Bobbie and my mother and I were round to Tanera Beag again for coral sand at the next low spring tide. This beautiful stuff is pure calcium carbonate and has fertilised hundreds of acres of this countryside. It is necessary to apply it heavily, at the rate of about ten tons to the acre of black ground, but when this is done, the ground will need no more lime for twenty years. I seem to be the only man using it at the present time, though there is not an acre in Coigach but what would do with a good dressing. When I applied a mere two tons of ground limestone to a bit of our ground in that spring of 1940 it was because I wanted the quick results it could give, until I could back it up with some loads of coral sand.

On this day the weather seemed perfect and we loaded up with over two tons. The labour was heavy for a man and a woman, so we left the last five hundredweight in the dinghy which we had in tow. But I did not trim that five hundredweight as carefully as I might have. This was an example of carelessness when one is tired. It would not have mattered at all had the weather stayed as it was, and had we been coming from Eilean a' Chlèirich we should certainly not have been careless, but here we were in narrow waters never more than a few yards from shore and we did not think.

Then a south-easterly breeze sprang up as we made for the north point of Tanera and was quite strong as we turned south into the sound. I began to be a little concerned for my mother, who does not like the sea and is the one person easier made seasick than myself. I need not have bothered. As we passed Iolla Chapuill, a rock in the sound north-east of Tanera, we had to go farther out from shore, and off that rock the waves are often steep because of the shelving of the sea floor. Two such steep waves hit us plumb and the heavily laden launch took a lot of water. That did not matter much, but the dinghy in tow could not rise so easily; the waves also caught her and filled her. I put the gear in neutral to stop the boat, but I dared not stop the engine just off that rock with this wind. My mother took the tiller quite calmly and kept the boat's head to the sea while Bobbie and I were reaching over the stern for our dinghy. She suddenly sank and held for a moment or two by the painter, but the still slowly moving propeller cut the painter like a knife and our dinghy disappeared. Those five hundredweights of sand had slipped down under the thwarts to make so firm a ballast that there was no hope of the dinghy emptying and rising to the surface again. Bobbie and I were numbed with this loss. We said nothing, but took the tiller from my mother and came on home.

The loss of that dinghy cast a gloom over the next week or two. She was only a year old, a cheap white-pine flattie such as the Orkney yards turned out for less than £1 a foot before the war. She was 13 feet 6 inches long and 5 feet 6 inches in the beam, very light to haul and extraordinarily easy to row. You could tread about in her and she would remain steady, and even if I stood on the gunwale where she was widest there would still be two or three inches of freeboard. She was particularly useful for carrying sheep, holding up to a dozen comfortably, and so steady when they tended to pack to one side or the other.

I telegraphed to Orkney to see if another boat could be got, but no. There is only one yard building small boats on the north-west Highland coast, and their tradition is one of strength and weight rather than lightness. The once prosperous Gairloch boat building industry has now quite gone. We were lucky to get a 13-foot dinghy by steamer from Colquhouns' of Dunoon for £14. This little boat is 5 feet in the beam and seems very much smaller than our flattie. I would not like to move sheep about in her, for it would be sheer cruelty to the boat.

Having completed the fencing of the big park to the state of being cattle proof, we got our first cow. She was a rather ugly black beast belonging to our old friend Mrs Fraser of Raon Mor. The cow had certain qualities which I knew: first, she had the virtue of youth, being less than four years old; she was a persistent milker, which is worth a lot under our conditions, and she was exceptionally good as a butter cow. This does not mean that she gave milk as rich as a Jersey's – it contains probably not more than 4.25 per cent of butter fat – but her milk has the idiosyncrasy of containing large fat globules. Thus, the cream rises quickly and almost completely and can be skimmed off in one thick blanket. When you have just two or three cows of your own and milk is an important item of diet you learn that milk is not just milk, but a fluid of varied qualities depending on the individuality of the cow, the period of the lactation and the time of year.

This black cow, which we called Bluebell because she came here when the wild hyacinths had begun to bloom, yields the milk which we like to set for butter. Not only does the cream rise so completely, but the texture and colour of her butter are very good. We do *not* like her milk for the tea, because the quick rising of the cream means an excellent first cup and the lower half of the milk jug contains a thin, blue skim milk which gives no body to the tea. The next cow we bought gave a milk of small

fat globules which did not rise readily and formed no sharply demarcated layer of cream in the setting bowls. Thus she is not particularly economical as a butter cow, but for tea and all other purposes her milk is preferable.

Milk is sweetest and fullest of flavour when the cows are freshly calved and at grass. A stale cow gives a flavourless milk. All these points are watched by the household living on their own produce. You become most decidedly epicurean when you feed largely on what you grow, and it is a right and sound development. We are meant to enjoy our food, and it is right that the simplicity and innate flavour of fresh homegrown foods should provide that enjoyment rather than the complex spicy kind of cookery necessary to titillate the jaded palate to stale ordinary food. I shall have cause to return to this subject because we found it so important, but given what I have said about the qualities of milk, there still remains technique in drinking it, almost as if it were wine. Milk is at its best as it comes from the cow, having lost none of its natural heat and not having been agitated by straining or overmuch pouring. When I was a lad I knew the taste of the milk of all the cows I milked and had my favourites. As I finished one of these favourites I would lift the bucket, twist round a quarter of a turn on my stool and take a long pull. It was glorious. Milk is both sweet and salty, but the sweetness masks the saltiness when the cow is fresh. If you drink milk at lunch as we do, it should be taken with the savoury course, for once the sweet pudding has passed through your mouth milk tastes thin and flavourless.

Well now, this cow: the worst thing about her was her looks. She was no good advertisement of herself. The only nice thing in her appearance was her eyes, which were soft and violet and highly intelligent. As I have come to know and love her I have come to watch those eyes closely, but I watch them nothing like so closely as they watch me. That cow knows me as well as my mother does.

We brought her over in the launch one calm day, from a rock just north of Badentarbet Pier where, at half tide, the boat could be brought alongside – cows and sheep are always loaded from traditional convenient rocks which were there long before the piers. We had covered the floor of the forward part of the launch with turves and we had plenty of old sacks to put over the gunwale as the cow was lifted inboard. Bluebell is in many ways a sensitive, nervous cow, but she is neither foolish nor hysterical. She did not like getting into the launch – what cow would? But no one could have had greater consideration. The Badentarbet salmon fishing crew came along to help, petting the cow so much and showing her a sheaf of corn in the boat, that between greed and fussing she was lifted bodily into the launch before she fully knew what was happening. There she stood quiet, with Murdo Macleod sitting on the forepeak holding the halter and patting her neck.

It was quite easy going ashore on our own quay, for the end of it was still unfinished and sloped down six feet from its proper level. Bluebell knew the idea was to go ashore and that the chances were there would be more doing ashore than standing here in a strange wobbly thing in which there was the continuous noise of an engine. She stepped out of the boat herself, climbed carefully up the steep ramp of stones to the finished part of the quay and looked around with her ears forward. We took her along to the walled garden where a crop of fresh grass was growing on the limy rubble. Phew! What stuff! she said, and wasted no more time looking about. That would come in an hour's time when her belly was full.

She was pretty thin then, scurfy in the skin and showing every sign that it was the end of the winter. May is the time when the owner of cattle is not overproud of his stock and takes no great delight in showing them to people. The weather is bright then, saying it is summer, but grass is still scarce. The bellies of the cattle are held high through having had dry food, and that food itself is past its best by the end of April, so that the poor things look worse than they are in the brilliant sunshine and greening grass.

There was no grazing in Achiltibuie to equal what we could offer Bluebell this summer. After calving on 10th June she milked better than I expected – up to three and a half gallons a day. But she dropped to two and a half in August, at which time I was spending less time working in the big park, and in addition to the grass lessening in value she was lonely. A cow is a sociable creature, and if there is no other bovine animal for company she is well satisfied with a human being. To many men cattle are just so much property, to be properly treated because that is the way they pay best, but I look at cattle in a different way. A cow is my favourite beast as a pet, for she has many nicer characteristics than a dog has and much more intelligence than a horse. There is more to it than that also: let me set it down in all seriousness, with Bluebell as the example.

She came to us and had no other beast near her; we petted her and she liked it. There was a lot of dyke building and fencing with barbed wire to be done in her park and she would come to inspect it all and lie down beside us as we worked. Then she calved and this bull calf was taken away from her before she got any notion of it at all. But I smelt of that calf and it was I who drew the milk from her. Her flood of mother love had to go somewhere and it was spent on me. And yet she knew me as a giver of food and she knew I had power over her. Thus do a man and a cow attain to an almost mystical union and relationship. The man is both child and lord to the animal, and for the man the animal becomes the object before which he lays the fruits of his labours in the fields and from which he draws through his hands the very stream of life.

Bluebell in her loneliness came to rely on me unduly. Wherever I moved about the place she wished to follow, and though she might not see me the wind would carry my scent and her muzzle would go up to assess my position before she would trot over to find me. It was a nuisance altogether, so I looked about for a second cow in self-defence. Bluebell, also, was a gate-crasher. She has been responsible for my making most of the gates about the place, which would otherwise have had to wait till I had more time. Apart from me, food is her other passion. She is the greediest cow I have ever struck, and has an eye for ever cocked on the chance of seeing something to eat. She will look into any unclosed door on the chance of finding something, because experience has led her to remember that many edible things are to be found in places where cows are not supposed to go. Whereas I merely make sure with the other cattle, and know there are some liberties I can take because animals are not quite as smart as men, I must make doubly sure with Bluebell and remember that she is not as absent-minded as I am.

Our ground is heavily infested with ticks; from all I can hear, Tanera always has been noted for its millions of ticks. Bluebell began to collect them about her body before the end of July. These loathsome bloodsuckers hang mainly on the parts where the skin is thinnest – under the throat, between and behind the forelegs, along the milk vein, in the crease made by the forward part of the udder and the belly, between the quarters of the udder and between it and each hind leg. Larval forms, known as seed ticks, would cling in serried ranks on her eyelids. Bluebell knew she was being irritated, but she also knew that a man could help to stop that irritation. How often has she come and shoved her great behind into me, asking for the ticks to be removed!

Bluebell is with us still, having now had three calves while in our care. They have all been black bull calves and therefore not worth our keeping, but they have been good ones and have fetched high prices. Each year I say I will get rid of her, because she is so ugly and so naughty, but I love the cow dearly and more than the others, so I dare say she will stay a while longer. The poor beast would be deeply hurt if I dumped her on someone else, for she feels tied to us and this place far closer than the other cattle do.

The sun kept on shining, telling us it was the best of all worlds. We lived in a land of beauty unscarred by war, yet all we held dear was in the direst danger. It was a fantastic world, this of 1940.

We had to think about Alasdair, who was at school near the Moray coast. A way home must be explained and maps given him so that in an emergency he could find his way through the hills. I had confidence in the boy that he could do this in a fortnight. There was a suggestion from his school that he might join a party of children being evacuated to Canada. But Alasdair's home was not on the east or south-east coast of England; he was not living in a tenement or crowded area of London; why should he go away? We decided he should remain here. It was not for children of people in our position to leave Britain.

And since my mother's home was now in the south-east corner of England, I had to think of her too. I was in no position to say yes or no to her, and she, being without fear, said she was going back and would not evacuate her home unless compelled by our own military authorities. It was hard saying goodbye to her, though I was warmed by her tremendous faith. Events justified it.

Alasdair came home in due course for his summer holidays; the Battle of Britain was fought and won; we got our hay in without a shower, and my hard labour of the spring looked as if it would result in a heavy crop of swedes for the cows, of potatoes and vegetables for ourselves, and in growing promise for the year ahead. The news steadied. We could not share their immediate danger; we could only admire our fellows from a safety we almost despised.

The rushes in the big park looked a formidable forest of dark green viewed from the gateway at the west end of the walled garden. They were waist-high, the result of many years' unchecked growth. Rushes increase rapidly in pasture because the grazing animals carefully clip the grass all round the clumps and thus remove all competition. The clumps spread and join until grass almost disappears. One grass does seem to persist in an attenuated form – that awful weed of arable land, onion couch grass. Normally it would disappear from a pasture, for the conditions of close turf do not favour its spread, but it can grow in the heart of a thick clump of rushes, using the fibrous mat as one would plant bulbs in compost. I did not know this until I made a positive attack on the rushes by buying a short, heavy, wrought iron scythe blade which I fixed to an American snath, and cutting them. When I say cutting them I do not mean running the blade through them an inch or two from the ground. That is not cutting rushes, it is pruning them with a view to getting a stronger growth next year.

I have an idea that only a strongish man in his prime can cut rushes as they should be done with intent to eradicate them, and even then that man would need to be cutting his own rushes rather than someone else's or he would tend to lose heart. It is work which either breaks your back or develops its strength to unimagined endurance. When a man uses a scythe in grass he maintains a steady sweep and the sharpness of his blade and the sweetness of his action takes the scythe through with comparatively little effort. That is as it should be, but when attacking a high, clumpy crop of rushes the steady sweep gets you nowhere. The blade must go in level, but deep, so that the crown is taken off the clump entirely and you look down on to a lovely pattern of densely packed circles and ovals of white pith. The rushes do not like such exposure: sun and rain beating into their heart sap their strength. But they are not dead, only weakened. If the ground is then heavily grazed by cattle, the young growth of the rushes will be plucked off and the already injured crowns are not helped by heavy feet cutting into their middles. Next year the ground may be cut for hay, which means that the rushes have to compete with the grass on what are now rather less than equal terms. They make a poor show and the presence of a few rush stems among the hay is an advantage rather than a nuisance in a wet climate, for their stiffness keeps the grass springy so that it dries better in the field and can be carried as hay to the barn in a wetter condition than if it was all grass. The rushes prevent heating in the stack.

One more experiment was successful: I put a good layer of coral sand over the newly exposed crowns of the rush clumps in one patch of the park. This practice did two jobs at once, liming the soil as well as rush killing. The clumps were reduced to raised places in the sward by the next year, through which the plough cut with ease. I should like to have done this over the whole park, but, as always, time prevents many of the farmer's good intentions.

That rushy ground should be in such condition that it can be ploughed the following year, assuming that it has been made dry enough by draining. But rushes are as much an indication of sour land as wet. I have seen them spreading fast in dry, well-drained fields which were short of lime.

A good man working twelve hours of the day can cut about an acre of grass, but he would not get more than a quarter of an acre of fifty-year-old rushes cut through the crown. And he would not work twelve hours a day on the job. I would spend five or six hours hacking the rushes and I did about two acres in 1940. Some of the ground is now growing oats – but that is running ahead. The immense bulk of cut rushes dried quickly in that wonderful year of early summer weather and gave us a biggish job carrying them into a stack at the foot of Cnoc an-t-Sidhe. We have no horses here, for the nature of the ground is such that they would be uneconomical to keep; all carrying of light bulky stuff such as rushes, hay or corn is done in a sheet of sacking, Norwegian fashion. In this way I can manage sixteen to twenty sheaves of corn at a load, and as much dry rushes as can be packed into the sheet. It is quite an economical way of transport as long as barn or stack is not too far from the job; otherwise too much time is spent walking back empty. But there is no better way open to us, so whether we like it or not we have to do it.

This stack of rushes gave us excellent bedding for the cows all winter. How happy I was to see them standing belly-deep in their stalls in the sweet-smelling stuff, their coats shining clean and with a feed of hay at their heads! But I am not sure that rushes help to make such good manure as I had intended they should. They do not rot down in the manure heap like straw, and as far as I can see, the manure heap made from rush bedding does not get hot at all. I have used the manure in the rows on which I have grown cabbages and swedes, and when the ground has been dug in the following year the manure has turned up again apparently very little rotted.

In 1941 I moved one manure heap and sprinkled sulphate of ammonia over each layer as I rebuilt it. Such treatment should result in heating and rotting of the bedding as the heap was open to the rain, but the rushes were still quite rushlike and stiff when I used the heap in the mangold rows. Given the rushes, I should still use them for bedding and they are the best possible stuff for covering potato and other root clamps, but the problem has ceased to interest me so much since our farm will produce no more heavy crops of rushes. Had the choice been open to me, I think the best way of turning the rushes into manure would be by putting them into a yard or building in which young cattle were being wintered untied. The constant and even treading would have broken them down mechanically, as well as the chemical effect of the urine on the ever-thickening layer.

A dry store was an absolute necessity to us before we did any other constructional job on the farm. We decided to roof in a building on the northern side of the Planestones, measuring 20 feet by 10 feet, for which we had bought corrugated iron before the war had become serious. Like all such jobs, it meant a lot of getting ready before doing the actual work. The front wall had to be lowered and levelled to a height of eight feet. This bit of wall is unique in the toughness of its mortar. Coral sand does not appear to have been used, only hot lime in a manner which I have been told by natives of the North West is not known now. It is extremely hard work to part stone from stone, or indeed to get the point of a pick into the junction. The jarring was sufficient to bring blisters even to my hands, which I had thought long past that stage. I made a hole in the back wall for a window – a foolish thing to do as I soon found out, for that wall was mortared only with a poor clay without any lime. I nearly let the whole lot down about my ears.

The wood for this building came from the old house. Now that we were living on the Planestones it had become unsafe to move about near Tigh an Quay. If the weather was wild, slates would fly and dig into the earth when they whizzed down. The quickest way of getting the slates off was to punch the sarking off from below, standing on the uppermost floor of the building and using a pole as a ram. Most of the slates were flaked and rotten round the nail hole, so they shook off fairly easily before the sarking itself was clear of the rafters. This technique worked splendidly till we neared the ridge of the roof, which called for our standing more to the middle of the floor. A young friend, Edward Booth, was staying with us at the time, helping with the work of the place until he was to join the Navy in the autumn. He was standing in the middle of the floor in the haunted room battering at the sarking with his pole when every floor joist collapsed at once at its junction with the wall. I happened to be on the first joist of the adjacent room when this happened, and saw the whole floor going down like a lift, but rather faster. Edward was going down also, in a sitting posture, but with thin air as his seat. The whole outfit fetched up on the next floor but one with a great crash and an incredible uprising of dust. Edward climbed out a little shaken and with a bruise on his hip where he had managed to strike the edge of a mantelpiece on the way down. That was the end of the haunted room of Tigh an Quay. A thrush nested in one of the joist holes in the wall last year and its mate sang joyously from the gaunt chimney stack above.

As the summer wore on I had to think seriously about a byre. Bluebell had herself chosen the most westerly compartment of the main range of buildings as the place where she preferred to stand when being milked. It also seemed the most sensible place to build the byre if I could get the roofing material, but before the roofing there was a three-foot layer of soil and rubble on the floor. There was nothing for it but steady work. The August rains had come, and as we dug into that sixteen-foot square mass we were disagreeably surprised to find the earthy part of the rubble was clay. Where did it come from? How did it get into there? There are many mysteries about this place in the way of accumulation of rubbish. At this time we did no more than sling the stuff out of the window and wheel the stones into two heaps in the desolation of the walled garden. We have done a good deal of clearing before and since then, but nothing has been so hard. The one bright spot was when we found there was a floor of red brick underneath all the rubbish.

Once more the old house became Crusoe's ship in providing wood for the cow stalls and calf pen. I had to splice rafters to make them reach across the building and supported the splice by running a length of timber vertically from the floor. These vertical supports to the roof were so arranged that they played their part in forming the stalls. The corrugated iron for the roof had not come yet, so I lashed and tacked a roof of canvas and boards on to the rafters just above the cow stalls, and if the truth be told the animals lay there comfortably until 22nd November, when I fetched the roofing from Badentarbet Pier and got it fixed the same afternoon. I got a window from the house and cemented it into the upper half of the window hole of the byre, the lower half being walled up and cemented. Then I brought in a lot of rushes and stacked them in the corner. The byre became then what it has been ever since, a quiet and delightful place where our guests love to congregate. I would as soon sit in a byre in which there is plenty of hay or bedding and where contented animals are eating or chewing the cud as I would sit in an armchair in the house. Indeed I would rather do so, for the body can relax utterly laid in the straw in such quiet company. Milking times are sheer pleasure, for the byre and its occupants extend a feeling of welcome.

Some day soon I shall have to build raised concrete standings for the cows, but so far I have had no time for the job – nor any great inclination if the truth be known. Who would have thought that I, the exponent of clean milk production and adviser on cow shed floor construction at the age of twenty-one, would have descended to this state of a primitive peasant before he was forty, content to see his cows lying on a level brick floor, on a great compacting bed of rushes? There are neither regrets nor remorse; the cows are healthy and comfortable and they will develop no big knees or calloused hocks from cold hard concrete!

The cows lie in winter on their thick bed of rushes and straw which is dry at the top where it is against their skins but wet and urine-soaked below. That bed is not disturbed till May, when it goes out into the drills for the root crop. Disturbance would make that bed insanitary and there would be loss of ammonia. As it lies there it develops some heat of its own – which fact the cat also discovered, for she would come down from the hay to lie on the cows' bed each day while they were out grazing. This practice of mine with the cows' bed conserves plant food in a way I cannot hope to equal when I get concrete stalls.

The udders of the cows are not washed before each milking as they should be. They get a good rub with my hand, which rubbing not only detaches loose particles of bedding, hair and scurf, but pleases the cow and brings down her milk. I milk and strip carefully and weigh the milk (for recording is one of the joys of keeping cows), but when I pour out from the pail into the tin setting pan in the dairy I pour from the side of the bucket which was nearest me because a few hairs and specks collect on the inside of the bucket farthest away. Bobbie scalds each setting bowl every day, but the milking pail rarely gets a scald. The milk is poured from it in less than a minute after it comes from the cow, and immediately I go to the rainwater butt to let the water run all round the inside and outside of the bucket. By never letting it stand, there is never a hint of semi-dried milk adhering to the bucket. Our milk keeps sweet for thirty-six hours and more even in the height of a thundery August. It does not get a chance to keep longer than that.

We bought our second cow in October 1940, from a man who was giving up his croft and going to work on munitions in Glasgow. I do not suppose he looked upon the change of occupation as a misfortune, but I was certainly sorry to see him go, for it meant one more croft going to ruin. His cow was a blue-polled one, probably the best in Coigach. She was not only outstanding as a milker but of such shape as would grace the best herds of dual-purpose cattle. She moved with an action equal to that of a Highland cow. The only fault I could see in her was a touch of sullenness in the eye.

The same ritual was followed in ferrying over this cow, but even more care was taken as she was a heavier beast. Alec Mathieson, from whom I bought her, provided a little light relief by backing across the launch with the sheaf of corn and not realising he had not more than seven feet to go. He clung to the gunwale with the crook of his knees and escaped with no more than a wet seat. The cow was lifted out safely on this side and left on a good patch of grass while Bobbie and I took the men back to the mainland.

She was called Rainbow and has been a good servant to us. She is never naughty like Bluebell, but is downright bad in one respect, which is denoted by that sullenness I had seen in her eye. Rainbow will not let her milk down unless there is food in front of her, and that food must be something she likes well enough. Suppose you put nothing for her: well, there will be no milk and she will stretch her neck round, looking at you with sardonic interest. Suppose you try hay: any beast gets hay; she will push it about with her muzzle, get her head under it and throw it about and eat none. This she will do though she might eat it gladly either before or after she was being milked. Such a cow as this has the whip hand of you and as far as I know there is no way of curing her. She is conscious about it all, so conscious that it is no good trying Pavlov's technique of breaking down a conditioned reflex. There are some cows with which you can gradually cut down the food given under such circumstances until it is sufficient to leave an empty pail in front of them, but Rainbow is not to be caught like that. What I have to do is to find the least sumptuous food that will produce the results and stick to that or its equivalent for feeding at milking time. You must never feed anything very attractive like oilcake, or you have no shots in your locker. Rainbow has roots at milking time, and in summer an armful of new-mown grass or kale. She must have had this habit since her first calving, but if she had been mine since her heifer days I should be heartily ashamed of having let her develop it. The moral is to take the calf away from a heifer before she so much as sees it and never to give her any feed at milking time.

Rainbow calved on 14th December 1940, and looked at that time as bonny a beast as any man could wish to see. She had improved in condition, was as sleek as a mole and had such a bag as I never expected. Her calf was black and a bull, a sore disappointment to me at that time. Little did I know then that I was to get six bull calves in succession; in fact, I have not had a cow calf on the place yet. This calf was a beauty, so square and deep. I had to have a bull anyway, and as Rainbow showed herself such an outstanding cow I felt I could do no better than rear this Tommy Tittlemouse and use him.

There is some risk in importing cattle from outside the West Highland area to a place like Tanera which is so heavily infested with ticks. These parasites carry the protozoan, which, in the bloodstream of cattle, causes a breaking down of the red blood cells and results in Redwater fever. It is better, therefore, to rear your own cattle and your own bull. Even so, the heavy tick infestation of Tanera was too much for Rainbow. She had an attack of the disease in May 1941, when the ticks were invading grazing animals particularly badly. The illness pulled her down in condition and gave her a staring coat, though her milk did not go down markedly. Her twelvemonth record of 845 gallons on wartime feeding gave me great satisfaction. She was mated to her son Tommy as soon as he came fit for service, and I waited a long nine and a half months for a cow calf from this union. Bluebell was already in calf to Tommy and produced a bull, so I felt the chances of a cow calf from Rainbow were pretty good. And when the calf did come it was a big white one with black muzzle, eyelashes, feet and ears – one of my favourite colours in cattle. But it was a bull, and I had a good quarter of an hour's curse.

I was interested to observe Tommy from his birth upwards, for my eyes are now not altogether those of a farmer as they were years ago when many a dozen calves passed through my hands. I am supposed to be a biologist and have some work on the study of animal behaviour to my credit. Tommy was no less interesting because he was a farm animal being reared for purely practical ends. As a boy I taught a calf to drink without thinking out the problem, but now I saw it analytically. The calf naturally sucks milk and does not drink, and when it sucks its head is in an upward-reaching position. Now, to be pail-fed, this calf, which has never seen its mother and will only know me as parent, must learn to overcome the instinct of a million years which makes it reach upward and suck. I put my finger in its mouth, the middle finger, simulating a teat, and gently incline its head downwards into a quart of the first milk of the cow. Little Tommy is as yet unsteady on his legs and there is not much of him anyway. He has no experience, only inborn instinct. As soon as his muzzle touches the milk his head jerks up with surprising strength. His little organism revolts at immersing his muzzle in liquid though till a few hours ago he had bathed perpetually in a dark sea of it. We try again, wetting the finger with milk afresh and letting him take the finger for a few moments between his upper lip and questing, experimental tongue. Down, down I draw his head and he sucks perhaps a pint through the gap in his lips each side of my finger. He staggers with exhaustion and gives a tiny grunt.

For three days the finger is necessary to guide his muzzle downwards to the milk, the quantity of which has now risen to a total of a gallon a day given in two or three meals. The finger is gradually withdrawn as he sucks, until the fourth day it is withheld altogether, and after a little time of impatient reaching for it he plunges his muzzle deep into the milk and drinks. The finger is gone for good.

Tommy is in his little pen five feet square, knowing little of the world, which to him cannot be bigger than the byre itself. Then one day when he is three weeks old I open the door to let him come out and move about this world of the byre. But he has never been out and how can he know this is a door? The fact that there is space where there has formerly been something solid does not convey to his speck of brain that he can walk into that space and through something which is a door. But it is at least the characteristic of the young animal to be inquisitive, and that teller of his brain, his muzzle, goes pushing into space. He almost falls out of the pen into the byre, and then all is strange and Tommy is frightened. He jumps forward on uncoordinated legs and comes into sharp contact with a wall. More fright. He barges sideways and is further upset by the brick floor, which is strange to his feet. He slips and slithers and comes by chance on to the cows' bed. Ah, here is what to him is firm ground. He stands and holds on as it were.

Yes, there he stands all alone and lonely, legs splayed, his head held uncertainly. One foot is knuckled over at the pastern and the whole limb is trembling. His ribs are heaving and in that byre I can hear his heart pounding. No more for now, I say, and put my hands on him. These he knows as I guide him back to the door of his pen, push him in and turn the snib. And now Tommy is in his little home again which he knows, and becomes immediately a bumptious and cocksure little calf.

Thereafter, each day when the cows are at grass I open the door of the calf pen and Tommy comes forth boldly. His little games are set ones, just like a child's. There is the preliminary romp which follows the same pattern time after time and day after day – round to the cows' bed, kick up the heels; jump; run across to a heap of bedding in the corner and try to climb up it; fail to do so, half fall back but land on the feet; run across to the cows' bed again; kick up the heels – and the same again. Now he is puffed and stands a minute before he goes on to his inquisitive games. These include pushing everything off a bench, curry comb, dandy brush, heavy turnip knife and so on; he pulls a box away from a wall and turns it upside down. I do not wonder if I shall have to clear up this litter after his capers each day; I *know* I shall, for he observes a close and constant pattern. Usually when I go to put him in his pen I find him lying quiet on the cows' bed.

Always Tommy is pleased to see me, for I mean food to him and all the companionship he has ever known. I shall never forget how one wet day when he was four months old I went into the byre to write as there were visitors in the house. I curled up in the corner on the dry rushes. Tommy rose from the cows' bed, came over to play with my ears and the corner of the manuscript book, and then, with some effort and great deliberation, he climbed on to the heap of rushes and lay down with a sigh, his weight against my body. Tommy was at peace and began to chew the cud.

A WILD WINTER

B Y AUGUST 1940, the farm work necessary to keep the cows for the winter was pretty well done. The hay was in, the swedes were all singled and hoed, and the plot of cow cabbages was already green all over, showing no brown earth. The garden was yielding a wealth of food, and apart from hoeing there was not much more we could do in it before the winter. My leg was now sound enough to allow me to work with the big boulders and dressed stones still lying in the harbour at the foot of the quay. The derrick was set afresh, and with enthusiasm, for it was nine months since a stone had been moved. Raising the big stones was not the only job to do; there was the accumulation of gravel to move in the bend of the quay where ultimately the boat would lie, and there was the seemingly endless quantity of filling to be thrown up into the middle of the structure, tons and tons of it. We did reach the foundation of the quay at its seaward end, but halfway up the harbour we think there must be several feet of shingle lying above the original level of the harbour floor. A stone there has XII cut in its face, where the edge of the quay is seven feet above the present floor. If there were originally twelve feet of depth at that place there can have been but little dry time in the harbour.

It is the seaweed and the east wind together which are mainly responsible for filling the harbour with unwanted shingle. The bladder wrack fastens to a bit of shingle beyond the foot of the quay and the bladders are almost enough to float the stone; the east wind is sufficient to raise it from its bed when the break of the sea is on it, so that with the rise of the tide stone and weed are washed forward into the harbour. Once there, the bladder wrack slowly rots off because it is now out of its optimum conditions of growth. The stone is left.

The job went ahead slowly for a few days round each spring tide, for we could now work only at low water at such times. Not a day was missed even when visitors came; they were pressed into service and always the response was one of pleasure at joining in the work, especially as it involved playing with water and with pulleys. A doctor of medicine rowed over to see us one morning; we had never seen him before, but by lunch we were good friends. We got the first stone to the final level at the inside end of the quay on that day – a huge Caithness blue mudstone which had lain buried below for perhaps fifty years. That stone has come to be called Blue Martin, in remembrance of this friend of a day who may yet return to find pleasure in the finished work.

Bobbie and I were working alone through October and November because there were no visitors then and Alasdair was at school. Some of the stones were too heavy for us to raise on the chain, which was not intended to lift more than half a ton. Those that were twice this weight had their final bed made ready for them in the afternoon. Then we would lever them with crowbars to the foot of the pole, put the chain about them, lower the pulley block and hitch it to the chain. At each end of the stone a float would be fastened with rope, after which there was nothing else to do until almost high tide when it was practically dark. The great stone would come up easily under water, the floats would be detached and the stone swung into position. Then lower a little, remove the chain, and there it was, needing little more than a touch here and there with the crowbar on the following day. Sometimes the chain blocks would jam when the stone was part way up: the heaviest stone of the lot got jammed three times on its vertical journey of twelve feet, which meant unhitching it to release the blocks and waiting till next day to do it again. This in turn meant working three-quarters of an hour later each day when the tide was high. I remember working waist-deep in the water at the end of the quay, and having to come out and run about every two or three minutes because of the cold.

At last that quay was levelled, and its middle filled and the parapet carried along to the end and halfway along the end. No physical job we have ever done has given me the feeling which the quay did at its finish. There were certainly odd jobs to do yet, concreting the surface and the top of the parapet, but the main fabric was built and as I sat in the window of the little house on the Planestones I could not take my eyes off it. How often had I imagined its shape as I now saw it, when there was only open sea overlying an ugly heap of boulders! I walked the length of the quay in the dark on that first evening not once but half a dozen times, feeling the firmness beneath my feet and enjoying the sight of the water just an inch or two below the level at the end where I leaned over the parapet. It was Sunday 17th November 1940, only two and a half years after we had bought the place, and when we had estimated it would take us three years to do it. But in this place of Tigh an Quay there is more to do than we can cope with in our lifetime. The finish of one job merely releases us for the next. All the same, the quay remains a thing of pride to me, possibly more to me than it does to Bobbie. Little did we know on that first night it was finished how soon the strength of our work was to be tried by the ordeal of tempest.

We enlarged the house just before Christmas 1940, by getting another small hut of Canadian red cedar, lined with Cellotex. But we did not attach it to the existing house on the Planestones. It was erected in the garden under the high wall of the main range of buildings and facing north up the garden. What a way to face! I can hear someone saying. I like sun in a place as well as anybody else, but if I have to choose between having sun and having wind as well, and having no sun and shelter from the wind, then I go for no wind and put up with the loss of the sun. If your house faces south in the North West Highlands it means you get all the terrors of the south-east wind, the miserable greyness of the south wind and the terrific gales of south-west weather, which is the commonest of all, especially in summer. Northerly winds are uncommon except in early summer when they are fine-weather winds. We are relatively sheltered from the north wind at Tigh an Quay and experience little discomfort from it, but with the bulk of Meall Mòr immediately to the south it might be thought we should be sheltered from the south and open to the north. This place is not unique: only ten miles away the House of Gruinard faces due north to the open Minch, yet good timber grows, the gardens grow verbena, escallonia and many another tender shrub. The rose trees show no sign of having suffered from wind. After all, anything here which faces north does get a good deal of sun in summer, when it rises high to the north-east and sets well above the north-west.

The Garden House becomes a haven when the searing easterly and south-easterly gales are blowing, and another good reason for having it well away from the house on the Planestones was that it gave our visitors and ourselves much more privacy, a factor which becomes most necessary on an island or where your house is small and of wood. Everybody has liked the Garden House, winter and summer, even with its restricted view of the sea. It was a great liberation for us in Alasdair's holidays, and he could go into a tent in summer if a friend were staying with us. But a year later we were feeling the pinch again and I needed a study where I could write and leave my stuff lying about. I loathe having to tidy up every day because I happen to be working on the one and only table.

I had done a piece of writing for exactly £50, so I invested most of it in another red cedar hut which was divided into two, the smaller part being Alasdair's room and the larger part my study and office. Other household improvements have been a storm porch to the house on the Planestones and another very big one to the Garden House. Oilskins and rubber boots can now lie to hand without littering the little rooms. The study may be a blessing to me but it is equally so for Bobbie, because it has got rid of piles of books, papers, a filing cabinet and innumerable masculine oddments which she would consider no ornaments to the house. The long and wide fitted bench in the study is a bulkhead which we picked up from the sea near Eilean a' Chlèirich. An east wind dried this batten beautifully, and when I had built it into the study I polished it with wax. It is a lovely thing. The window of the study looks forth to the apple trees and over the garden; when I sit in there my eyes rise from work and see the small birds of the land – blackbirds industriously scratching a manure heap flat or making holes in it almost like a rat would; hedge sparrows following in the wake of the blackbirds, going in and out of the holes as if they were caves from which to sing their soft undersong; thrushes perch in the apple trees, singing increasingly from January to June, and the wren and robin are there too. Sometimes the birds scatter and the blackbirds cry with alarm – as well they might, for the sparrowhawk has flashed into the garden seeking a panic-stricken blackbird. This bird cannot see me as she perches for a minute on the top of the apple trees and I enjoy a close look at that fierce, cold face and athletic form. How beautiful is the fine barring across the chest, of brown on a field of cream! I wish the bird were not one of our residents, for we have too few small birds here to spare for the hawk. And when an island loses its stock of small birds it may have to wait too for recolonisation.

The winter of 1940-41 was hard on our few land birds. It was a winter of east wind with one great blizzard which must have buried many a small creature. It began on the afternoon of 18th January when Bobbie and I were going over to the mainland in the launch. There had been heavy snow the day before, though now it was calm and brilliantly clear in the pale winter sunlight. We left the harbour halfway through the ebb tide, which meant we should hardly get back again before the berth for the launch was dry. But it did seem such a good afternoon.

When we were less than halfway over to Badentarbet Pier we could see big white-capped waves a mile away to the south in the sound of Horse Island, though we were in calm water. And on Ben More there were huge plumes of driven snow flying from the several summits and ridges and shining in the sunlight in amazing beauty. Sea, sky and air – all reached a pinnacle of beauty in that moment, but contemplation of it was not my job: I turned back and berthed before the harbour dried. But this was not done before the wind was up, biting cold and flurrying the dry snow from the quay.

A blizzard in Scotland means east wind, for the snow is never in the physical condition to drive horizontally when the wind is in any other airt. We on the Planestones of Tanera could not rightly experience a blizzard because we are at the very sea's edge facing east. The wind could not carry the snow from the mainland across two miles of sea. But it carried the cold and penetrating power gathered in its journey over the mountains, and up the park the blizzard was real. Our few Shetland wethers kept at home made for an exposed place, thus showing their innate wisdom, for the snow was blown clear and they were not in danger of being buried. A blanket of driven snow was coming off the top of Meall Mòr, hurrying eastwards with the sun gleaming through it and lighting the millions of separate seething particles three hundred feet above us.

The low sun died and left the menace of night.

The henhouse at the top of the park, built of turf and stone on a summer's day, was quickly filling with drift and the birds themselves huddled in uncomprehending misery. We picked them up and brought them to the shelter of the ruin and gave them a heavy feed of hot mash for the night.

The mainland was an indistinct blur in the dusk, for the flying snow over there removed all detail of houses and crofting ground near the sea. Our shutters were put up for the night because they saved the windows, but they could do nothing to prevent the terrible noise of sea and the shaking and creaking of the little house. The byre was filling with snow when I went out to milk, and poor little Tommy Tittlemouse, then just over a month old, was black no more, but white the length of his back and telling me he was feeling chilled. I made his pen like a little tent with sacks over the top; then I gave him more rushes for his bed and with wisps of them gave his sides and back a good rubbing.

After one more day of rather easier wind the weather settled for twenty-four hours. Many of the gullies of the mountains had disappeared under an unbroken carpet of white, and some of the houses at Achiltibuie were half buried. How many sheep, I wondered, were buried beneath that whiteness? It was disastrous.

Three days after this, on 22nd January, we had a hurricane from the east: the gale increased all day, reaching its pitch at high tide at half-past three in the afternoon. The waves broke over the quay and fell into the launch at her berth on the inside bend. Would our drystone work on the quay stand up to this bombardment? Ought we to bring the launch up to the head of the harbour and let her dry out there, so that she would be free of the torture of the sea for twelve hours?

Bobbie and I got into our Grenfell suits, thinking we would try to beach the launch within the shelter of the harbour. The water breaking over the quay went through our Grenfells and woollen clothes underneath as if it were solid beads of shot. We hauled the launch alongside the quay almost up to the Planestones, but we had not realised how big the sea was even inside the harbour and what force was in these lessened waves. The keel would have been pounded out of her in a quarter of an hour. So we hauled her back again, fighting the wind this time and finding it no easy job to get ropes fast on bollards and samson post. We ran new ropes from her port side right across the harbour and bent them to projecting rocks and anchors.

I noticed Bobbie had lost all activity: her face was blue and expressionless and her hands hung in front of her belly like helpless useless things. I took her by the arm and led her back up the quay. She neither resisted nor responded but came like some quiet broken animal that had no will. I was doing that rare thing, gasping with cold, but because I had to do more of the heavy work my body had not felt it so badly.

Bobbie came indoors. I lit methylated spirit in the Primus burner cup, put on a quart of water, pulled the wet things off Bobbie and wrapped her in blankets on the settee, ran back to the Primus and gave it fifty pumps or so. Two minutes later the quart of water was singing and poured into the hot-water bottle. This went to Bobbie inside the blankets and another quart went on the stove for tea, which was infused inside another three minutes and cups poured out in four. Bobbie was blue no longer and she was perking up. Neither she nor I have ever been colder than we were that afternoon, yet as we swallowed that tea I could not help thinking that here were we, able to come in and get warm, while at that very moment there were probably men sitting astride upturned boats in the Atlantic Ocean without hope of warm tea and little of rescue. I think our life on this fringe of the ocean has given Bobbie and me the deepest possible sense of responsibility about the use of imported things, whether petrol, paraffin, flour or wheat. The island years impressed on us most surely the sin of waste, but the war years of trying to make a home on Tanera have been an education in making do on the least possible, in being resourceful and in never taking goods from a needy outside world if we could help it.

The east wind blew hard for well over a third of the total time from
January to April 1941. Such a year was not remembered in these parts. It
had still one more surprise for us, a demonstration of what an east wind
can do over a mere two miles of sea. Many days of March had been that
perfect calm, sunny weather which can be some of the best of the Highland
year, but towards the end of the month there were signs of the returning
offensive of Auster. He came in increasing strength from the 24th of the
month, and on the night of the 26th-27th gave us the most terrible hours
we have ever spent in this little wooden house. When I went out in the
morning I felt dazed, but things of interest revived me in a very short time.
I was seeing things I might not see again – at least I hope I shan't. There
were wrinkled crabs in the walled garden, not one but a dozen or so, and
some were six inches across the carapace. How on earth did they get there?
Then I went into the park and found more crabs and many starfish, and my
collie bitch Trimmie found a ballan wrasse, weighing a pound and a half.
This fish, and the crabs, are denizens of the sea just below low-tide mark,
and here they lay about the grass two hundred yards from the high-tide
mark. I remembered reading as a child how tropical storms sometimes raise
water from the sea in such volume as to shower fish on the inhabitants of
adjacent shores, but I had never thought to experience the phenomenon in
Scotland. Sometimes I wish I could have seen that great disturbance of the
waters of the Anchorage which caused this to happen, and at others I feel
it was just as well to have been in bed.

A few days later I was telling some men at Polbain about the shower of
crabs and fish, and heard then that once before a small shower of herring
had come down on Ard-na-goine in a big easterly gale. But no herring
weighs one and a half pounds and few are as heavy as some of those crabs
which were hurled two hundred yards inland. It was not until low tide that
I found a deep wave of gravel had been moved from the bed of the sea and
deposited in the mouth of the harbour. Oh! the work in clearing it. When
I told an old man on the overshore about this he thought it over well: 'Ah
no, Doctor,' he said, 'that wouldn't be the wind itself, now. I'm thinking it

wasn't the wind at all. It was afther being in the nature of an eruption.'

I would not need to be much more credulous to believe him.

The garden is not very demonstrative in a Highland March, but the evidences of devastation were obvious on this awful morning. The smaller branches on the eastern side of the old apple trees were reddish-brown, for the bark had been rubbed from them and hung like the velvet from a stag's antlers in August. The fruit buds had been knocked off entirely, which made the little short fruit spurs look like the handless wrists of little children.

I was deeply moved by all I saw and for a few hours was disheartened. The mood passed, though the east wind blew for another fortnight without rain. That in itself meant that the killing salt spray was not washed off trees and shrubs. The buds of the blackcurrant bushes blackened and fell off so that it was July before they gained a half-hearted foliage. The beech and thorn hedge up the middle of the garden, planted but four days earlier, was blasted for the year. Such kale plants as had escaped earlier buffetings and were now putting forth a much-needed bite of green for the cows were blackened afresh and rendered useless. It was at this time I decided I would build up the east wall of the garden to ten feet. The fact that it is still to be done does not matter overmuch; the effort was in the decision to undertake the job.

Disappointments in this spring were not yet at an end. In the optimism of early January I had decided to buy a two-wheeled *Trusty* tractor, for I knew I could not hope to get much farther in working this place without some form of mechanical traction. I had made many enquiries, hoping to find out the capabilities of the two-wheeled tractor driven by an air-cooled engine of 4-6 hp. Replies were most disappointing. Some said not enough was known about their performance and the rest said they were all right for a level market garden on light soil but no good for farm conditions. And yet, I thought, a firm cannot go on for long selling a dud machine to sapheads. Then the Director of the Agricultural Engineering Research Institute gave me an opinion on small tractors, plainly doubting. But he added a postscript to say he had just had a call from the manufacturer of the *Trusty*, who had said objectively that he thought the Director's opinion unduly pessimistic. I liked that touch of objectivity on the part of a manufacturer and wrote him a long letter explaining where I was, what I was, what Tigh an Quay was like and what was expected of a small tractor. Could it tackle very old ley riddled with roots of rush clumps?

I got the straightest of letters back and a lot of explanatory pamphlets. The manufacturer stuck to the point that the *Trusty* would go wherever a pair of horses could plough. He went so far as to say if I bought one he would come and give a demonstration of the machine's capabilities. That is confidence. I should have to pay about £175 for the tractor, plough, cultivator, harrows and roller, a lot of money for a man who had his living cut from under his feet less than eighteen months ago. But I felt if I was going to show it was possible to develop a distinctive crofting husbandry in the West Highlands I must be prepared to be the one to make an expensive experiment. It was wartime, I was not fighting as so many of my friends. So I took the plunge.

MacBraynes' kindly allowed their steamer to come into the Anchorage with the tractor on board, on 30th March. It was already too late in the season to get very much ploughing done, but you can contemplate doing things in the West Highlands at which one would be aghast in any other agricultural district. I have seen old ley turned in May and sown with oats about the 20th of the month and there has been a good crop by September. One man I knew of went the length of sowing oats the first week in June, and with a confidence which was justified by results. Such a practice would be more than heresy in a farming district; it would be insanity. It seems that the long daylight of this far North and the moist August is enough to hasten growth so far as to make ripening possible by the end of September.

But I was not to get going at all in the spring of 1941. The captain of the steamer called me inboard to see the machine. One of the long handles of tubular steel was pointing skywards and the engine ports were broken. It was a perfect day and a perfect tide for landing the machine on our quay and I could not expect the steamer to come twice in such good conditions. So I decided to take delivery and have the new parts sent on. This was a time when air raids were dislocating traffic in England, so I did not curse the railways as I certainly should have done in peacetime; also I thought it hardly fair in such a period to decline delivery. So the *Trusty* swung out on the steamer's derrick and was lowered gently on to a staging I had put across the coaming of the launch. Unloading on our quay was easy: planks were put from the gunwale to the quay, the launch securely tied fore and aft; the tractor was turned through ninety degrees and wheeled off. Eight and a half hundredweights could not have been moved more easily.

The manufacturer sent me the new parts quickly, but the carburettor had evidently been so much disturbed that I could not get the machine going. The *Trusty* lay unused until 5th September, when the manufacturer made good his promise and came this great distance to set me going: Mr Reach of Tractors (London) Limited and Pat Murphy the journalist came together. I picked them up in the launch at Badentarbet Pier. I had no need to ask who was the Yorkshireman and who the Irishman, and Reach almost immediately said to me, 'Why, you were brought up in Yorkshire,' which, of course, is a fact, though only half of me is Yorkshire blood – the romantic half – for it is my sincere contention that the Yorkshireman is a romantic. He will pursue an ideal, and it is no detraction from romance to follow an ideal with acumen and common sense. Reach was a romantic too – full of faith in his invention.

Reach and Murphy fell upon the engine and had it going in about five

minutes, but I thought the carburettor rather a chancy thing all the same. The machine trotted into the park, leapt an open drain and galloped up the steep slope of Cnoc an-t-Sidhe. That alone was an amazing performance.

'It's all in the balance,' said Mr Reach, 'in the distribution of weight.'

Then he adjusted the plough and started. It was set far too deep, but at least it showed what the *Trusty* could do. A wide furrow slice nine inches deep lay inverted on the grass; black and fat it was, and we all marvelled at this soil which is despised the length and breadth of Scotland.

Reach the enthusiast rattled off instructions to me which he had to repeat half a dozen times during the day. It was difficult for me to take them in and at the same time be as wonderstruck as I was watching the soil of Tigh an Quay being turned. We raised the ploughshare and widened the furrow slice so that we were ploughing between four and five inches deep and laying each slice beautifully flat so that no grass was showing through at the edges. The top of Cnoc an-t-Sidhe is the residue of some old-time glacier. Below the first nine inches of soil is a couple of feet of glacial silt in which rest large boulders partly polished by glaciation. The tractor plough soon found the tops of these and we were able to see how the machine checked at them without snatching and went out of gear. Murphy and Alasdair and I went to work with pick and crowbar and raised many a dozen boulders in the course of two days' work. Later we moved some of the really big ones, but some will have to wait for the end of the war and the free use of explosives.

Mr Reach was not satisfied with the performance, and before the ploughing season of 1942 he sent me a brand new tractor which has run most sweetly. Such is pride in the thing one makes as judged by a Yorkshireman. 'What's the good of me calling it a *Trusty* if it isn't?' he said.

ISLAND HOME

DURING THAT WINTER OF 1940-41 we thought the summer would be barren of the joy of friends. The war was not very old yet and all of us were still in a serious mood. But when spring came folk were tired with air raids and overwork and needed just that break of remoteness which Tanera could give. Letters from friends came increasingly often, asking with some hesitation whether they might come to see us during the summer. There were also letters from people we had never seen who would like to call. Well, it is difficult to 'call' in the Highlands: in peacetime a call meant lunch and tea in our part of the world, and it was common for us and our acquaintances to make the double journey of twenty to fifty miles to pay such a visit of courtesy. An island is more difficult to reach than even the scattered households of the north-western mainland, so when we say we shall be glad for anyone to call, it usually means that our open house extends the traditional Highland hospitality of forty-eight hours. Whether chance acquaintances stay beyond that time is for us to say. Our family has no piper who, on the second morning, can play *Lochiel's Farewell to His Guest* before breakfast, but there are equally courteous ways.

Friends have come in these two years whom we have not seen since the war began. Within a week of each other there came Ivan Hulberd, now married and a Captain in the Army, and Alec and Beryl Valentine much Blitzed; now there was no mad party in *Southseaman* like the one three years before. They got down to singling carrots and helping us catch Shetland sheep on the islands. When Bobbie's sister and brother-in-law came again, veterans also of the London raids, they took eagerly to work as if such use of the hands was necessary to them. Their work consisted of a barbed wire fence the whole length of our cliff. Another friend, who had not been farther than a mile from Gower Street throughout the London raids, coming in the dry weather of May 1941, saw the great quantities of seaweed washed on our shore by the easterly gales. He occupied himself burning the lot and pounding the clinker so that we could use it as a potash dressing on the potatoes. 'The last kelp-burner of the Isles, and all that,' he said, and ever afterwards has signed his letters James McKelpie.

One girl came from England whose passion was gardening. She was a mistress of her craft. It was something worthwhile to see those hands dip into earth and touch the roots of plants. She shaped our ideas and taught us much, and got me down to helping her clear that terribly shabby corner of the garden beneath the old buildings. We cleared a dozen cartloads or so of broken slates and crockery, and such weeds as dockens, nettles and fool's parsley. It is now called Miss Muffet's corner, edged with a hedge of cotoneasters and filled with fruit bushes.

Whatever Tanera was doing before the war towards making good talk and fun, it has done much more since in a happy spirit of hard work. There are limits physically to the things Bobbie and I can do together, and the coming of friends is our opportunity to get certain big jobs done; especially so when they have some distinctive ability. The chimney stacks at either end of the old house and main range of buildings were themselves seven feet high and showing signs of crumbling. And the foot of those chimneys was thirty-six feet above the ground on a gaunt roofless gable. We thought a lot about those chimneys in the big gales. When Geordie Leslie arrived on a borrowed rowing boat, he and I managed to lower the chimney above the little house on the Planestones, but I was not man enough for the one at the other end and I would not endanger the life of one of His Majesty's serving officers by letting Geordie try it. It was different when James Fisher the birdwatcher and Alan Pullinger, Editor of the *Climbers' Club Journal*, came for a few days. Alan was a climber, and if he thought it fit to get on top of that chimney above the byre I was satisfied to let him. James Fisher and I acted as labourers, boarding over the byre roof below as a protection and getting ready to clear the rubble. Alan climbed that seven feet of bare chimney and stood on top of it with the calmest skill I have ever seen. Then

he lowered the stack stone by stone to the level of the gable, put two flat slabs over the flues and came down.

Thus has our house been full each summer from March or April till October, and I believe Tanera has had its place for these few in healing war-worn bodies and minds. We have had fresh food in plenty for them from garden and dairy; we have seen lines soften in their faces and frames toughen, and it has been joy for Bobbie and me. A journey to the islands to gather the Shetland sheep for clipping or marking makes a good outing for our friends, and we almost rely on their help now for the necessary numbers in working the sheep on to a small promontory where the animals can be caught. What happy days they can be, these shepherding trips to the islands! They are good, fine, calm days of necessity and the islands are looking their best. Perhaps there are six or eight of us and Trimmie the collie, all able to run. The sheep are always troublesome to catch, sometimes a tup puts one of us on our back or a strong wether drags a fellow along the slippery rocks to the sea. What a yell of joy there was when I fell over backwards into the sea with a struggling sheep in my arms from the forepeak of the launch! The sheep was captured with a boathook and I came round to the stern of the boat to climb up the rudder. Clipping is no orderly business of having a sheep brought to you as you sit astride a clipping form in comfort. We have to clip where we can catch the sheep on the serrated rocks of the steep promontory. Sometimes a ewe will leap off into the sea, swim across to the main mass of the island and be lost to us for the year.

Alasdair has grown up to almost fifteen years old in a world in which these exciting things for a boy are real and serious, and not play. The island years of the Chlèirich, Treshnish and Rona were not holidays and glimpses for him, but the wholeness of his life; now on Tanera his school holidays are spent helping to carve a home and a farm on a rough island.

In the autumn of 1941 I was sitting on the hillside looking down on our ruin. How different it was from two years before! There were the trim lines of the quay and the Planestones terrace, the increasing amount of dark dug ground in the garden, the greenness of the hill and the attenuation of the rushes in the park. The ruin itself was no great eyesore from up there, neither is it as we live about the walls themselves, but that place we had called the walled garden in an optimistic moment was depressing from wherever it could be seen. As you came up the quay and looked through the arch there were desolation, decrepitude, dockens, ragwort and twitch – a jumble of rubble and weed two or three feet deep over the whole courtyard. The only beautiful thing in there needed looking for; a little wild geranium which bloomed nine months of the twelve.

I believed we should feel happier if that place were cleared, but how could we undertake such a job now when so much of our labour must go to immediately productive ends? The walled garden would be a pleasaunce only. Then, as I sat up there looking down on the place as on a plan, I got a new conception of what the walled garden should be. It should be divided into two, the larger part inside the archway being 22 yards by 12 yards and the smaller part near the byre 14 yards by 12 yards. This latter should be the farmyard, and instead of dropping the remaining bit of the factory wall which fell seventy-five years ago, I would build it up and make it the side of an open-fronted haybarn. The guttering of this barn could lead the rainwater to a cistern which, being opposite the byre door, would be useful for watering the cows at night in winter. The south wall of the farmyard could be the back of a lean-to shed for implements.

I knew there was an immense amount of stone in that courtyard, especially where the wall of the many arches had fallen. The removal of the earth, slates and rubble would be job enough without carrying out all the stones as well, which would only make another unsightly heap until I could use them. It would be an economy of labour to make the division between walled garden and farmyard a drystone wall five feet high, of the best workmanship I could produce. As the whole courtyard was so long, the walled-garden part would look better for being shortened and bounded by my own drystone work.

The decision to undertake a job is the most difficult part of it for me, but once undertaken I feel eager to get on with the hard work. Much as I should have liked to begin at the archway and work back, I put that desire aside and began at the farmyard end because that was where the labour would first ease the general working of the farm. I cleared a strip six feet wide right across the place where the new drystone wall was to be built, and was delighted to find that below all the rubbish there was an excellent paving. A job of wholesale clearance like this one cannot be undertaken until there is somewhere available for a tip. You cannot waste your time clearing one place and littering up another. We were fortunate in having decided to extend the Planestones terrace southwards across the head of the harbour to our boundary. Any big ugly stones we found which were unsuitable for a drystone wall – the sort which the dyker describes in the term that 'it wouldna sit in a bog' – we carried or rolled out to use in the extension of the terrace, which was to be several yards wide. The main 'eye drain' from the park opened where the terrace was to come, so we built a stone culvert through to the sea. It is our intention, when this terrace is full and the filling well settled, to build a high wall on it which will protect that odd corner of ground, which the old people called the calf park, from the worst of the east wind. We hope to make a water garden there at the mouth of the drain and grow some of the royal fern which is so common about the lochs of Eilean a' Chlèirich but is not found on Tanera.

That piece of ground, the calf park, is the foot of the steep northern slope of Meall Mòr and the poorest bit we have. It is continually wet with seepage from above, and yet it drains rapidly because the soil is thin and mixed with rock detritus from the cliffs above. The wind through there is truly terrible whether east or west. We planted it with a good many trees of one sort or another, but those which are not already dead we are moving elsewhere because the wind has reduced them to thin struggling sticks.

Beginning the clearance of the walled garden, then, was also the beginning of the extended terrace, and we had the double thrill of seeing the one place coming clean and the other growing. Perhaps I should say there were three exciting things, for as I brought to light the big stones of the fallen wall of the arches I set them as the foundation of the new drystone wall across the courtyard. It was an economy of labour to keep this going as well. All the small stone from the rubble went into the middle of that new wall, and when we found our barrows full of limy soil only, and not of slates and stone, we ran the loads into the garden instead of to the terrace and thus limed a big piece of ground in the course of the winter.

The farmyard was cleared by December and my new wall built. I was satisfied with that drystone wall and proud of it. I had done my best to get any lichened faces of the stones to the outside so that the finished job should not look raw.

The winter of 1941-42 was remarkable here for its dryness. This had two distinct effects on the complex of our life: it meant that the labour of clearing the walled garden was much lightened, indeed a wet season like the following winter would have made the work impossible; and the weather meant that I was drawn outside every day. There was so much to do anyway, and so much could be done because the ground was dry, that I worked my fill each day and was too tired to write anything but necessary letters in the evenings. The bank balance dwindled, therefore. If I let my enthusiasm for work overcome my good sense, it would mean an end to the development of this property as a self-contained farm, which was the job I felt it incumbent on me to do as a contribution to solving the West Highland problem.

Bobbie said, now I had built the wall across I could come inside more and get some writing done. I entirely agreed, but laid the foundation of a baffle wall in the walled garden to prevent a straight draught of east wind going into the farmyard, and once the foundation was there my hands would go to the job in every spare moment, so that also was finished and the writing left. But there is always a swing of the pendulum and the intensely wet winter of 1942-43 has enabled me to finish this book and other work as well. Oh, for the spring and fresh air again! And for the end of the war when I shall feel justified in writing outside on a fine day!

As we reached the eastern corner of the courtyard the rubbish grew deeper, and when we almost reached the wall the paving suddenly stopped. It was the edge of the kiln where peat was burnt to produce the red herrings for which Tanera was famous. The kiln was three feet wide, nearly three feet deep and nine feet long, and even now was full of ash. We mixed this with soil and lime mortar to form the body of what is now a herbaceous bed overlying the kiln and the few feet of paving west of it. When the wall was finally cleared there still remained the foundations of the piers of masonry which had supported the wall of the arches which fell so long ago.

If the foundations could be got out without too much damage to the paving round about, the holes could be made into flowerbeds, 8 feet by 2 feet 6 inches. The stones were very big ones, well mortared in and deep, but we got them out in time and used them as the first courses of other baffles which we have built against the wall of the main range of buildings to check the sweep of east wind through the archway. At last those holes were filled with good earth, the flagging of all that courtyard well brushed with a hard broom during a heavy rain, and the order had been given for some standard rose trees which were to form a line in this row of beds where the foundations had been. I moved an Albertin rose which had not done very well on the Planestones and set it against my new transverse wall, and an Excelsior rambler was put by the main baffle. Bobbie and I agreed that we needed one good standard tree of some kind in the middle of the walled garden, or courtyard as it looked now. A flowering cherry would probably die, a weeping willow or wych elm was hardly the right thing, nor was a standard fruit tree. We decided on a sycamore as being hardy and likely to form a compact close-topped tree. The nurserymen unfortunately sent us a bad tree – eight feet of stick and three little twigs at the top. This we endured for six months and then replaced it with a handsome specimen laburnum which I chose for myself when in Inverness.

The standard rose trees were another disappointment. They came late, unheralded by an advice note, and had spent a fortnight on the journey. The weather was intensely dry at the time, so they reached us in a desiccated condition from which we were unable to revive them. The nurserymen have now replaced them and we have added a few more rambler roses which are intended to adorn the walls. Once more we are being optimistic, but this time conditions for the growth of these trees are as good as we can make them. We have even planted a fan-trained apricot tree against the wall of the house facing south and flanked by a baffle wall to east and west. I have heard of this courtyard being called the hottest place in Coigach, and if apricots were grown here a hundred and fifty years ago, why not now? Perhaps we are at a stage in the cycle of weather when it is worsening, when there is more east wind than there was a century ago. Certain it is that all the plum and apricot trees have been gone many a long year, and in the few years we have had Tigh an Quay the old apple trees have tended to lose some of their canopy rather than add to it.

Several of our friends have brought rock plants which we have put in the interstices of the paving of the courtyard. Dwarf phloxes, saxifrages, tiny irises and aubretias will gradually fill those earthy niches and the dockens and annual poa grass will come no more. Desolation has left the place and we feel no shame now as we come up the quay with friends and look through the arch. The immensity of the job of clearing has but added to our enjoyment of this separate and distinctive garden.

Birds seem to love it though the plant cover in there must necessarily remain sparse. Bird song sounds loud there and the many holes in the walls are an attraction to thrushes, pied wagtails and hedge sparrows. The robin has nested here in 1943, for the first time since we came. The former habit of these birds was to leave us in March and return in October. It is for the sake of the birds about the farmyard and walled garden that I have had reluctantly to part with the cat – for which I had a particularly high regard.

Miss Purcell came to us in the winter of 1940-41. Bobbie called me into the dairy one day to look at a pan of milk of which the cream had been disturbed: Was it a rat? No, but I could not see how it could be a cat as there was no such animal here on our side of the island. I reserved judgement. Then one day after a night of rain the cream was disturbed again and on the bench where the pans were set were several little round footmarks. It was certainly a cat; and another day I found those prints on a bit of soft smooth earth. But we never saw the cat. Various contraptions of fish netting failed either to catch the cat or prevent her going into the dairy. Cats tread delicately and with precision.

In July I had two tons of baled hay at the back of the byre. My mother had sent gooseberries to Bobbie by post, which meant they were rather the worse for wear when they reached us. Bobbie laid them out on dishes and newspapers on the lower tier of bales in the byre because she had so little room in the house. As she worked there she heard a loud purring but thought it must be the muffled sound of a starling on the chimney stack. Then she looked up and saw a tortoiseshell-and-white face keeking over the uppermost bales of hay. Bobbie quietly left the byre and fetched me.

'I've found the cat,' she said.

When I came in, all my animosity to the creature evaporated. I saw the cat now as a homeless thing which much wanted a home but was in doubt about asking for one. 'Ah, little pussy,' I said, and climbed on to the first tier of bales. The cat recognised the kindliness I was extending; she stood up and reached forward her head to my uplifted hand. What purring! And what a cat! She was immense. She was tortoiseshell and white in colour and had a coat in glorious condition. Not a fluffy coat but a short one through which the rippling movements of her muscles gleamed as she strode to and fro. Here was a real cat, embodying and expressing the whole notion of cat. Bobbie fetched a saucer of milk and the cat came down to the first tier of hay, still purring her pleasure.

Here was an animal which had been about the place for six months and had most carefully avoided being seen by us. Apart from the milk she had taken she had hunted her food and had become to all intents and purposes wild. Now she had decided to be seen, and having shown herself had thrown off completely all idea of shyness or hiding.

The cat said, 'Here is my place and I will stay with you.'

And I said, 'Stay you shall until I see you catch a bird in this garden and then you will go.'

Had we been living on the mainland I would have given her some little licence with the birds, though not much, because there is a continuity there: but on an island where there are no rabbits or mice a cat is more likely to for the birds, and an island population of small birds is a finite thing which cannot endure the predations of an imported animal.

I do not think the cat took any birds during the autumn or winter. Her days were spent curled asleep on top of the hay or sitting in the cows' bed. She came down from there each milking time and strode purposefully about the floor of the byre. As I rose from the cow she would leap to the weighing machine and rub against it, for she knew the bucket went on it before a saucerful of warm milk was poured out for her. All robberies from the dairy now stopped and this cat never came near the house. We never saw signs of her catching a rat except that one was laid in the middle of the byre floor one morning, killed but little damaged.

I believe she must once have caught or eaten a poisoned rat, for she did not come down from her lair one morning. She lay there curled up for five days, eating nothing. Then she was better and came down for her milk as usual. No one could have been ill with more dignity.

My collie bitch, Trimmie, dislikes cats intensely. Miss Purcell knew this quite well and trod with the greater circumspection when Trimmie was around. Trimmie with all her sharpness never caught Miss Purcell off her guard, yet you never found the cat making a sudden or undignified movement of escape. And when Trimmie had a pup of eleven weeks old when, although it was marked exactly like Trimmie, the cat realised the harmlessness of the pup and would allow it to rough play. When the pup grew as big as Trimmie and looked so very like her, the cat still knew from a good distance who was who. The pup would be allowed to romp up and even climb the bales of hay to where Miss Purcell had her lair. Trimmie certainly got the worst of it in all conversation with the cat.

But this winter no robins dared to hop about the byre floor at milking time and I noticed the number of birds to be very low. It might have been the three hard winters which had reduced them – or it might be the cat. I could not blame her yet. And then in April I found her with a chaffinch, a species of which we had very few. Then I found a few more feathers on top of the hay. It was no good being sentimental. I put Miss Purcell in an openly woven sack and took her to the mainland. She neither struggled nor complained, which made it all the harder for me. I went to a collection of rabbit-holes in some rocks and put the cat down there. She strode with all her characteristic precision and purposefulness into the largest hole and disappeared. That was the last I saw of her. Rabbits, I fancy, were more desirable game to her than small birds. I missed her, and still do; and perhaps this year, when rats are common about the place as a result of my corn-growing operations, she would have had game enough without the birds. But I have made the final decision not to have a cat here again. The birds are much more numerous now and far tamer than before. And small birds collectively will do more good about this place than a cat, and give much more pleasure. I have been going for the rats with break-back traps and find them most efficient, but more rats pour in from the cliffs as fast as I clear them about the buildings.

Thus far have we come: what was a roofless ruin in 1939 is now a home where there is a fair standard of comfort. A good boat lies inside a safe quay. Those bare, rough acres which provided only a bite of summer grazing are now wintering six head of cattle from their own produce and so far feeding three people that their weekly outgoings for food do not amount to four shillings each a week in cash. There is also a surplus of produce to export from Tigh an Quay. The ground is fenced so that we can turn the cattle into different enclosures and rest content about them. We

are clothed in tweed and knitted things made from the undyed wool of our Shetland sheep. Not much money has been spent, but that which has gone into the place has been earned during the period of our work. The cost in the labour of our own bodies has been great, though I believe it has been a charge on the income of our strength and not on its capital. And we have not finished yet. We shall lose a few more finger-nails from getting them trapped between the big stones, and many another day shall we have to stop working with stone because the blood is showing pink through our fingertips.

Perhaps we shall never finish Tigh an Quay and it will remain a road on which we have travelled hopefully. The place and our work on it have had their influence on the outside world, for good or ill. A wind-swept doom-ridden island property has begun to flower again and the principles we have used can be applied elsewhere. My own life here is on the point of enlarging and changing, in that the Department of Agriculture for Scotland has asked me to devote some of my time to travel in the crofting areas with a view to establishing demonstration crofts and advising crofters how to improve their holdings. For over three years Bobbie and I have worked alone, sometimes with discouraged monotony, sometimes with doubts as to whether it was worth while unless the idea went farther than Tigh an Quay, but usually with a deep enthusiasm.

Bobbie and I set out to make this ruin of Tanera. It seemed to fight us for a while, two human beings attempting to clear a century of gathering doom; then we felt the weight lift, and though life held just as much hard work as before, life was easier a little. We were still novices during the island years on the Chlèirich, the Treshnish and Rona. And if the red stones and rough acres of Tanera could talk they might tell another tale – of what all these islands have done to us.

Little Toller Books
FORD, PINEAPPLE LANE, DORSET
w. littletoller.co.uk   e. books@littletoller.co.uk